DATE DUE

FRANCISCO ARIAS
The Judge
1621

The Scolar Press
1977

ISBN 0 85967 372 3

Published and printed in Great Britain by
The Scolar Press Limited, 59-61 East Parade,
Ilkley, Yorkshire and
39 Great Russell Street,
London WC1

NOTE

The following works are reproduced (original size) with permission:

1) Francisco Arias, *The judge*, 1621, from a copy in the library of St. Edmund's College, Ware, by permission of the President.

References: Allison and Rogers 37; STC 741/ 14833.

2) John Heigham, *The gagge of the reformed gospell*, 1623, from a copy in the library of St. Edmund's College, Ware, by permission of the President.

References: Allison and Rogers 423 (under Kellison); STC 14907.

THE IVDGE

WHEREIN IS SHEWED,
how Chriſt our Lord is to *Iudge* the
World at the laſt Day ; to the extreme Terrour of the Wicked,
and to the exceſſiue Com-
fort of the Good.

*With a Preface, which it willbe neceſſary
to read before the Booke.*

Tranſlated into Engliſh.

*Nolite errare, Deus non irridetur : Quæ enim ſe-
minauerit homo, hæc & metet.*

Gal. 6. verſ. 7.

Be not deceaued, God will not be mocked; for
the thinges which a man ſhall ſow, the
ſame he ſhall reape.

Permiſſu Superiorum, 1621,

TO
MY NOBLE,
FAITHFVLL,
WORTHY,
and moſt deare Friend,
Mr. G. T.

SYR,
Since I had
the Ioy to ſee
you laſt, I hauc
looked a little
into the next Life, as deſpay-
ring
A 2

ring that in this, I should be able to find any thing which might be worthy to fill vp that place , which is made empty by your ABSENCE. And now by chance, or rather by Gods good Prouidence, I haue met with a Prospe-ctiue-Glasse, which giues me a view of *Heauen*, and *Hell* , in a very expresse & cleare manner, though the Countreyes theselues be far off . I should neuer haue beene able to fit the Instrument towardes any eye; but finding now, that all was ready made (and that , so excellently) to my hand , I haue aduentured to frame a

case

cafe for it, after the English fashion. The thing in it felf, you will not chufe but like, for it is excellent; and I am but too fure, that you wil loue the part that I haue therein; becaufe the fame Loue hath ceeled vp the eyes of your iudgement concerning me. But if (abftracting from that) you chance to like it, I shall ftand in little feare of the cenfure of others, who muft giue me leaue to belieue, that ther liuesnot amõgft them all (for ought I know) a man that can outftrippe you in *Tranflating*. Heerein I haue feene pretious things of your doing; both in

A 3   Profe,

Profe, and Verfe, and in feuerall Languages. And I neuer
mifliked any *Tranflation* of
yours, but that one, when you
traflated your Prefence, from
the eyes of my body, bywhofe
Abfece, I am in part depriued
of being able to *tranflate* fome
of your vertues into my foule.
The leaft that I can do againft
Abfence & *Diftance*, for fo great
a wrong, is to fend them a *Defi-
ance*; and to bid them be fure,
that if they mean to make me
loue you one haires breadth
the leffe, they shal loofe their
labour. Nay they kindle me
rather, to make this expreffi-
on of my felfe; and to *acknow-
ledge*

ledge (as I may fay) *this Statute* of my hart, before the World. For I am fixt in giuing you all power ouer me, and I glory in being fubiect to fuch a Friend.

Your, *what you will*

G. M.

A 4

ENGLISH RECUSANT LITERATURE
1558–1640

Selected and Edited by
D. M. ROGERS

Volume 336

FRANCISCO ARIAS
The Judge
1621

JOHN HEIGHAM
The Gagge of the Reformed Gospell
1623

THE PREFACE·

A Learned and holy man of this age, be-sides the odour of his Sanctity , hath left furuiuing , di-uers Monuments of his writing ; and, amongſt the reſt , three bookes *Of the Imitation of Chriſt our Lord* . In the firſt of theſe , he ſheweth, vnder ſeuerall Titles , the ſeuerall Offices which his diuine Ma-ieſty is performing to the ſoules of men ; as he is our *God* ; our *Redeemer* ; our *King* ; our *Sauiour* ; our *Mediatour* ;

A 5

our

our *Aduocate* ; our *Captaine* : our *Sa-crifice* ; our *Spouse* ; our *Doctour* ; our *Law-giuer* ; our *Pastour* ; our *Light* ; our *Life* ; &, to conclude , our *Iudge*. The whole booke is large ; and not only should I haue felt the paines in tranſlating it all , but I might haue doubted of your Patience , whether or no it would haue reached, to the reading of it ouer , with due intention. The laſt of the *Tytles* , deliuered to vs by our Authour , I haue heere tranſlated ; and you may ſee, that he is a Lyon by his nayles .

In this diſcourſe of *Iudge*, which is not founded vpon priuate contemplations, and much leſſe, either vpon looſe coniections , or ſtreyned conceipts ; but euen wholy in effect , vpon the paſſages of holy Scriptures (though not cyted word for word , but duely pondered, and truly para-phraſed, as the beſt ſpirituall wryters are wont to do) he doth admirably deſcribe

deſcribe the ſoueraigne Maieſty , the incomparable Mercy , and the inuiolable Iuſtice of our *Iudge.* And (as incident heerunto) he deliuers vs ſuch a Mappe of the next world ; and doth ſo deſcribe the *Paradiſe* of heauen , & the *Zona Torrida* of hell, as may ſerue, either to rauiſh vs with ioy , or ſtrike vs through with horrour , and make vs euen wither , for woe ; according to the ſeueral ſtate that we may be in. If wĕ be members of the true Church of Chriſt our Lord ; and if , withall , we be in the ſtate of grace, we ſhall looke with more hope vpon the ioyes of heauen, then with feare, vpon the torments of hell; and ſo, we ſhall get courage in the good courſe begun . But if, on the other ſide, we be cut off from the communion of the true Church of Chriſt our Lord, by any one errour in beliefe; or if yet, being Catholikes, we be remaining in ſtate of mortal ſinne, this Treatiſe, I hope,

will

wil help to guide vs by the hād out of thoſe Labyrinths; & place vs in that high way of Fayth & Charity, without which we can haue no tytle to heauē; but the iaws of hel, wilbe ſure to ſucke, & ſwallow, & deuoure vs.

Let no man therfore be deceaued, or rather let no man deceaue himſelfe. God is God, and he wilbe ſerued. And it is all reaſon, that, by our beleeuing, and liuing as we ought, true Homage may be done to that infinite, inuiſible, immortall, and moſt pure Maieſty of his. And man is man; a thing of nothing, for of nothing he was made. And as now he is, what is he, but a Pedlars-ſhop full of traſh; or rather a very ſincke full of filth; and to what height of honour ought he eſteeme himſelfe to be aduanced, if he had but euen a ſingle leaue, to ſerue & loue ſuch an omnipotent Creator? But now, ſince beſides this, he is to be rewarded

with

with an immortall Crowne of glory
for fo doing (the fublime excellency
wherof , no created power can comprehend) what meruayle can it be ,
that the torments be alfo infinite, to
which he fhalbe adiudged and chayned ; if infteed of doing reuerence to
God , by imbracing an incorrupted
faith , & leading either an innocent,
or penitent life, he enter into rebellió
and treafon againft him , by imbracing any errour in beleefe , or falling
into fenfuality , or any one other
mortall fin, if withall, he dye therin,
without repentance.

It is not want of Charity , in
them who fay , That all fuch as dye
with any mortall finne vpon their
foules fhall eternally be tormented in
the fyre of hell ; but it is true Charity
to declare this truth, that fo , in tyme
men may know to what to truft . *S.*
Paul abounded, and ouerflowed with
Charity ; and that very *Charity* it
was

was, which obliged him to proclaim
Gal. 5. v. this doctrine ; That, *the workes of the*
10. *flesh be manifest* , and he saith they are
these, *Fornication* , *Vncleanes* , *Impudi-
city* , *Luxury* , *Seruing of Idolls* , *Witch-
crafts* , *Emnities* , *Contentions* , *Emula-
tions* , *Angers* , *Brawles* , *Dissentions* ,
Sects , *Enuies* , *Murthers* , *Ebrieties* ,
Commessations , *and such like. Of these*
(saith he) *I foretell you* , *as I haue fore-
told you* , *that they which do such things
as these* , *shall not obtaine the kingdome of
God.*

Now if these Sinnes doe exclude men from heauen , others also
which are as grieuous , wilbe as sure
to exclude them ; and the more certainly will they exclude them , the
more grieuous , and enormous they
fall out to be . For if simple fornication doe make a soule lyable to the
paines of hell , what will not Adul-
try do? If for a priuate emnity with a
mans neighbour, he shalbe adiudged
to

to thofe eternall and vnquenchable
flames, what fhall he not be, for deuiding the Church of Chrift our
Lord, by vnbeleeuing any doctrine,
or difobeying the gouernement therof?

I fay the vnbeleeuing of any
doctrine, as before I faid of the committing any other mortall finne. For
this is as true, in the law of our faith,
as it is, in the law of our life, That,
Qui in vno peccat omniũ factus eſt reus;
he that offends in one, is made guilty of
all. Not that he who offends in all,
fhall not be more deepely damned,
then he that doth it but in one; but
becaufe whofoeuer fhall haue offended mortally againft any one commandment of our Lord God, which
concerneth good life, or any erroneous doctrine, in difference from the
Catholike beliefe, is moft truely declared to be a breaker of the Law of
God, and a corruptour of his truth;
and

and that as such a one, he shall perish,
except he repent . Woe be therefore
to them (and of woe they will be one
day sure) who bringe such false
weights into the world ; and who
prophane the law of God , and not
onely the law, but the law-giuer himselfe ; In that they allow him not to
be a perfect hater , and a seuere punisher of all mortall sinne , in what soule
soeuer it be found . Whereas yet he
protesteth himselfe (throughout the
whole Current of holy Scripture)
not onely to hate , but to abhorre it .
The (1) *impious man, and his impiety are*
hated by Almighty God . The (2) *scoffer,*
the (3) *Lyer, and the* (4) *Arrogant per-*
son , is an abomination to God . The (5)
way of the wicked man, and euery wicked
thought of man, is abhorred of God . Thou
(6) *wicked man, thou shalt dye the death.*
Behould (7) *the whirlewind of the indig-*
nation of God shall go forth (sayth the
Lord of Hosts) and it shall come vpon the
head

(1) Sap.
14. 10.
(2) Prou.
3. 32.
(3) Prou.
12. 22.
(4) Prou.
16. 5.
(5) Prou.
15. 9 .
(6) Ezech.
33. 8
(7) Ierem.
23. 19 .

head of finners , like a furious tempeſt.

Now, if any man perhaps fhall tell me, that thefe places, & the like, are only meant of Infidels, or fuch other wicked men, as fhall haue fpent their whole life in the offence of God ; but that chriſtiãs & fuch as lead not a life fo prophanly wicked as thofe others, are not meant heereby, howfoeuer they may commit fome mortal finne, and continue therein ; let fuch a one behould, how the holy Ghoſt taketh care to anfwere his obiection, by af-furing vs, That, *If a man, who had been neuer fo iuſt, fhould yet forfake that iu-ſtice by committing finne, he fhould dye therein.* And then he can looke for nothing, but that *Day,* whereof ano-ther Prophet fayth : *That it fhall come burning, like a fornace, where all proud men and all other perfons working wic-kednes, fhould be like ſtubble, and that this day, fhall fet them on fire.* Nay it is a feareful thing to fee, in the Prophet

*Ezech. 18.
26*.

Mal. 4. 1.

B   *Ieremy,*

Ieremy, how our Lord doth fweare, That how full of priuiledge foeuer, & how deare foeuer a man may haue beene to him, yet if he fall to finne, & dye therein, he will reiect him. For fpeaking of a finner he expreffeth it, in thefe wordes of Terrour: *As I liue* (fayth our Lord) *if Iechonias the fonne of Ioachim the king of Iuda, were a ring, which I did weare vpon myne owne right hand, I would plucke it off.*

Ierem: 22. 24.

So deadly doth Almighty God hate finne, and finners; and fo infallibly will he iudge them to be tormē-ted for the fame, in thofe eternall ardours of hell, if they repent not cordially thereof before their death. And what a fit of phrenfy then, muft that be, which can poffeffe vs fo far, as to make vs, for any temporal and bafe delight, to forfake, and be forlorne by that God of eternall Maiefty, and of infinite beauty.

But in the felfe fame manner, the

the Fathers and Doctours of the holy Church, haue testifyed this truth vpon all occasions. They were not Infidells, but faythfull Christians to whome *S. Chrysostome* sayd (when withall, he tooke himselfe into the number:) *Consider that without fayle, We must all departe, to stand before that Iudge, Whome it will not be possible for vs to deceaue; and Where, not only our actions shallbe iudged, but euen our very Wordes, and thoughts; and Where We shal endure extreme punishment for those things, which heer haue seemed but smal. Be alwayes remembring these thinges; & see thou neuer forget that fire Which is neuer to be extinguished.* Let vs therefore (sayth S. *Ambrose*) *lament our sinnes that We may deserue pardon If our sinnes be not forgiuen in this life, We shal haue no rest in the next.* The (a) *burning of such as shal be damned, Wilbe eternall, as the fire is to be Which shal burne them:* and *Truth affirmeth, that not they only*

Hom. 22. ad pop. Antioch. tom. 5.

Ambr. in psal 38.

(a) *Aug. de fide & oper. cap. 15. tom. 4.*

B 2   are

are to be sent vnto it who *wanted Fayth,
but they also who* wanted good workes .
This last is sayd by *S. Augustine*, and
he also affirmeth thus in another place: *No one good deed is left vnrewarded,
nor no one sinne vnpunished . At the last
Day* (sayth (b) S . Gregory) *that de-
uouring flame shal burne such as are* now
polluted with carnall pleasures; *then shall
the infinitely* wide mouth of hell, *swallow
downe such persons, as heere are puffed vp*
with pride. *And they,* who through their
*fault haue heer performed the wil of their
crafty Tempter, shall fall like reprobates
into those torments, togeather* with that
guide of theirs. And (c) *according to the
quality of their sinne , the punishment
thereof shallbe ordayned, and euery damned soule shallbe tormented in the fire of
hell, after the rate of her demerit .*

(b) Greg.
l.9. Moral.

(c) Greg.
l.5. Moral.

　　This is then the verdict of the Fathers and Saints of the holy Catholik
Church , and of the Apostle Saint
Paul; yea and so the holy Ghost himselfe

felfe, who wrote by his penne, and which is euery where cleerly giuen, to proue this certaine truth, That *any one mortall finne, whether it might be against good life, or true beliefe,* doth shut vp the gates of heauen against vs, & set open the bottomlesse Abyffe of hell to swallow vs, vnlesse we repent thereof sincerely, before our death.

The hower of which death, because it is so wholy hidden from vs, it will infinitely concerne vs, both instantly and exactly, to cast vp all the accompts of our Conscience; to be cordially sorry for all our finns; to confesse them distinctly; to purpose an amendment firmely; and to satiffy for them intierly. For this is a busines which must not be difpatcht after a curfory and fuperficiall manner; but we are to confider with what care we would confult about our estats, if they were in danger; or about our liues, if they lay on bleeding. And

B 3   heere

heer we muſt not faile to vſe ſo much
more deligéce then there, as *Eternity*
is of more importance, then a moment of *Tyme* . And in fine, we are to
do it ſo, as, at the hower of our death,
(when we ſhall go to ſtand before
our *Iudge*) we would be glad that we
had done it . For without this true
repentance which ſignifieth a flight
from ſinne with griefe; and ſuppo-
ſeth a flight towards God with loue,
it is no Faith in Chriſt our Lord ,
which will ſerue the turne to pre-
ſerue vs out of that lake of eternall
torment. But rather, the more knowledge we ſhall haue had of him by
Faith , the greater will our torment
be, if we do not pénance for the ſinns
which weſhal haue cómitted againſt
that Maieſty of his Which , the ſame
Fayth telleth vs to be infinite ; and
that his hatred againſt ſinne is alſo
infinite ; and that as , with ſtrange
mercy, he will aſſume to incompre-
                              henſi-

henſible, immortall ioy, the ſoule, which at that day he ſhall find to be free from ſinne; ſo in whomſoeuer he he ſhall perceaue, that ſin remaines, the ſame ſoule will he then inſtantly adiudg to that ſea of fire & brimſton, where it will ſaile in ſorrow, & blaſpheme, and rage, for all eternity.

To the pretious *Death*, & *Paſſion* of Chriſt our Lord, we owe & muſt acknowledg (amongſt innumerable others) this vnſpeakeable benefit(for which let all the Angells for euer bleſſe & praiſe his holy name), That through the infinite merit therof, we may be receiued to grace, by meanes of true contrition and pēnance; how often, and how wickedly ſoeuer, we ſhall haue offēded that high Maieſty. But that *Death* & *Paſſion*, will neuer ſaue the ſoule of any one creature, vnleſſe both that myſtery, and all the other myſteries of Catholike faith, be well belecued, & al ſinne be cordially

B 4   dete‹

deteſted; which ſinne, is a monſter, ſo fierce and cruell, as that it did coſt the very ſonne of God his life. By that life, and by that death I begge, that thou wilt giue ouer to trample with thy durty feete, in the ſacred Bloud Royall of our B. Sauiour, which he ſhed for thee vpon the Croſſe. For ſo thou doſt, preferring *Barabbas* before him, as often as thou cómitteſt any mortall ſinne; and ſo long thou haſt continued to doe it, as thy ſoule hath beene ſpotted with that crime.

Or if thou haue ſo little of the noble in thee, as to be moued more by thine owne intereſt, then by the conſideration of that immenſe benefit, which the foũtain of Maieſty vouch_ſafed, with ſuch exceſſe of loue, to this wicked creature man; then, do I coniure thee, euen by that very intereſt of thine owne, that inſtantly thou make haſt into thy ſelfe; and that, diſcharging thy ſoule by pénance,

ce, of whatsoeuer may be offensiue to the pure eyes of God, thou implore his mercy now, which may saue thee from that inflexible iustice of his, in the last dreadful day. At which tyme, euen this very paper will appeare to thy extreme, and euerlasting confusion, if thou forbeare to serue thy selfe of this admonition. *Heauen and earth shall passe away, but the word of God shall remayne for euer.* And that word hath thus aduised vs, and thus assured vs by the mouth of the most B. Apostle S. Paul, speaking to the Galathias: *Nolite errare, Deus non irridetur: Quæ enim seminauerit homo, hæc & metet. Quoniam qui seminat in carne sua, de carne & metet corruptionem; qui autem seminat in spiritu, de spiritu metet vitam æternam.* The plaine and cleere sense whereof, is as followeth: *Take heed you frame not certaine fantasticall, and false opinions to your selues, as if you could ouer-reach Almighty God, & eua-*

Matth. 24. v. 30.

Gal. 6. 7.

B 5   *euate*

cuate his truth, & make him belieue that he gaue you a free law wherby to liue, thē indeed he gaue. But be well assured that the very truth is this: Let euery man a- liue, consider seriously what he sowes, for iust so, and no otherwise, shall he reape. If yow sow works of flesh (which are par- ticulerly cited before, in this Preface, out of a former Chapter of S. Paul to the same Galathians) yow shall reape nothing but corruption, but destruction, but euerlasting damnation. But if yow sowe workes of the spirit, which are wholy contrary to those others, and are there expressed to be Charity, Ioy, Peace, Pa- tience, Benignity, Goodnes, Longanimi- ty, Meekenes, Faith, Modesty, Conti- nency &, Chastity, yow shall in vertue of that spirit (wherewith you liue, and whereby you are to walk) passe on from this transitory to an eternall life; & then at the most liberal hands of God you shal receaue a most precious crowne of immor- tall glory.*

A

A
TABLE OF
THE CHAPTERS
OF THIS
DISCOVRSE.

Of

THE

THE IVDGE

CHAP. I.

How the office of being our Iudge, doth belong to Christ our Lord, as he is man; and of the great benefit which God imparteth to vs, in giuing him to vs, to be our Iudge.

LTHOVGH the indignation, & wrath of Christ our Lord against the wicked, and the punishment which he inflicteth vpon their sins, do belong to the office which he hath of being a *Iudge*; yet so also doth it belong to him, vnder the same Title, to doe fauour to such as are *Good*, to defend them, to imparte benefites to them; and both to expresse mercy to-

C   wardes

wardes them in the *Iudgment* which
he exerciseth vpon their faults, & to
giuethē reward for their good deeds,
and for this reason it is that I wil declare the benefits and fauours which
we obtaine by Christ our Lord, in
respect that he is our *Iudge*. It (ᵃ) belongeth to Christ our Lord, that he
be our *Iudge*, in regard that he is a
man, and because he tooke the nature
of man vpon him; as being a most
conuenient thing, that the *Iudge* be
seene by all such as are to be iudged
by him; and that the guilty may wel
vnderstand, and heare the sentence
that shalbe giuē against them; & that
for as much as men are composed of
a body & a soule, they may perceaue
it with their soule, and heare it with
the senses of their body. Now if
Christ our Lord, as he is only God,
were to be the *Iudge*, he could not
then be seene by the wicked; and the
sentence which immediatly he should
pro-

(a) Why
it was
wholy fit
for the
second
Person of
the most
holy Tri
nity to be
our Iudg
at the last
day.

pronounce would not interiourly be
perceaued by them; and therefore it
was fit that he should be our *Iudge* as
man, and should passe his *Iudgment*
vpon men, that so he might be seene,
and heard by all.

This Mystery was discouered
to vs, by Christ our Lord, and Saui-
our himselfe, whilest he was saying : *The Father iudgeth no man, but he hath* Ioan. 5. *giuen all iudgement to the Sonne, and he gaue him authority to exercise Iudge-ment, as the sonne of man.* That is to say, Although the eternal Father haue the supreme authority, and power of *Iudging*, & that to him it doth prin-cipally belong to approue, & reward that which is good, as also to repro-ue and punish that which is euill (& the same also hath the Sonne; and the holy Ghost the same, as being one & the same God with the Father) yet the office of *Iudging* exteriourly, and after a visible manner to be seene, in

the

the Tribunall, and with the authority & Maiefty of a *Iudge* ; to giue exteriourly a *fentence* which may fenfi-
bly be perceaued by fuch as are *iudged*, this doth only belong to the perfon of the Sonne of God . Who by
meanes of the moft facred humanity
which he hath immediatly vnited to
himfelfe , & by the power which frō
all eternity he hath as God ; and by
that which in Tyme was communicated to him as man; he is to make
this vifible and exteriour *Iudgment* ,
this being an execution of the interiour inuifible *Iudgmēt*, which is made
of all the moft Bleffed Trinity . And
although this exteriour *Iudgment*, be
alfo afcribed to the Father , and to all
the Bleffed Trinity , as to the prime
caufe of all things, yet he who is the
immediate executour of this *Iudgement*, is Iefus Chrift the Sonne of the
liuing God ; becaufe the facred Humanity is only vnited immediatly to
the

the perfon of the Sonne , & that Humanity doth make this *Iudgment* , as
the inftrument of Diuinity.

Now (b) an immenfe benefit, and
an imcomprehenfible mercy it was,
for God the *Father* to giue vs Chrift
Iefus for the *Iu ge* of our caufe, as he
is man, as he is our brother, and our
Sauiour If a delinquent were in prifon for greiuous Crymes , deferuing
death, and that he had a brother who
moft tenderly loued him , and efteemed him , and did fo much defire his
liberty , and his good , that to deliuer
him out of prifon , and from death,
he had fpent his fortune, and had ex-
pofed himfelfe to many troubles, and
euen to the hazard of death; and if
the king fhould affigne that brother
of the party for the *Iudge* of his caufe,
with Soueraigne power , to *Iudge*
him without appeale; what kind of
fauour , what clemency would it be,
which heerin fhould be vfed towards

(marginal note:) (b) An vnfpeak-able be-nefit of God who gaue vs Chrift our Lord for our Iudge.

C 3   that

that man ? How full of ioy and comfort would he be, vpō the naming of such a *Iudge* ? How confident and secure would he make himself, that the sentence would be full of pitty , and as fauourable to him , as possible his cause might beare ? Well therfore , since all men , according to the (c) ordinary law are faulty and guilty, & it being necessary , according to the diuine Iustice and wisedome , that *Iudgment* be giuen vpon them ; & the cause of all them , who haue comitted mortall sinne, being so important, that either they must be condemned to immense & euerlasting torments , or be declared not guilty , but worthy to enioy the kingdome of heauē; what greater fauour, what clemency could be desired, or euen thought of , then that God the *Father* should be pleased to giue vs, for our *Iudg, Christ Iesus*, who is our brother , and of the selfesame nature with vs ; and who

loues

(c) From which Christ our Lord & his B. Mother are excepted .

loues vs with an vnfpeakeable loue;
and who doth fo much efteeme, and
defire both our liberty, & our glory,
that for the procuring therof, he hath
offered himfelf to moft bitter paines,
and fcornes, and euen to the death
of the Croffe? O how great a comfort, O how incomparable a ioy is
this, for thofe fonnes of *Adam*, who
feele the greatnes of this benefit? O
how confident, and fecure ought
they to be, that *Iudgment* fhall goe
vpon them with greate mercy; and
that the rigour of *Iuftice*, fhalbe té-
pered with much pitty; and that the
fentéce fhall paffe in fauour of them,
for as much as fhalbe poffible, without impeachment of the holy law, &
moft fweet ordination of Almighty
God.

CHAP.

CHAP. II.

Of the great desire, which Christ our
Lord hath (for as much as concerneth
him) not to condemne any one, in his
Iudgment, *but to saue them all.*

THIS most mercifull *Iudg*, hath
giuen vs some most euident testimonies, of the most ardent desire
which he hath, not to condemne
vs in his diuine *Iudgment*; but to deliuer vs as free & safe, & that the sentence may wholy passe in fauour of
vs. One of these testimonies, and that
a very admirable one, is this; That
before he would come, the second
tyme, to make an *vniuersall Iudgment*
of sinners, & to condemne & punish
(a) Marke such as he should finde to be faulty,
this excel-
lent do-   (a) he came, in that first cõming of
ctrine, for his, to passe a *Iudgment* vpon sinns
it is ful of
truth and themselues; to destroy, and to con-
comfort. sume, and to depriue them of being,
                                          and

and life; and in like manner alfo to
paſſe a *Iudgement* , againſt all the enimies of our ſoules : namely the *World,*
the *Fleſh*, and the *Diuell* ; and to ouercome, and diſpoſſeſſe them of all
power, and Tytle, which they might
make to men; and to defeate thoſe
forces which they mainteyned to the
preiudice of mens ſoules; and to giue
men ſtrength , and meanes , wherby
they might defend themſelues, and
obteine perfect victory againſt them
all . That ſo , when he ſhould come
to paſſe a *Iudgment* vpon men , he
might finde them free from ſinne ;
and if not all of them , yet ſo many,
at leaſt , as would take profit by the
grace he gaue them; and conſequently
that he might haue nothing to puniſh
in them . Yea and moreouer, that he
might finde them conquerours ouer
their enemies , that ſo he might giue
them that reward of glory , for their
victory, which he had promiſed to

ſuch

such as should ouercome.

This is that high *Mystery* which Christ our Lord discouered to vs in the Ghospell, somtyme saying, *That he came not to Iudge the world, but to saue the world.* At other times he saith, that he came to make iudgment vpō the world, as he teacheth vs by the *E-uangelist* saying, *I came into the world to Iudge it.* And yet in another place: *Now is Iudgmēt to passe vpon the world.* Our Lord meanes to say heerby, as himself declares, That at his first cō-ming when he came, in a mortal and passible body, he came not to passe a *Iudgement* vpon men, to chastise & condemne the wicked, by doing Iustice, and pronouncing a sentence of condemnation against them. For if he had come to this end, and that he would haue passed this *Iudgement* at his first comming; he would, in effect, haue bin obliged to comdem-ne all the world; for, in effect he
found

Ioan. 3.

Ioan. 12.

Ioan. 8.

found them all in fin ; and euen thofe few Iuſt perſōs who were free, were ſo, in vertue of his being come to ſaue them. And if that firſt coming of his, had beene to *Iudge* men , euen thoſe few had alſo bene in ſtate of ſinne, and had beene condemned . He therfore explicates himſelfe by ſaying, *I came not to iudg the world, but to ſaue it*, That is, I came not as a Iudge, but as a Sauiour, I came not to condemne ſinners by doing Iuſtice on them , & by paſſing a ſentence of condemnation againſt them ; But (b) I came to ſaue them , by ſuffering and dying for them, and by communicating my Iuſtice and merits to them ; that ſo I might free them from ſinne , and Iuſtify them ; and giue them the ſpirituall health of grace , and of eternall glory . And to this very office of ſauing men, is ordeyned that *Iudgement*, which he ſaith he came to make in that firſt comming, and which he

was

(b) Chriſt our Lord deliuereth no man from the paynes of hell , by his ſacred Paſſion, but ſuch as firſt are deliuered by it from ſinne.

was to paſſe againſt ſinnes,& againſt the diuell alſo in fauour of men. So doth he declare himſelfe, ſaying: Through my Paſſion and Death, Iudgment is now to paſſe, and ſentence is to be giuen, in fauour of the men of this world, againſt the diuell. For till now, he held men ſubiect, and captiued vnder his power and tyranny; but now, by the payment which I am making for thē, they are to remaine ſafe and free. Now, the diuell, who is the Prince of this world, who held men ſubiect vnder ſinne, is to be depoſed from that dominion which he held in the world; for innumerable ſoules, which were captiued in error and ſinne, are to be conuerted and ſaued; and remedy ſhalbe imparted to them all, wherby they may be deliuered from him, and may obtaine eternall glory.

So alſo, in that firſt cōming of Chriſt our Lord to ſaue mankind, he

he made a kind of diftinguifhing and
deuiding *Iudgement*, betweene the
good, and the bad; the ele&t, and the
reprobate. For when he was preaching, and working miracles, and
procuring the faluatiõ of the world;
fome did profit by his comming, re-
ceauing his fayth, and obeying his
Ghofpell, & participating of his merits. And others againe, becaufe they
would not belieue in him, nor ferue
themfelues of his remedyes, did ftill
remaine in their fins; yea, & through
their ingratitude, and the hardnes of
their harts, they grew therein. And
thus by the occafion of the comming
of Chrift our Lord, the diftinction
grew more apparent, betweene the
faythful & the vnfaithfull; between
Iuft perfons, and finners; betweene
the elect, and fuch as were reproued
by God.

For they who receaued the faith
of Chrift, & did follow him, by the
imitation

imitation of his life, & by the taking vp of his Crosse, according to their (c) present iustice, were iust persons; & as long as they did perseuere, they had signes in them, of being predestinated; and they who receaued not the fayth, according to their then present state, were wicked & reprobate. This did our Lord declare, whē he sayd : *I came into this world, that they who see not, might see; & they who see might be blind.* Whichwas as much to say, Vpon my comming, did this iudgment follow, and this distinction was made amongst men; that many who in their soules were blind, through ignorance and errour, and vice, and who did not see the truth, nor did walke in the right way to heauen, by beleeuing in me, with a liuely fayth, they I say, might see the truth, and follow it. And that many others, who saw, and had knowledg of the Scriptures, and did know the law,

(c) That is according to the state, wherein they were at that tyme.

law, and the Prophets; & who both in their own, and in the peoples opinion, & estimation, were held wise, and had a spirituall light wherwith to looke into diuine things; they, I say, for their pride and ingratitude, should remaine blind; and, going astray from the right way, should not find their errour and perdition.

Another diuine and most singular testimony, which Chrift our Lord hath giuen vs, of the desire which he hath, in this iudgment of his, not to finde any sinnes which he might punish, nor any sinners whom he should be so obliged to condemne, is, That (d) at his first comming he made a law, which was to laft till the end of the world, wherby he gaue faculty to all sinners, that during the whole tyme whilst their life should last, they might passe a *Iudgement* vpon themselues; acknowledging their sinns, and accusing themselues there-

(d) Let all Angells adore him for this ineftimable benefit to men.

therof with greefe , and confeſſing them to a Prieſt , who ſhould hould the place of Chriſt our Lord ; and ſatiſſying for them, according to the iudgment of the ſame Ghoſtly father, and that they performing this , he would not , in his *Iudgment*, either cõdemne or puniſh them , but would declare them to be *not Guilty* , and would impart the kingdome of heauen to thẽ . And that ,if hauing once paſſed this *Iudgement* vpon themſelues , they ſhould yet return againe to ſinne , & become abnoxious *her*by to eternall condemnation ; yet ſtil as long as their life ſhould laſt , they might returne to paſſe the ſame *Iudgment* vpon themſelus ,as often as they would ; and that if they ſhould do it according to (e) *Truth*,he would not condemne them , but would admit them into his company , and make them happy . O *Iudgment* which is ſo deerely ſweet ! O *Iudge*, who is ſo ful of

(e) Confeſſing them all clearely with great ſorrow & firme purpoſe of amendmẽt

of mercy ! and how vnanſwerable is it proued by this moſt pitteous *Iudge*, that his intention and deſire, is not to puniſh but to pardon; nor to condemne, but to abſolue and ſaue; ſince before he comes to paſſe his *Iudgment*, he vſeth ſo many meanes, & applyes ſo many remedies, to the end that he may finde no ſinnes to puniſh, nor no ſinners to condemne.

If an earthly *Iudge*, had his priſon ful of delinquents & theeues, & murtherers, and ſhould make a kind of agreement and bargaine with them, that (f) euery one of them might chooſe what friend or kinſman of his owne he would, and in ſecret ſhould declare his offence to him, deliuering to him the whole truth, and vndergoing but that penalty which he ſhould impoſe vpon him for the ſame; And that, vpon ſome day of the ſame yeare, himſelfe would come to the priſon to *Iudge* them; and that he

(f) Conſider ſeriouſly heerof & admire the infinit goodnes of God in that, wherein the blind world thinkes it hath hard meaſure, namely in the Inſtitution of the Sacrament of Conteſſion.

would

would pronounce them to be free,
who had declared their offences to
friend or kinfman of theirs; & who
had performed the penalty which he
had impofed; and that he would only cōdemne thofe others, who would
not haue recourfe to that remedy ;
what would you fay of this *Iudge*, &
of this agreement ? You would fay ,
that there nether is,nor euer was,nor
euer will be in the world any Iudge,
who fheweth , or is to fhew any fuch
mercy; nor who euer made , or will
euer make any fuch Capitulation ,
with perfons who had deferued to
dye; nor are there any laws on earth,
which can permit any fuch thinge.
And if there were any *Iudge*, who
would fubmit himfelfe to the like cō-
dition , there would no delinquent
be found , who would not ioyfully
performe this agreement , and fo be
declared for not guilty .

     Well then, Chrift Iefus, the E-
ternall

ternall *Iudge*, and who is of infinite
power and Maiesty, doth shew this
mercy to all such sinners as are worthy of eternall death. And he hath
made this bargaine, and agreement
with them all; and that is yielded to
by the laws of heaue, which the laws
of earth will not endure. Let vs therfore serue our selues of this mercy,
let vs performe the articles of this a-
greement; and let vs, in tyme, passe a
Iudgment vpon our selues; let vs confesse our sinnes with true sorrow; &
let vs amend our liues, to the end that
when at the houre of our death, in
the *particuler Iudgment*; and at the end
of the world in the *Vniuersal iudgment*
we shal come before this great *Iudge*,
he may find no sinnes to punish or
condemne in vs. For it is sayd by S.
Iohn the Apostle, concerning this
Lord: *If we confesse our sins, repenting* ᵗ. Ioan, ᵗⱼ
our selues truly of them, before God and
his substitute, God is iust, and faithfull,

in

52 THE IVDGE.

in fulfilling the promises, and rewarding the merits of Chri our Sauiour; and so he will pardon vs our sinnes, through his merits, and will cleanse vs from all wickednes, as he hath promised.

O most vnhappy men who deferring to do pennance, and to make amendment of their liues, despise this mercy of God, as S. Paul sayth by making ill vse thereof; *And (g) by this meanes they treasure vp the wrath and punishment of God for themselues, against the day of his wrath, which is, that, of his Iudgement.* These lawes of mercy were not made, nor are they proclaimed vnto men, to the end that thereupon, they should take such a wicked strange presumption to sinne; but that, if they haue sinned, they should not be dismaid: but that in hope of this diuine mercy, they should instantly correct themselues, and reforme their liues and obtaine pardon. So doth the glorious Apostle

S. iohn

Rom. 2.

(g) Woe be to thē who will needes be wicked euen because God is so infinitely good.

S Iohn aduertife vs; for hauing fayd:
*That if we confeffe our felues well, God
will pardon vs,* he inftatly addeth this, 1. Ioan. 2.
*Thefe thinges haue I written, to you my
children, to the end, that you may not
finne but that you may fly from finne at
full fpeed but yet if any man do finne,
we haue an aduocate before the Father.*
That is to fay, let him not be difmaid,
nor out of hope; but let him inftantly be conuerted to God, confeffing
his finnes, and doing pennance for
the fame; becaufe we haue an Aduocate and Mediatour before the e-
ternall Father, which is Iefus Chrift
the Iuft, and the very fountaine of
Iuftice, who made fatisfaction for al
our finnes.

D 3   CHAP.

CHAP. III.

Of the benefit which Christ our Lord im-
parteth to vs , in giuing vs to vnder-
stand, and feele the grieuousnes of
sinne , by the meanes & manner of his
Iudgement, to the end , that we may
in tyme do pennance for it .

ANOTHER most singular be-
nefit , which Christ our Lord
imparteth to vs , vnder the quality
of his being our *Iudge* ; is to make vs
know and feele, the grieuousnes of
of sinne, that so we may be drawne
to abhorre it greatly , & to conceaue
a true feare of falling into any offence of God . This knowledg, and this
holy *Feare* do we fetch from the consideration of that diuine Iudgment ,
since notwithstanding that Christ
our Sauiour , is of his owne Nature
most pitteous, and most benigne ; &
be-

being the very fountaine of pitty and
mercy; and being most profoundly
meeke, and sweet, and the very fountaine of sweetnes; and being so great
a louer of men, that he dyes for them;
and so much desiring, and esteeming
the saluation of their soules, that he
giues his life for the same; we (a) yet
see, that in his *iudgment* he will come
extremely full of cause, to make vs
horribly feare; and most terrible wil
he be in the highest degree, and full
of wrath and fury, & for zeale of iustice against sinners He will come
sitting downe, vpon those horses of
the heauen which are the cloudes; he
will come in a warlike manner., accompanyed by all the squadrons and
armies of heauen; he will draw with
him the whole world of creatures,
being all ranged & placed in forme
of battaile against sinners . Yea, and
euen the very Saintes, and Blessed
soules themselues, who are so full of

(a) The
terrour
wherwith
Christ
our Lord
will ap-
peare, at
the later
day .

Matt. 25.

Sap. 5.

Sopho.c.1.

D 4   pitty

pitty, and haue beene the Aduocates
of sinners, will come armed, & shall
be made both Iudges, and the Ministers of diuine Iustice against them.
He shall haue, for the Messenger
Psal. 96. which speakes of his comming, a
most furious fire, which shall burne
and purge all corporeall creatures; &
a most hideous frightfull sound of
mysterious trumpets, which shal sped
themselues ouer the whole world; &
shall make all creatures tremble; and
shal passe and pierce euen to the low-
est bottome of hell, and shall make
those soules spring out of those infernall habitations of theirs, full of horrible confusion, to resume their bodyes and appeare in *Iudgment*. In this
manner doth the Scripture describe
the comming of Christ our Lord to
Iudgement.

Let vs now consider, who it is
that causeth this mutation of Christ
our Lord. Who changeth him in so
strange

strang a fashion? Who maketh him,
of most pittifull, so extremly fierce?
Who, of most profoundly meeke, so
full of wrath? Of must delightfully
sweet, so full of fury and terrour? Of
peaceable, so giuen to warre? Of a
refuge and shelter for sinners, to be
growne such a seuere punisher of the
faulty? Sinnes (b) they are which
cause this great mutation, and which
do so farre estrange him from that
most benigne, and sweet condition
of his. The hatred and profound
detestation which he hath of sinne;
the liuely feeling he hath, to see himselfe so foulely offended; the greiuous
weight which our faultes do carry
in his diuine presence, wherby his
will is transgrest, and his law despised, do make him grow so frightfull,
and so very fierce, towards the doing of iustice, and taking vengance
vpon sinners. So saith the Apostle of
Christ, *Iudas Thadæus*, speaking of

(b) See heere, if sinne be not a dangerous companion to liue withall.

Iud. 1.

D 5   this

this *Iudgment* : *Marke well, for our Lord doth come accompanied with the innumerable troupes of holy Angells to passe a iudgment vpon all wicked men; to conuince them of all the euil workes which they haue comitted, and of all the euill words which they haue spoken, contrary to the law of God ; and to pronounce a sentence of condemnation against them*

Since then the hatred which God doth carry againſt ſinne , is ſo very great ; ſince the puniſhment which he will execute vpon ſinners in that *Iudgment* of his is ſo immenſe; O it is full of reaſon , that from the faith and infallible notice which we haue of this truth , all we , who are beleeuers, ſhould fetch a knowledge of the grieuouſnes of ſinne ; and a perfect deteſtation of the ſame, and a profound griefe and ſorrow for ſuch ſinne as we haue already comitted; & much feare in reſpect of them which

we

we may commit heerafter. That fo
we may fly them, and be freed from
the fury of that diuine *Iudgment*, and
from that fentence of eternal damna
tion, which is to be thundered out
against finners. For *(c)* this is the true
reafon, why this *Iudgment* is difco-
uered, and notified to vs, as *S. Paul*
affirmed whilft he was preaching to
the *Athenians* to this effect: *God doth
now anounce the truth of his Ghofpell, to men; to the end that all men, and
in all places, may do penance of their fins;
fince he hath, with firme deliberation,
ordeyned a day, at which tyme he will
iudg the whol world with great vprightnes of iuftice; giuing to euery one, that
reward and punifhment which his workes
deferue. And this Iudgment he will
paffe vpon the world, by the meanes of
Chrift our Lord; who, as man, hath authority from the eternall Father, to giue
vifible Iudgment vpon all men.*

(c) The
true vfe
which we
are to
make of
confide-
ring the
terrour of
the day
of Iudge-
ment.

Act. 17.

CHAP.

CHAP. IIII.

How we are to haue great feeling, of the grieuousnes of sinne, by reason of the demonstrations which shall be made by all the creatures of God before the Iudgement.

TO the end that from the declaration of the office which Christ our Lord hath of being the *Iudge*; & of the *Iudgement* which is to passe vpon the whole world, we may draw the great fruite of knowing and feeling the greiuousnes of sinne, and of abhorring it, and doing penance for it; and, that we may also draw from thence, a feare of sinne, and of the punishment therof, we will go declaring those points, and misteries of this diuine *Iudgment*; which may best discouer to vs the immensnes of the hate, which God doth carry towardes

wards finne; and of the punifhment
which he inflicteth vpon finners. The
firft point which doth difcouer to vs
the hate which God doth carry toward finne, is, that in this his terrible *Iudgment*, he will not onely punifh the finners who did offend him
by their fins, but (a) he will, after a
fort, punifh all the Creatures of the
whole world, wherby finners were
affifted and ferued. The *Sunne* fhall
grow darke; not as now it doth fom-
tymes, by naturall caufes; or in refpect
that any cloude may ouerfhadow it;
or becaufe the Moone may caft it felf
betweene it, and the earth, (as it
hapneth in the cafe of an Eclipfe)
but it is to be obfcured, by a fupernaturall and miraculous caufe; and fo it
is to be vnderftood, that for a while it
fhall loofe the whole light it had. The
Moone fhall alfo loofe her light. The
Stars fhall fall from heauen either becaufe when they are without light,

it

Matt. 24.

(a) How
infenfible
creatures,
fhall after
a fort be
punifhed,
for ha-
uing been
made the
inftrumēt
of mans
fiane.

Ioel. 2.

it shall seeme to be , as if they were
fallen , or els for that , in very deed,
they shall dislodge themselues from
that high firmament , where they are
fixt, and for some tyme shall fall from
thence, and deteine themselues in the
ayre , till they returne againe into
their place.

The *powers* of the heauen shalbe
moued, that is, those celestiall bodies,
with their naturall vertue shall tremble, and so shift their places, as in an
earthquake the earth is wont to do;
or if it be vnderstood of *Angells*, the
meaning is , how in that day , they
shall make some kind of spiritual de-
mostration, & motion of great admi-
ratio. The *Sea* shalbe troubled, & shalbe moued in a most woderful maner,
and with the waues thereof, shall
make such a hideous noyse, as will a-
stonish the whole world ; & oppresse
and afflict with excessiue feare and
horrour, the harts of mortall men , &
                                    will

will make them euen whither againe
with woe. The *Earth*, shall tremble, *2. Pet. 3l*
and shalbe open in many partes, and
shall disclose euen the pits of hel. The
Ayre, with the same *Earth*, and *Sea*,
shall burne by that most ardent ouerflowing of fire, which shall consume
al the liuing bodyes, of fishes, beasts,
and men. God in his law, comman- *Deut. c. 13.*
ded the children of *Israel*, that when *v. 20.*
they should be to fight against the I-
dolatours, and Pagans (who dwelt
in the Land of Promise, and whome
he was pleased to punish for their
sinnes) not only that they should kill
the men, but euen the very beasts,
which did them seruice; and so in
particuler he (ᵇ) exacted this of
Saul, when he went to fight against (b) A sign
the *Amalecites*; and because he did of this
not punctually comply with this cō- truth in
mandment, but suffered some of the Testamēt
Cattle to liue, God was offended, & *1. Reg. 3.*
Saul was punished.

Let

Let vs now fee why God did not content himfelfe, with caufing the men who had finned to be put to death, but the beafts alfo, which had no fault. It was to make men vnderftand and feele, that finne is fo great a mifcheife, and is fo worthy to be abhorred and punifht, and that God doth indeed, fo much abhor it, that it is a moft côuenient thing, not onely to punifh finners with eternall tormēts & death, but to deftroy alfo, and confume, and as it were to cha-ftice, the creatures wherof they did ferue & help thēfelues towards their finnes. Therfore is it, that refoluing in the *Vniuerfall iudgment* to chaftice the wickednes of all men, in a moft complete manner, he will not content himfelfe to deliuer ouer finners themfelues to thofe eternall ardours of fire, & thofe other immenfe paines of hell; but to the creaturs alfo wher-of they made fome vfe in finning, he

giues

giues as it were a kind of payne, and
punishment, in detestation of the sins
themselues ; as also, to the end that
they may be purged, and cleered frō
that indecency, and deformity which
grewto them, by the seruice, which
they did to sinners. For thus it is, that
the *Sunne*, the *Moone*, & *Stars*, which
did illuminate sinners whilest they
were committing their sinnes, shalbe
depriued by him for a whyle, of all
the light, & beauty which they haue,
& he shall conuert it into thick darknes. And as for the *Sea*, & the *Earth*,
& *Ayre*, which gaue food to sinners,
& did maintaine them, whilest they
were offending God, he will make
them as it were feare, and tremble, &
will depriue them, for a tyme, of the
naturall quality and disposition they
haue ; and will consume, and kill all
those liuing creatures, and plantes,
which were the food of sinners ; and
wil destroy al those buildings, which
E   were

were the habitation of wicked men.
And thus, through the mutation, &
demonstration, & desolation which
in the *Iudgment*, God will shew in al
the creatures which serued sinners, he
doth teach and testify the infinite hatred which he hath against sin . And
he doth induce, & perswade vs , that
now, through the knowledge of this
truth, we may be drawn to abhor &
detest them; and that with a peniten-
tiall & holy life, we may cleanse our
soules, as well as possibly we can, frō
al fault & offence of his diuine Maiesty . *S . Peter* (c) doth admonish vs of
the good effect which we are to draw
from the change which is to be made
vpon the creatures, by saying to this
effect : *Since there is a day of the vni-*
uersall Iudgement to come wherin all the
creatures, for hauing serued sinners are
to be purged with fire and burnt ; inferre
my brethren from hence, how diligent ,
and constant it is fit for you to be , in the
leading

2. *Pet.*3.

(c) This
truth is
insinua-
ted by S.
Peter.

leading of a good life; and how holily and
purely you are to converse in this world,
and how vigilant, and carefull, it will
becom you to be, in erforming the works
of piety towards God; and of mercy tow-
ards your Neighbour; expecting with a
liuely fayth, that day of our Lord; and
approaching and drawing neere to him
with speed, not with paces of the body, but
with the desires & affections of the soule,
desiring and louing this day, and prepa-
ring to see your selues at that tyme, ac-
companyed with purity of life, and with
the exercise of vertue.

CHAP. V.

How Christ our Lord, discouereth the
hate, which he carryeth towardes sin,
by the so particuler account which he
taketh of them all.

ANOTHER mystery of this diuine *Iudgement*, discouering the
E 2   mighty

mighty demonſtration, and deteſta-
tiõ which God doth expreſſe againſt
the faults whereby he is offended; is
the ſo particuler accompt which he
will take of vs, & which we all muſt
giue, of all the facultyes or powers,
& al the ſenſes, both of our body and
ſoule; & of all the creaturs which we

(a) If you
beleeue
this point
of fayth
to be true
I ſhall not
need to
wiſh you
to looke
wel about
you.

haue vſed; and (a) of all the workes
which we haue performed, all the
wordes which we haue ſpoken, and
all the thoughts which we haue conceaued, how little ſoeuer they fall
out to haue beene; without leauing
out, ſo much as any one idle word, or
any one idle thought. We ſhall giue
accompt of how we imployed our
Vnderſtanding; if we did ſet it on
worke, vpon the inquiry and ſearch
of God, and his truth, and in contemplating on him, & his holy Cõ-
mandments, and the workes of his
handes, and the diuine words of his
mouth. As for the memory, we ſhalbe

be queſtioned, if we haue vſed it, in
calling our Lord God to mind, togeather with his preſence, his goodnes, his power, and all his benefits,
and mercies. We ſhalbe arraigned v-
pon the point of our Will, if perhaps
it haue beene buſyed, in the loue, and
eſtimation, and deſire of God, and
the accompliſhment of his Law, and
of his will ; and in the ſearch of all
thoſe thinges, which concerne the
glory of our Lord God.

We ſhall (b) giue account, of
how we put the ſenſes of our body
on worke ; if we imployed our eyes
vpon behoulding this fabrike of the
world, and theſe Heauens, and Elements, and the other works of God,
that ſo, behoulding in theſe creaturs,
the trace, and ſent which they carry
in them, of all his diuine perfections,
we may raiſe our ſelues vp by them :
So to conſider with our ſoules, the
power, and the wiſedome, and the

(b) We
ſhall not
only giue
account
of our
ſinnes, &
the facul-
ties of our
mind, but
alſo of the
ſenſes of
our body
and of the
vſe of all
Gods cre-
atures.

E 3   good-

goodnes, and the beauty of God, and
by this meanes, to loue and praise him
with our whole harts. So also, if we
imployed our ears, to hear the words
of the true God; and those instructi-
ons, and doctrines, & admonitions,
and examples, which were profitable to the soule; and in hearing the
sweet musicke of mans voice; and of
the instruments which he can vse, &
of the birds also of the ayre, so to stir
our selues vp, towardes deuotion, &
to contemplate the much sweetnes
of that Celestiall musicke; and so to
loue and esteeme the blessinges of
heauen. And concerning the Smell,
if we imployed it onely, vpon those
things which are necessary for mans
life; & through the sent of creaturs if
we aspir'd towardes the sweet sauour
of vertues, and of good example; &
of the glory of the next life. So also
for the Tongue, if it was mouing in
the prayse of our Lord God, & in offering

ring him deuout prayers, & in lear-
ning and teaching those thinges,
which are necessary both for our selues and our Neighbours; and in discouering, and confessing our sinnes
for the obtayning of pardon, and re-
dresse thereof, and in taking but that
food, which was necessary for the
sustenance of our life; and in drawing out of the gust & sauour of corporal meate, a consideration and feeling of the vnspeakeable sweetnes,
and sauour of those spirituall foods of
grace, and glory. So also, if we haue
imployed the sense of Feeling with
our handes, and all the rest of our body, vpon the onely taking of those
thinges, which were necessary for
the same body; and profitable for our
soule, and for our Neighbours, and
for the vse of our life, and for the exercise of the workes of Charity and
Mercy.

This good vse of all the powers

of

of our ſouls & ſenſes of our body doth
our Lord God demaund of vs , when
he ſaith , *Keepe thy ſelfe , and keepe thy*
ſoule , with great care ; and of this are
we to make a very exact accompt ,
in his diuine *Iudgement* . Wee ſhall
alſo giue accompt in the ſame *Iudg-*
ment of all our ſinnes of ſpeach ; ſuch
as are vaine Oathes , Reproaches ,
murmurations , curſings , ſcoffing of
our neighbours , and words of anger
and impatience , of lying, of ſowing
diſcord : Of theſe and others which
are either laſciuious , or curious, or
vaine, *of euery idle word* , ſaith Chriſt
our Redeemer , *ſhall men giue a compt*
in the day of Iudgment ; and that word
goeth for *idle* which is neither neceſſary, nor profitable . Accompt muſt
alſo be giuen of all ſinnes of deed ;
ſuch as are diſobedience to parents ,
and other Superiours , reuenge , ill
intreaty of our neighbours, diſhone-
ſty, iniuſtice, vſurping & detayning
                                    the

Deut . 4.

Matt . 12 .

the good, of others againſt right, vnlawfull bargaines, pride in gouernement, exceſſe in the furniture of houſes, of clothes, of expences otherwiſe, and in the intertainemēt of ſeruants; exceſſe alſo in dyet, in play, and in other ſuperfluous and vaine things: Of all theſe, and of all other euill deeds, accompt muſt be giuen, as *Ecceſiaſtes* ſaith; *All things* Ecclef. 12. *which are done by man, both good & bad, ſhall be preſented in that diuine Iudgemēt, to be there examined*; & for euery work which ſhalbe found erroneous and ill, he ſhalbe puniſhed. We ſhall giue accompt of al our thoughts, ſuch as are raſh Iudgmēt; conſents which are giuen to reuenge, or els vncleanes or voluntary delights, in any thing which is ill; or to inward hatred; or in fine, to thoughts which are vnprofitable For as the Wiſe man ſaith, *God will examine, & iudge the thoughts* Sap. 1 *of the wicked.*

E 5   Beſides

Besides this, we shall giue (c) accompt of our sinnes of Omission, which are the most in number, and ly most hidden from our sight. For hauing forborne to pray, to read good bookes, to fast, to performe other penances, and mortifications, and to confesse, and communicate. For hauing omitted to do the workes of Iustice, and mercy, in certaine cases, and at certaine tymes, when either some particuler precept, or the great necessity of doing those workes, did oblige vs to them. For hauing fayled to comply with many dutyes of our calling, and offices, to which we were bound by the obligations either of God or man. We shall giue accompt, how we haue profited by those spirituall and supernaturall graces, which God hath giuen vs; such as are his *Sacraments*; the guifte of *Fayth*; the Doctrine of the *Ghospell*; good *Sermons*, holy exampls, vertuous

(c) A point of great moment and little thought on.

vertuous conuerſations, the admonitions, and reprehenſions of our
Superiours, and Ghoſtly Fathers;
and the interiour inſpirations which
God hath giuen vs. We ſhall giue account, how we haue vſed our naturall and temporall benefits, as namely
our *Health*; if we haue imployed it
vpon the ſeruice of that Lord who
gaue it; Our *Tyme*, if we haue ſpent
it profitably; our *Reputation*, if we
vſed it to the glory of God, and the
good of our Neighbour. Our *Eſtate* &
temporal goods, if we haue imployed
them, onely to the ſuccour of the true
neceſſities of our ſelues, our family,
and our neighbours, and of thoſe
things which are profitable to the
life of a Chriſtian man, and to the
honeſt Condition of euery one.

The accompt which is to be giuen for theſe ſinnes of *Omiſſion*, and
the puniſhment which is allotted to
them, Chriſt our Lord declared in
that

that *Parable* of the *Talents*, when he told that vnprofitable seruant, that the *Talent* which God gaue him, (which are his naturall and spirituall guifts, as also his temporall goods) was not well imployed by him, nor vsed in those workes which were agreable to God; and he said thus to him; *Thou negligent and wicked seruant, since thou sayst that I am rigorous, and that I expect more then I laid out, why didst thou not put out that* Talent, *to profit which I gaue thee?* That is, *why didst thou not make the right vse of what I gaue thee, imploying it well in the exercise of vertue, in the increase of merit, and in the multiplication of good works?* And so, when he had rebuked this sloathfull seruant, he commaunds the ministers of his Iustice, to execute the sentence, which he giues against him, when he sayth, *Take that vnprofitable seruant, and cast him into exteriour darknes, which is that of Hell; where*

Matt. 25.

where there is lamentation, and euerlasting torment, through the paines of
intollerable both heat and could, & other
torments also, which are to be endured
there.

CHAP. VI.

*How Christ our Lord declares the dete-
station which he carryeth against the
sinnes of wicked men ; whereof they
are conuinced, by the sentence which he
pronounceth against them.*

THESE are the things, wherof
a man is to giue accompt in that
diuine *Iudgment* of God. And this is
that, which now is to be considered,
that so he may know how deeply
God doth feele the weight of sinne,
and consequently how to moue himselfe to detest it. And withall let him
ponder, how after, that Christ our
Lord hath demāded this accompt, of
the

thē whom he findeth to be culpable, for not hauing complyed with these obligations; but proceeded contrary to his commaundements: How, I say, that most iust *Iudge* will conuince them in that terrible *Tribunall*, before all the Inhabitants both of heauen and earth, saying to them in his man. ner.

(a) If this do not mooue thee, pray to God that it may, for els thou art in ill case.

You (a) *men*, *why haue you thus offended mee? why haue your done me so many Iniuries*, *I being your God, of infinity Maiesty, Goodnes, and wisedome? I being your Creatour, your Father, and your Sauiour, who for you did giue my life, and shed my bloud? Why haue you spoken so many wordes in affront of me? Why haue you wrought so many wicked deeds, in dishonour and disobedience to my Law? Why did you consent to those bad desires, and thoughts, whereby you came to cast me vnder the feet of those creatures, esteeming & louing them more then me? Me, whom you ought to haue*

pray-

prayſed, & glorifyed with your tongues;
whome you ſhould haue ſerued, and obeyed with your workes ; whome you ſhould
alwayes haue deſired and loued with your
whole harts; for whom you ought to haue
giuē your liues & a thouſand liues, if you
had been Maiſters of ſo many. Why haue
you ſo diſhonoured me, tranſgreſſing &
trāpling vpō my Precepts? Why haue you
exchāged me, with ſo extreme contempt,
for thoſe moſt baſe aduantages and gayns
of earth, and for thoſe moſt vaine delights, & guifts of creatures? Since you
confeſſed me by your wordes, to be your
Lord and God, why would you deny me
by your workes? Tell me you men ſince I
haue imparted to you ſo many ſupernaturall guifts, which I gayned for you, by
my Paſſion, & Death; A guift of Fayth,
and Baptiſme, whereby I made you
Chriſtians; a guift of Grace, whereby
I adopted you for my Children; ſo many Vertues, whereby you might adorne
your ſoules, & be enabled to worke well;
The

The guift of Sacraments *, which might conferre and conuey my* Grace *into your soules ; and innumerable inspirations, which might quicken you vp towardes vertue: and so many most high, and most pretious guifts, which I purchased at my so great cost ; why haue you set them at so low a rate? VVhy haue you despised thē, and permitted them to passe away, without being of any profit to you at all? More account did you make of the vanity of your descent, according to your linage of flesh & bloud, then of the fayth of Christians, and the adoption of the sonnes of God.*

More account did you make of money, which is made of dead mettall; & of the goods of this life, and of the vaine punctillios of honour, then of the blessing of my grace, and of those immense, eternall treasures of my glory: I hauing giuen you such a holy Law, a Doctrine so pure, so profitable, and so celestiall, that you might obserue and keepe it; hauing

giuen

giuen you so many Prophets, Apostles, holy Doctours, & so many Preachers, and
teachers of my Ghospell, to the end that
they all might counsaile, & perswade you
to the obseruation of my Commandmēts,
and to the accomplishment of my will; yea
and my selfe, being come visibly downe to
earth in flesh & bloud, to teach & preach
this Law to you, by the very wordes of
myne owne mouth, why haue you made
no more account of this law, nor complyed with my will, nor obeyed my wordes?
Why would you rather do that which Sa-
thā that did tempt you to, thē that which
was commanded you by me? VVhy would
you rather follow, and obey that peruerse
enemy, who abhorred you, and endeauoured nothing but your damnation, then
me, who am your God, & who was your
Father, & who loued you, and did procure your saluation & euerlasting glory?
Tel me yet further, O you vngratefull mē,
since it is I who gaue you life, & health,
and temporal goods, & space of tyme,

F   that

that you might sacrifice it all to my seruice; how commeth it to passe, that you
would needs imploy it in offence of me? I
gaue you life, I say, and health, and
strength, whereby you might haue ac-
quired vertues, and haue exercised good
workes, and so you might haue (b) meri-
ted eternall happines. And you on the o-
ther side, haue imploied it in the pursuite
of vaine honour, & of pleasing men, for
certaine interests which passe and perish;
and in the search of those deadly delights
which now are carrying you on, towards
eternall torments. I gaue you temporall
meanes, for the necessary supply of this
life, and that you might relieue the miseries of your Neighbours; and you haue
wasted them, vpon the foolish complements
of the world, and vpon banquets, which
serued not for necessitie but for gluttony;
and vpon certaine attires, & ornaments,
which did but serue for vanity; and vpon
sports, and other vicious imployments. I
gaue you Tyme, to the end that you
might

(b) throgh
the passiō
& promise
of Chriſt
our Lord
good
workes
arriue to
be meri-
torious,
and not of
themsel-
ues.

might imploy it vpon praying, and rumi-
nating, and meditating vpon my benefits
and mercyes, and vpon the Mysteryes of
my law, and in performing workes which
might haue relation to euerlasting life;
but you haue wasted it vpon vnprofitable
conuersations, and vpon wicked deedes,
which deserue to be rewarded with eternall fire.

These complaintes doth God
make against sinners, by his Prophet;
and there will he make them at that
day, with greater demonstration of
mislike, then euer, till that tyme, he
will haue shewed. And thereby he
will conuince them all, & they shalbe able to make no excuse or deféce,
nor haue so much as one word to answere; and so shall that be fullfilled
which the *Psalmist* sayth, *All wicked-* Psal, 106.
nes, that is, all wicked men, shal haue
the mouth stopped vp.

Let vs now consider, what e-
uery one of these sinners will thinke
F 2   with-

within himfelfe, in that point of the
diuine *Iudgement*, when (c) he fhall
see a Theater made round about him,
of all the creatures, both of heauen
and earth; and that himfelfe is placed
in the middeft of them; & that both
all the Angells, and men, and Diuels
are looking on him. And when he
fhall obferue, that his finnes are pu-
blifhed, and proclaymed before them
all; and not only his wicked words,
and workes, but euen all his bad defires, and thoughts; & when he fhall
perceaue that all that lewdnes which
he committed in the moft retyred
corners; yea and thofe impurityes,
which did not fo much as iffue out of
his hart, fhall then be cleare and pa-
tent to all the world. To fee that all
thofe Diuels fhal ftand accufing him,
& that his own very confcience is ftil
vpbraiding & códemning him. And
to fee the *Iudge* himfelfe offended, &
enraged againft him; and that he behoulds

(c) Make
this cafe
thyne
owne be-
tymes;for
one day it
wilbe thy
cafe,whe-
ther thou
wilt or no

houlds him with a countenance full
of terrour, and of reuenge, for iniu-
ryes receaued; and to see that hideous
pitt of hell, all open, in expectation
to swallow him vp; and to see himselfe so euidently conuinced, & that
he hath no word to plead for himself.
And (d) that finding himselfe hem-
med in, by such an excesse of afflictions, & such incomparable miseryes,
he cannot fly away, nor hath he any
one hole wherein to hide his head;
nor any one thing to alleadge, nor a-
ny one person to whome he may appeale, or by whom he may be succoured. For to defend himselfe against
the *Iudge*, is impossible, since he is of
infinite power. To deceaue him with
false informations, cannot be, since
he is of infinite Wisedome. To work
vpon him by way of presents or pe-
titions, is not to be thought of, since
he is infinitely iust. To goe in search
after Patrons, and Aduocats, is losse

(d) A sad
conside-
ration but
most cer-
tainely
true.

of

of labour. For in that day, neither
the Angels, nor the Apostles can intercede for any one, no nor euen the
(e) A hea- Queene (e) of heauen, and the mother
uy and of mercy, can plead the cause of sin-
moft def- ners in that day. The gate of pardon
perate and sauing mercy, is then closed vp,
cafe. against all the wicked; & all the iust
and blessed soules, shall approue of
the diuine Iustice, in that day; and
shall reioyce, in that it is to be executed; because so it is fit for the glory
of God our Redeemer. And then shal
that be perfectly fullfilled, which the
Pfalm. 57. Psalmist sayth: The Iust man, seeing the
punishment, and vengeance which is to be
taken vpon the wicked shall reioyce, not
for the payne which those sinners
shallbe subiect to; nor out of any desire of reuenge; but only for the zeale
they haue to the glory of God, & for
the loue they beare to his diuine Iustice.

CHAP.

CHAP. VII.

How Chriſt our Lord, diſcouereth the grieuouſnes of ſinne, and the hatred which he carryeth againſt it, by the laſt ſentence wherby he is to condemne the wicked, and the puniſhment which he inflicteth vpon them.

ANOTHER Article of the diuine *Iudgement*, which doth admirably diſcouer the exceſſiue hatred which Chriſt our Lord doth carry againſt ſin, is the laſt ſentence which he will thunder out againſt the wicked. As ſoone as he ſhall haue publiſhed their ſinnes, & conuinced them thereof, he wil deuide them from the company of the Iuſt ; and then turning his terrible and fierce countenance towardes them, he will pronounce this moſt hideous ſentence againſt them. *Depart* (ᵃ) *from me, you accur-*

(a) Our Lord deliuer vs from ſo great a miſery,

F 4

accurfed into that eternall fire which is prepared for the Diuell and the wicked Angells. Depart from me, who am an infinite good, and the fountaine of all benediction, of grace, of comfort, of ioy, of life, of faluation, & of glory. If then, they be deuided from that only fountaine of al Good, what kind of miferable thinges will they find themfelues to be? It is plaine that they muft find themfelues without comfort, without grace, without ioy, without repofe, or eafe; and ful, on the contrary fide, of all mifery, of all mifchiefe, & of all paine. Depart all you accurfed; becaufe *curfed are they, who breake the Commandments of the true God*; for the greateft ill of all ill, is fin, and to this ill do they fubmit themfelues who do any thing againft that which our Lord cōmads. So fayth *Dauid,* & fo doth the church fing euery day, when fhe fpeakes to God, *Curfed are they, O Lord, who depart*

part from keeping of thy Comandmentes. Pfal. 118.
In particuler manner are they *accurfed*
in the Law, who doe not offer the
firft fruits, and tithes of thofe things,
which God had giuen to them; and Matt. 3. 1.
curfed alfo are thofe others, who hauing promifed fome beaft, in facrifice, to Almighty God, do offer him
fuch a one, as is leane and lame, and
worth nothing Into all thefe curfes
haue you fallen, becaufe you haue
broken the Commandmēts of God,
and gaue him not the honour, and
glory, of all the good deeds which
once you wrought, nor of all the benefits which you receaued. And hauing confecrated and dedicated your
foules to our true God, by *Faith*, and
Baptifme; and being obliged to giue
him the beft and chiefe part thereof,
which is your loue, and obedience, &
fidelity, and a watchfull care to doe
him feruice; you did not giue this to
God, but to the world, and to your

owne will; and for thefe reafons you
are indeed accurfed, and your felues
are the authors of your malediction.

(b) Be at-
tentiue,to
fee whi-
ther the
wicked
are to be
fent, whé
they are
once dri-
uen from
God.

　　Let (b) vs now confider, whither
it is, that he fends them, when once
he driues them from himfelfe. *Go*,
faith he, *you accurfed, into euerlafting
fier*; & becaufe in this life you fought
for contentments, for delights, and
gufts according to your owne will,
againft the will of God, you fhal now
be burnt, body, and foule, with a
moft furious and impetuous fier, a-
gainft your will. And becaufe by finning you haue offended and defpifed
God, who is infinite Good, and an
infinite Maiefty, that fier fhall be infinite in the continuance therof. And
who now fhalbe the minifters of Iuftice, to torment thefe accurfed creatures? And with what companions
fhall they be forted, in that torment of eternall fire? *Go*, faith our
Lord, *into eternal fire, which is prepa-*
red

red for the diuell and his wicked Angells .
For the principall authors of any wickednes , the punifhement is princi
pally to be prouided ; and becaufe the
deuill , was the firft author of finne ,
therfore was the torment of eternall
fier , prouided firft for him . And becaufe wicked men did follow the
deuill in the fault , they fhall follow
him alfo in the paine . And becaufe
they chofe to obey the perfwafion &
will of the deuill , rather then the
commaundement and will of God ;
they fhall therfore haue him for their
tormentor , and companion , in that
euerlafting fier .

O what kind of paine , what
kind of torment is this which is prepared for the wicked! O what an (c)
huge Sea of paines and torments is (c) It is
this ; fo very incomprehenfible , tho- fad fwim-
rough the intenfenes and fiercenes , this fea.
and fo infinite in the continuance
therof ! The thing, which in this life
doth

doth moſt of all torment, and doth cauſe moſt exceſſiue paine, is fire. But the fire of this life, doth worke after a limitted manner; according to the naturail power which it hath; & it cannot paſſe beyonde thoſe confines. Wheras the fire of hell, howſoeuer it be of the ſame nature with this of ours, yet worketh it as a ſupernaturall inſtrument of God; and ſo it receiuesno other tax or limit, but the onely will of God. And (d) as the thinges which God doth take for Inſtruments, whereby he ſheweth mercy to ſuch as ſerue him, are ſublymed by himſelfe, aboue the power which they had in nature; and are enabled to produce admirable effects; As namely he exalteth the *water* of *baptiſme*, ſo farre as to be the inſtrument of iuſtifying a ſoule; and the *Balſamum* of *Confirmation*, and the **Oyle** of *Extreme Vnction*, to giue ſtrength and increaſe of grace; ſo the
                                    fire

(d) An excellent conſideration.

fire of hell, which is so deadly fierce
of his owne nature, is supernaturally
strecht vp, to inflict a kind of paine
and torment which is incomparably
more great, and fierce, then that to
which the whole power of nature
can arriue. And so it shall not onely
torment the body, but the soule with
all. And it shall not leaue anie one
part, or power either of body or soule vntormented; and the torment &
greife which it will cause, shalbe
greater then all, which either we can
say, or thinke.

The Prophet (e) *Isay* doth signify thus much when he saith, That
Topheth, which is hell, *is prepared for*
the wicked by God the eternall king, from
the begining of the world. It is mightily
deepe, for it is in the very Center of
the earth. It is mightily wide and
capable, for the receiuing of all such
as shalbe damned. The nourishment
and food which shall maintaine it, is
fier

fier, which shall neuer be quencht (as euen heere, the fier doth neuer go out, if alwaies it haue matter to intertaine it,) for the breath of God, as if it were some torrent of brimstone, doth inflame it. His meaning is, that as a mighty quantity of brimstone will inflame this fier which we haue, & as longe as the brimstone lasteth, so longe, doth the fyre also last; iust so, the will of God will kindle that fier of Hell; and as his will is eternall, so the fier can neuer haue an end. Now this fire, being supernaturally so fierce, and furious, to torment and burne; the wicked will not also faile to be very (f) well disposed, and prepared, to be tormented and burnt. Therefore doth the Prophet *Malachy* say, That they shalbe like straw. *The day of our Lord*, sayth he, *shall come burning like a fornace of fire: & such as are proud withall the workers of wickednes, shallbe like straw to be infla-*
                                        med

(f) How conbustible the wicked shallbe in the last day.

Malac. 4.

med; and the fire of that place shall burne
them. And *S. Iohn Baptist* saith, that
they shall be as straw; when he telleth
vs, that Christ our Lord shal come to
iudge. *He shall carry*, saith he, *in his*
hand his Fanne; and like a labourer he
shall cleanse his barn, which is his Church;
and he shall lay vp, in his granaryes, his
cleane and choice corne, which are the
iust : & the straw (which is the wicked)
he shall cast into vnquenchable fire. This
chaffe and straw, are thinges which
be easily kindled by the fire, & they
make a mighty flame; and so the wicked are made apt, and well disposed,
by the diuine iustice to be burnt, in
that eternall fire, both in body and
soule.

But yet, although they shall be
burnt like chaffe and straw, and to
be penetrated by the fire, from side
to side; yet are they neuer to be consumed, but they shall liue for euer,
and for euer shall their paine endure.
                                    The

Iob. 20.

The wicked man shall pay for his sinnes (sayth Sophar, the friend of Iob) but he shall not be consumed, nor shall he loose *either his being, or his life.* This

D. Thom. in additio- nibus q. 74.

fire, to which Christ our Lord will deliuer the wicked, is to be increased by that other fire, which shall come before him ; and wherewith, as hath been said, he will purge all the inferiour creatures. And he will also purge those iust persons, whome he shall finde aliue when he comes to iudge; which persons shal dye by that forerunning fire; and in a very short tyme they shal be purged, & they are to rise, with all the rest. And this very

(g) Marke now, or neuer.

(s) fire, when once the sentēce shalbe giuen, will wrap vp all the wicked, both in body and soule; and the earth opening it selfe, in many places, that fier, shall discend with them all, through those ouertures of the earth, into the bottomles pitt of hell; and the earth, shall then shut vp it selfe,

some

& some do hould, that the waters shal
then returne to couer the earth, as
they did when God first created the.
For the cause of his discouering the
earth from vnder the waters, was to
giue conuenient habitation to men,
and beasts ; and that cause growing
once to cease, the waters shall return
into their due place, and the wicked
shall remaine locked vp in the center
of the earth, enuironed vpon all sids,
with that fire of hell. And (h) being
couered first with the whole globe
of the earth, and next with the pro-
foundnes of the Sea , they are neuer
to get out, from that lamétable place,
and that euerlasting fire . *For as* S.
Iohn affirmeth, *They shalbe tormented*
in it day and night, for all eternity .

> *Titelm. l.*
> *7. de Cælo*
> *c. 4. Lauel,*
> *l. 4. Me-*
> *teor .*

> (h) The
> braue spi-
> rits of our
> tyme, will
> be might-
> ily to seek
> whenthey
> come hi-
> ther .

> *Apoc.* 20.
> 14 .

Nor shall this torment of fire ,
whereby the wicked are to be tormented go alone; but togeather with
that they shall suffer other most bitter paines ; whereof euery one wilbe

a kind

a kind of hell to the damned. They
shall haue such a cruell and fierce
rage of hunger, (¹) that if it were

(i) The
deadly
hunger of
hell.

possible, they would teare in peeces
and eate themselues ; and this so raging hunger they shall euer feele, in
all the moments of their tyme, nor
shall they euer be at peace. Withall,

(k) The
scalding
thirst of
hell.

they shall haue a most (k) scalding
thirst, which will afflict them in all
extremity. If a man who were sicke
of a burning feuer, should be, for
some dayes, denyed a draught of water, towardes the appeasing of his
thirst ; he would feele so much torment by it, that he would rather
chose death, then it. And what then
shall they feele, who burning in that
hideous fire, are possessed with such
a most raging thirst: wheras yet they
shall not get the least drop of water,

Apoc.14. for all eternity. For, as *S. Iohn* affirmeth, *The smoke of their torments shall
ascend, for euer and for euer ; and neuer
shall*

shall they rest, either by day or night.
They (1) shall also continue in that
euerlasting prison, bound hand and
foot; and so are they to be cast into
that fire, as Christ our Lord signifyeth, when giuing sentence against
him that came into the *Feast* (which
is the bosome of his Church) *without his wedding garment* (which is
charity and grace) he sayd thus to the
Ministers of his Iustice : *Bind him
hand & foot, and so cast him bound into
exteriour darknes, where shalbe weeping,
& gnashing of teeth.* That is, the wicked shall remaine obstinate, & hard-
ned for euer, without meanes of remedy, or deliuery. And this is, to
haue the hands and feet tyed vp; To
be incapable of doing any one work
or conceauing any one good desire;
in such sort, as that whatsoeuer they
shall do, or thinke for all eternity, is
to be wickednes and sinne. And as a
man, who being bound hand & foot

(l) The
indissolu-
ble chains
of hell.

Matt : 22.

G 2   and

and caft into the bottome of the fea, cannot fwimme nor fcape from being drowned ; fo thofe wretches can neuer wraftle out of thofe paynes . For if there could be any remedy, it muft be by pennance , and amendement of their liues ; but that can neuer be , becaufe they are to remaine obftinate in euill, and difabled to do any thing which is good .

These miferable damned crea- (m) The tures, fhal alfo be fubiect to moft (m) filthy offenfiue fmells, which fhall extrem- fmells of ly afflict and torment them. This is hel. fignifyed by S . Iohn who fayth, *That* Apoc. 14. *into that lake of fire* (*which is Hell*) *the* 19.20. *Diuell fhalbe caft* (who is the occafion of the paynes of Hell, and of death , (for which caufe he is called fometymes, by the name of death,and hel it fe fe) *& that into the fame lake, all* Aug . de *the wicked who are not written in the* ciuit. Dei *booke of life fhalbe alfo caft; and that this* l. 20.c.14 *lake of fire, shall burne with brimstone ;* which

which signifyeth the detestable smell of that horrible prison, which is caused supernaturally, either by brimstone, or some such thing.

These and innumerable other paynes there are, in that most hideous prison; and although they be all so immense, as that they exceed all expression; yet the ([n]) greatest of thē all, is hauing lost the glory of God; and then being to want it for al eternity. For as the greatest good, and suprem felicity of man, is to see God, and to enioy him : so the greatest misery, and mischiefe, and torment, is for euer to want the sight of God, & the possession of his celestiall Kingdome. This is that, which aboue all things, doth torment those most vnhappy soules of the damned; to see that they might haue gained an infinite good, and that they had tyme & commodity for it; and that through their owne fault, & negligence they

Riber . in Apoc.c.19 num.37.
(n) If thou belieue not this truth it is a sign that thou art extraordinarily in ill case.

G 3   gained

gained it not , nor did ferue themfelues well of their tyme , and of thofe
other meanes which were giuen thē
by our Lord for that purpofe . And
to fee , that innumerable other men
of their owne naturall condition, &
fraile like themfelues , doe , for the
good imployemēt which they made
of the guifts of God, obtaine to enioy fo great a good, and to poffeffe it
with a perpetuall fecurity ; whereas
they, by their negligence, or malice,
loft it : The remēbrāce heerof,which
for euer fhallbe imprinted in their
minds, will be fo liuely and frefh, as
that they will neuer be able to caft
it off ; and this will breed in them an
intollerable griefe beyond all griefs;
and a moft vehement indignation ,
& a hoat boyling rage againft themfelues, for hauing fo loft God . But
yet this torment doe they not feele ,
for the refpect of God ; for they doe
not loue,but do abhorre him, but on.
ly

only for the interest & profit which
they might haue had by his glory.
And this torment of indignation is
that, which Christ our Lord, did
signify by the gnashing of teeth,
which springeth from the inraged
wrath of the hart. That (º) excellent writer *Rusbrochius*, doth ponder
the grieuousnes of these torments very excellently well; and particulerly
he sayth, That the hauing lost the
glory of God, is the greatest of them
all; and he expresseth it, by these
wordes: *Belieue me, that whatsoeuer
can be sayd of the paynes of hell; if it be
compared with that which there is felt,
in very deed is lesse then a drop of water
is, in respect of the whole Sea; and yet
neuerthelesse, all those paynes of hell put
togeather, are nothing, in respect of that
one only payne, which is felt by hauing
for euer, lost the sight of God.* And of
this paine, S. Iohn Chrysostom said:
If thou put before me a thousand hells, they

G 4

(o) Note
this cer-
tain truth
so piously
deliuered.

Rusbroch.
Epist. 1.

Chrys. in
Matt. c.7.
hom. 14.

they are not all so great a mischiefe, as is to loose the glory of Christ our Lord, & to be abhorred and driuen away by him, with those (P) wordes: I know you not.

(p)O infinite affliction.

CHAP. VIII.

How the grieuousnes of sin is yet more discouered, by the causes, wh.ch Christ our Lord alleadgeth as the reasons of his Iudgment.

ANOTHER point very worthy of Consideration in this diuine *Iudgment* which discouereth also the mighty hatred which Christ our *Iudg* doth carry against sinne, which sheweth also the greiuousnes of those paines wherewith he is to punish the same, are the faults which he relates, and which he alledgeth at the tyme of his *Iudgment*, in the sentence of damnation, which he pronounceth
against

against the wicked, saying; (ᵃ) *I was hungry and you did not giue me to eate; I was thirsty and you did not giue me to drinke; I was a stranger and you did not harbour me; I was naked and you did not cloth me; I was sicke and in prison & you did not visit me.* For it is euident, that amongst all mortall sins, the very least, and they whereof men make least accompt and scruple, are the forbearing to succour their neighbours; euen in those cases of necessity wherin yet they are bound to do it, by the precept of Charity. And for this reason, Christ our Lord, who had no meaning in this relatiõ, which he makes at the tyme of his *Iudgment,* to reckon vp all those sins for which he is to cõdemne the wicked (for that would be a long (ᵇ)busines) did only speak of such as go for the lightest, & vpon which men vse to make the least reflection; wherby all men may gather and inferre concerning those

(a) So that men shall not be iustifyed by faith alone, since they are to be cãned for want of Charity,

(b) That is, it wold haue beene longe for Christ our Lord, to haue spoken of all a mans sinnes, in that speach of his.

Matt. 25

G 5   other

other great sins, for which he is to
passe the sentence of condemnation
vpon the wicked . And this following circumstance a man is to consider and ponder , euen in the very
bottome of his hart : If (c) these sins
of Omission, and negligence , in the
performing of the workes of mercy
(which in reason, and in the estimation and iudgment of all men are the
lightest of all mortall sins) be yet neuertheles so abhorred by Almighty
God , as that , in the vniuersall *Iudg-*
ment , he doth publish them in a particuler manner , as being very grieuous , and worthy of eternall condemnation ; and will complaine a-
gainst them , as against faults which
are full of iniury, and affront, against
his diuine and eternal Maiesty ; and
will proceed against such as fell into
them , as against his enemies ; and
will excommunicate them as *cursed*
people , dryuing them away for euer
out

(c) A most
necessary
consequē-
ce which
deserues
to be dee-
ply pon-
dered .

out of his company, and the communion of the Church triumphant; and
will deliuer them ouer into euerlasting fiers; and will execute the same
paines vpon them which are suffred
by the very Diuells themselues, in
whose infernall company they are to
be tormented, & that for euer; what
will he not be sure to do to wicked
men for the sins of cōmission, wherby
they offend their neighbours; which
are more expresse sinnes; and wherin, there is more malice shewed;
and which are committed by men v-
pon more deliberation. If the ouer-
sights and voluntary negligences in
not giuing bread to him who is hungry, or drinke to him who is thirsty,
or clothes to him who is naked, or
visits to him who is sicke & imprisoned, in cases when piety doth oblige
men to it, are yet so abhorred by
Christ our Lord, and so seuerely punished, what will he do to men for
those

those impieties, when a sinfull man will take from another the goods which he had honestly gayned; and if he robb him, or vsurpe it otherwise by vnlawfull and vnconscionable waies; and for those other sins, when one man takes the health and life from another, by wounding, and killing him, or doing it at least in his desire; and when he depriues him of his honour, and good name, by murmurations, detractions, and reproaches; or when he takes from him his wife, or his daughter, or his kinswoman by fornications or adultries, or the like? And (d) if negligence in releeuing the corporall necessities of ones neighbor when there is comodity for the same, be so abhorred and punished by Allmighty God; how much more will he abhorre and punish any slacknes in releiuing the necessities of soules, by teaching the ignorant, those things which are necessary

(d) The spirituall workes of charity are of farre more importance, then the sorporall

ceſſary to ſaluation; by reprehending
their vices; and by admoniſhing and
exhorting them to a good life, in
caſes of neceſſity and obligatiō. Thus
doth the bleſſed *Laurētius Iuſtinianus*
ponder this truth in theſe words: *If*
Chriſt our Lord in his Iudgment do ſo
exactly and preciſely examine & chaſtice »
the faults which are comitted, in failing »
to ſhew thoſe works of mercy which »
are expreſſed towards the bodies of »
men which dye; what kind of exa- »
men, and what kind of puniſhment »
wil he impoſe vpon their faults, who »
forbeare to ſhew the ſpirituall works »
of mercy which they ought to haue »
imparted, for the ſaluation of ſoules, »
which are immortall? Let him that »
readeth this conceaue rightly, and be
well aſſured that there is no doubt,
but that, as this latter fault is greater,
ſo ſhal the examen be more rigorous,
& the puniſhment more ſeuere. And
if the denying of any ſpirituall beni-
ſit

Laurenē á
Iuſtin l.
de humilit.

fit which is due to his neighbour for the good of his soule, be a fault of so high quality, how much more will it be so, to rob the soule of life, by giuing it wicked Counsell, and by teaching it false doctrine; and by inducing it to vice by all perswasions, and lewd examples. Let the good Christian passe on, and consider & ponder yet more deepely, that the sins which are (e) committed imediately against God, such as are the crimes of infidelity of seuerall kinds, of superstitions, and blasphemies, and Sacriledges in breaking vowes and promises made to God; and of periuries which draw God as a witnes of lyes, and falshood, be greater sins then they which are committed against our neighbours; and consequently the hatred which God doth carry against them, and the punishment which he wil execute for them, is incomparably greater.

(e) Sinnes cōmitted immediatly against God, are the greatest of all others.

From

From (f) hence the Christian man will gather the great necessity that he is in, to abhor in a most profound internall manner, all kinde of sins; and to flye them with a most watchfull care; & to feare them with his whole hart. For if the lighter sort of sinnes, and they wherof men are wont to make least accompt, are so publikely to be recorded & reproued in that diuine iudgment, & tobe sentenced as worthy of condemnation, and punished with eternall torments; the case is plaine, that the sins which are more greiuous, and in greater hurt & preiudice of our neighbours; and they againe which are of more imediate iniury, and affront to God himselfe, shalbe proclaimed in that diuine iudgment, to the greater confusion of sinners; & they shalbe more sharply rebuked by Christ our Lord, and more grieuously punished. And although the other torments were also

so

(f) The true vse which is to be made of this consideration.

fo eternall, yet thefe fhalbe greater
and more intenfe then they. For this
truth was reuealed to S . *Iohn* by the
Holy Ghoft, who fayth: *So much as*

Apoc. 18. *the wicked man hath glorified himfelfe*
and hath deliuered himfelfe ouer to vici-
ous pleafure: and fo much more, as he pre-
fumed of himfelfe , and lifted vp his face
of pride againft God, affronting his diuine
Maiefty with greater fins ; and fo much
more as he yeilded obedience to vice, in
contradiction to the law of God; fo much
greater torment shalbe impofed vpon his
body ; and fo much more greife and for-
row fhalbe inflicted vpon his foule .

CHAP.

CHAP. IX.

How a Christian is to draw a detestation of sinne, out of the consideration of this Iudgement of God; and great vigilancy in the leading of a good life.

THESE (a) are the points and articles of that diuine *Iudgment*, which discouer to vs the hatred, that God doth carry against sinne . And these we are to consider , with great attention; that so we also may gather this fruit out of the diuine *Iudgement* to abhorre sinne extremely, to grieue vnfaygnedly for those which we haue committed, to feare it with our whole harts, and to fly from it with cõtinual care. For it is all reason that we should abhorre that which God doth so highly abhorre ; and that we should be mightily grieued , for ha-

(a) For Iesus sake read ouer this Chapter with sober and sound attention,

H   uing

uing committed such things against
God, as he mislikes so much, & wherby he is so much offended. And it is
most iust, & fit, to feare a *Iudgment*,
which is so seuere, and ful of terrour;
and such torments as are so excessiue
and so without all end. And now,
that we may with the more efficacy,
rowse our selues vp towards a perfect
hatred of sinne, and a feare of the
diuine *Iudgement*, let euery one of vs
go casting vp his accompt, after this
manner.

(b) Resol-
ue thy
selfe to
suffereter-
nally in
hell if thou
refuse the
grace,
which
God is de-
sirous to
giue thee
euen very
now, if
thou wilt
concurre.

God (b) *who is my Creatour, hath
resolued, that the day shall come, when he
will* Iudge me, *and from this* Iudgment
*it is impossible for me to flye. So also hath
he resolued, that he will reward me in
this* Iudgment, *according to my works.
If he find me in the state of* Grace, *and
with the stocke of a good life in my hand,
he will giue me the reward of eternall felicity. If he find me in mortall sinne, and
that I haue ill imployed my life, he will*
                                          driue

driue me out of the sight of his glory, &
wil códemne me to euerlasting torments.
Now, that I consider my selfe, I see that
I haue lead a carelesse kind of life, & that
I haue committed many offences against
his holy Commaundmentes. If now, he
should call me to his Iudgment, I am
sure that I should be condemned; for I
haue not done pennance for the sinnes,
which I haue committed, nor haue I yet
reformed my life. At least I am in much
doubt of my saluation; for the pennance
which I haue done, was luke-warme; &
I haue sought to mend m life, but slack-
ly. It is necessary therefore, now, & euen
very now, that I change my course, that
I betake my selfe to my pennance, & that
I do it in good earnest. I will obey the
voyce of God, who commands me by Ecclesiasticus, saying: Before thou come
to the diuine Iudgement, prouide thy
selfe of workes, which may be holy
and iust, to the end that it may suc-
ceed well with thee. Before thou come

into the hāds of God, to be iudged by him, aske thy selfe the question, examine thy conscience well: passe an vpright Iudgement vpon thy selfe; reprouing thy selfe with griefe, & punishing thy faults with pennance; and so thou shalt find mercy in the sight of God; thou shalt find him a fauourable Iudge, and he will cast the sentence on thy side.

(c) Attention.

Let (c) the Christian man consider further, in the bottome of his hart, & let him reason thus within himselfe. If I (d) knew now that the end of the world and the Vniuersall Iudgment were to be held within ten or twenty yeares; it would more seriously worke vpon me, and would make me more carefull to do pennance, and to endeauour a totall renouation of my life; and I should more cordially feare the Iudgement, and eternall punishment of God, & the sinnes which make me subiect to euerlasting damnation. Yet certainly, for as much as concerns me, the day when I shall dye, is after a

(d) Of the litle difference, which there is to be for vs in substāce betweene the day of our death & the day of the last Iudgement.

sert

fort the very day of the Vniuersal Iudgement, *and of the end of the world.*
For the chiefe of that which passeth in the Vniuersall Iudgement, *and which maketh it to be feared so much, is the irreuocable sentence of eternall damnation which is then to passe vpon the wicked; &* (e) *that where a man shall then be lodged he shall lye for all eternity. And he shall then, no more, haue any vse of any creature of this world; or of tyme wherin he may do pennance, or procure saluation. Now this is, in effect, the same thing, which is to be done with me in the houre of my death. For then I shall be iudged; and if then I be found guilty, an irreuocable sentence of damnation shall passe vpon me; and where I shall then be cast, I shall remayne for euer; and in the* Vniuersall Iudgment, *there is no more to be done, but to confirme and proclaime the sentence, which was giuen in the particuler* Iudgment. *And in the houre of my death, for as much as concerneth me,*

(e) This maketh notagainst purgatory but shew-eth only that if a man dye in state of sinne, he shall continue so for euer: and if in state of grace, he shall also for euer continue so; thogh till all be satisfyed, he shal stay in purgatory and then he flyes vp to heauen.

the

the whole world is at an end; & so is the
vse of all the creaturs therof: since I shall
returne to it or them, no more; and so is
the Tyme also at an end, wherein pennance might haue beene performed, and
merit might haue been procured. If therfore it be so, that the houre of my death,
is to be the same thing for me, which the
Vniuersall Iudgment; and the end of
the world, and the same it is to be for all
men; and f since it is most certain that
the day of my death, will arriue eare
long; and that according to my age, and
to the tyme which men are wont to last
it cannot exceed twenty, or thirty years;
and since it is so casuall, as that perhaps it
may be care night; it followeth, as a most
iust and necessary consequence, that I
should, euen from this very instant, dispose my selfe to do pennance for my sins,
with greater care; and to make a totall a-
mendment of my life; & to do that which
Christ our Lord commandes me, saying:
Watch, for you know not the houre
when

(f) The
certainty
of death
and the
yncertain
ty of the
houre of
our
death.

Matt.24.

when your Lord will come; *and that
also which the Apostle* S . Peter , *in the* 2. Pet. 3.
*name of the same Lord , doth aduise me
saying*: Brethren the day of our Lord
will come like a theefe *Now the theef
who steales by night, comes without giuing any news of himselfe ; and then he
doth it, when he is lookt for least . Iust so
will christ our lord come to iudg vs in the
end of the world, and in the houre of our
death , and no man shall know when he is
to come; & the tyme willbe at hand when
many willbe least ready for it . Doe you
therefore earnestly labour to lead a vertuous life, that so you may be free from
sinne, and that . there be nothing in you
which may deserue reproofe ; but that ,
with a quiet and safe conscience you may
expect our Lord , when he shall come to
iudge .*

H 4   CHAP.

CHAP. X.

Of other Considerations, from which we may draw the detestation of sinne, & the care of leading a good life .

LET a man also consider with himself, the sentence, & punishment which followeth this *Iudgment* ; and let him be perswaded to feare God, vpon this ensuing reason. What (a) are those things, which a man in this life will not do, for the auoyding of paine and griefe ? A man who is in prison, and expects or feares a sentence of violent death , what doth he not, for the deliuering of himselfe ? He thinks of nothing , but how he may escape ; he neuer giues ouer to make friends, who may intercede for him ; he humbles himselfe to all such as are able to do him fauour , and to giue him helpe; he spends his meanes vpon Atturneyes & Lawyers, and in sending presents

(a) Is it possible that thou shouldest be so mad as not to be able to frame this argument in thyne owne person.

to

to such as may do him any good. A
mã who lyes sicke vnder great pains
which torment him day and night
without ceasing, being caused by
some surcharge of humours, which
he hath in his body, or by some sto -
ny grauell, which perhaps he hath
in his bladder, or by some Me-
lancholy, which is lodged at his
hart; what will he not do for his re-
couery? How willingly doth he imploy what he hath, in giuing fees to
Phisitians, and in paying of Apo-
thecaries bills, for druggs, which
way giue him ease? With what faci-
lity and diligence, doth he take pur-
ges; and permit that issues be made,
and buttons of fire be applyed; yea
and he endureth to be cut & opened,
offring himself to one extreme paine
& daunger, to excuse another which
is a greater, if he can tell how.

    If this be so, what then will it
be fit for me to do, that I may free my
H 5 self

selfe from thofe miferies & torments,
to which the wicked muft be fenten-
ced, in that diuine *Iudgement*. Which

(b) Tor-
ments
both into-
lerable, &
eternall.
(b) befides that they are, in thefelues,
extrem, beyond al that can be faid or
thought ; they are neuer to haue any
end , but in their contynuance , they
are to equall the eternity of God himfelfe. For as God , in his owne nature
is eternall , fo are thofe torments to
be eternall , by the determination of
God , which can neuer faile . Although thefe torments were no greater then for a man to be caft into fire,
fuch as heere we haue , (but fo as
that he fhold not dye of it for the fpace of thirty yeares) the very thinking
of it, would ftrike into him extreme
horrour; and there is nothing ima-
ginable which a man would not do
to keepe himfelfe from vndergoing
fuch a torment. Nay although it were
no more , but that a man were to remaine thirty yeares , laid in a bed ;
with-

without being able once to rife or
ftirre from thence , it would be of
intollerable paine to him ; and he
would performe things of very great
difficulty and labour, to deliuer himfelfe from the fame .

But what then will it be, to remaine in the fire of Hell , together
with all thofe other torments ,which
there are felt ; and that , for the fpace
of all eternity ; and what then will
it not be fit for a man to do,that fo he
may not be to endure thofe tormets?
And (c) to the end that a man may
haue fome little taft of this eternity,
let him thinke of fo many thoufands
of yeares which are to paffe ouer the
head of the damned , as there are
grains of duft in the whole world, or
drops of water in the fea , or moates
in the ayre ; and that at the end of all
thofe thoufands of yeares , they fhall
not get out of thofe torments , but
ftill fhalbe , as if they did but then
begin

(c) If thou
defire to
vnderftãd
eternity
thou muft
procure
to take it
thus in
funder.

beginne to suffer, and that then as many more thousands of years are so to passe; and then againe as many more; and that still, that wheele shalbe running round without any end. And let him also knowe, that by this so large contynuance, his torments are not yet to cease, nor to be in the diminution of a haires breadth; but that they shall be as (d) liuely felt at the end of so many thousandes of yeares, as at the first instant. Because those torments, do not worke after a naturall manner, that so they might be the lesse felt by custome, but they worke as instruments of the diuine Iustice, which is inuariable; and doth conserue them at the end of innumerable yeares, in the same force and fury which they had at the first. O with how great reason did the Prophet *Hieremy* exclaime to God & say : *Who is he that will not feare thee, O thou King of the Nations? Thyne is*

su-

(d) The tormentes of hell are not made more tollerable by a custome of enduring them a while.

Hier. 10.

supreme Dominion, and there is none like thee in wisedome and power.

By these Considerations, a Christian being assisted by God, will get, out of the diuine *Iudgement*, a great remorse and griefe for sinne, which doth so much offend God, and which is so greatly abhorred, and so greiuously punished by him. And (e) with this griefe, he is to accuse, and reprehend, and condemne, and with penances and mortifications, to inflict punishment, and take reuenge vpon himselfe. So did holy *Iob*, when he confessed saying : *Place me before God, and I will come to Iudgement, and consider what he is to do with me ; and I will loade my selfe with reprehensions.* For as *S. Gregory* (f) sayth vpon these wordes : *A man contemplating the so strict, and perfect examen, which God doth make of his sinnes in that terrible Iudgment of his, he turneth in, vpon, & against himself, & he reprehends himself*

with

(e) The cure of sin is pennance.

Iob. 23.

Greg. ibid. (f) Thus S. Gregory sayd & thus he did,

with griefe and sorrow, for the offences which he hath committed against God.

(g) A man is to carry a quick & watchfull eye ouer all his workes.

The (g) faithfull seruant of God, is also to drawe from this diuine *Iudge-ment*, a great watchfulnes and deligence, to consider well, and with attention, al the workes that he doth; and to see that they be good, and be wrought with a pure intention of pleasing God. Not being negligent in the performing of exteriour workes, & much lesse, giuing place in his hart to the desire or loue of any thing that is ill, or consenting to any thing which is contrary to the will of God; nor principally to seeke his owne interest in any thing, but onely the glory and good pleasure of God. To the end, that when our Lord shall come to iudge vs, he may find vs prepared, and may meete with nothing in vs which he will punish.

This Counsell was giuen vs by *Thess. 5.* S. Paul, who said, *You know well my bre-*

brethren, that the day of our Lord is to come vpon vs like a theefe in the night.
For although it be true, that when he will come to make the *vniuerſal Iudgment,* he will do it with great Maieſty and very manifeſtly to all the world; yet, for as much as concernes the tyme, the day, and houre, wherein he is to come, aſwell in the *vniuerſaU Iudgment,* as in the *particular,* he will do it ſuddenly and concealed; and ſo as that men ſhall not know either of the houre or day. He will come like a theefe, who hath a mind to robbe, when men are ſleeping and inconſiderat; ſo I ſay will he come, ſuddenly, & at vnawares to paſſe his *Iudgment,* vpon many when they liue careleſly in their ſinnes. Therefore (ʰ) we who are faithfull Chriſtians, and who by liuely faith are made the ſonnes of light; we, I ſay, muſt not ſlumber, nor giue place to the ſleepe of negligence and ſinne, as others are

con-

(h) **Take** heed of ſloath in Gods ſeruice.

content to do, who want this faith.
But let vs watch in prayers and good
workes, following the light of faith,
and the word of God; and let vs carry
our selues in al things, with sobriety:
That is, we muſt be very temperate
& moderate, as the Euãgelicall law,
& as the example of Chriſt our Lord,
and of his Saints doth exact at our
hands, both in our eating, drinking,
clothing, ſleeping, ſpeaking, and
whatſoeuer els. This fruit doth holy
Iob draw out of the conſideration of
of the diuine *Iudgement*, as himſelfe
expreſſed ſaying, *I did obſerue & exa-*
mine my workes, with much reflection &
care, to the end that none of them might
be wicked; and to the (¹) *end alſo, that*
all they which were good, might be well
done; for I know that in thy Iudgement,
thou art not to let any ſinne paſſe with-
out puniſhment. Which yet is to be vnderſtood of (k) ſinns, which formely
ſhall not haue beene purged and diſ-
charged by pennance.   CHAP.

Iob.19.

(i) It is not
Inough to
doe good
thinges,
but they
muſt alſo
be well
done.

(k) When
due pen-
nance is
done for
ſinne, it is
no longer
lyable to
any puni-
ſhment.

CHAP. XI.

How a Christian is to draw out of the Consideration of the diuine Iudgement, a great feare of offending God, that so he may fly far from it.

THE faythfull Christian, from the consideration of this diuine *Iudgement*, is to draw a very reall, & true feare of God. And this feare of God, and of his *Iudgment*, is the most particuler and proper fruite, which from that *Iudgment*, is to be drawn. So doth the Psalmist signify, when he speakes to God, and sayth: *O Lord* Psalm.118. *I haue feared thy Iudgments; and vpon the consideration how thou dost exercise them vpon the wicked, I haue conceaued an excessiue feare.* And *Salomon* his 2.Paral.6. Sonne, speaking to God in the prayer which he made in the Temple, declared the same truth by saying: *Giue*

I   *O Lord,*

O Lord, to euery one, in thy Iudgment,
*the reward which is fit for their workes;
& according to the desire of their harts,
to the end that they may feare thee, and
may walke in the way of thy Commandments, all the dayes of their liues.* And
the Angell, whome *S. Iohn* saw, did
say: *Feare our Lord, for the houre of his
Iudgement is come.* When a (ª) man
delights in wickednes, & yet calleth
to mind the diuine *Iudgment*, & the
punishment which God doth exercise vpon sinners, he doth conceaue
a *feare* of the payne; and being principally moued by that *feare* he abstai-
nes from sinning, which *feare* is a
feare of slaues, and therfore it is called *seruile* . And although this *feare*
be good, and doth grow from a root
which is supernaturall, it is yet imperfect, and insufficient for the obtayning of euerlasting life, or for the
iustification of a soule. Nor is it meritorious, but it is a ground from
whence

Apoc. 14.

(a) A ser-
uile feare.

whence iustification may rise, and it
is a disposition towards grace, wherby we may merit; and this it is wherof the Wiseman sayth: *That the* Feare
of God, is the beginning of Wisedome. Prouer. 2.
Which is as much as to say, That it
is a beginning for the obteyning of
an experimental knowledge of God,
which growes from Charity. And
so doth *Ecclesiasticus* declare it saying,
The feare of God, is the beginning of Cap. 25.
the loue of God. But (b) when a man (b) Of fi-
who loueth vertue, and is resolued lial feare.
to serue God, doth by cōsidering the
diuine *Iudgment*, ponder the grieuousnes of sinne, by meanes of the
seuerity of the same *Iudgment*, & the
excessiue greatnes of those paynes,
wherewith God doth punish it, and
therupon he doth incline himselfe to
a great feare of sin; and doth tremble to thinke of doing any thing,
which may offend the pure eyes of
God, this *feare* is a *feare* of sonnes; &

I 2   ther-

therfore it is called a *filiall feare*; because he feareth God his heauenly
Father , more then he doth the punishment , which otherwise is due to
him for the same .

So also, when a faithfull seruant
of God, through the desire which he
hath to flye from al offence of his diuine Maiesty , and in all thinges to
comply with his holy wil, doth settle
himselfe after a sincere , and serious
manner , to consider the *Iudgements*
of God , and those eternall punish-
ments and tormentes , whereby he is
to take vengance vpon the wicked,
thereby to moue himselfe so much
the more,to a feare of those *Iugdmēts*
and paynes; and the more to animate
himselfe to flye from all offence of
God , and to keep his diuine Commandments; this feare, howsoeuer it
carry a kind of respect to paine , is
not yet to be accōpted a *seruile feare*.
Nor doth it spring from selfe loue ,

but

but it is a *filiall loue* , and it growes
from Charity . Becaufe (c) in thefe
thinges which are morall , and voluntary, the nature and denominati-
on of the work, is principally taken
from the end at which it aymes. And
as a man who fhould fteale money
wherby he would enable himfelfe to
commit an adultery , were more to
be efteemed an adulterer then a theef;
fo the iuft man, who difpofeth himfelfe to feare the punifhment , due
to finne , that fo he may feare and
abhorre the finne , is rather to be ac-
compted to feare the finne , then the
punifhment. So therefore the feare
of this man , is a holy feare , and belongeth to a fonne, & friend of God;
& this very *feare* maketh a man iuft
and holy , yea it is euen iuftice and
fanctity it felfe This *feare* doth make
a man acceptable to God, and is meritorious of eternall life , and it maketh alfo the workes which proceed

(c) A clear
proofe of
the truth
which he
deliuered
before of
the two
Feares.

I 3   from

from thence, to be acceptable to God
and meritorious both of grace and
glory. Holy (P) *Iob* sayth of this *feare*,
The feare of God is wisedome it selfe.
And *Ecclesiasticus* sayth , *To feare God
is entire and perfect wisedome*. *A seruile
feare* is sayd to be *the beginning of wisedome*; because it disposeth a soule
towards *wisedome*: and so is this *filiall
feare* sayd, *to be very wisedome it selfe*,
because it imbraceth wisedom, it loc-
keth it vp , and it doth perfect, and
increase it. For he that hath this **feare**
hath the guift of holy wisedome togeather with it , which is that principall guift of the holy Ghost, wherby God is knowne and loued. And
through the exercise of this holy
feare, this guift is increased; and for
this reason the Wiseman sayth of this
feare : *That it is the fountaine of life* ,
because it giueth spirituall life to the
soule, and from thence do spring the
workes of life; since they be such
as

(d) The
places of
holy
scripture
reconci-
led which
seemed to
differ.
Iob . 18.
Eccles. 1.

Prou .14.

as are (^{e}) meritorious of eternall life.
For they, who after this manner do
feare God, as *Ecclesiasticus* sayth, do
procure with diligece, to pleafe God
in all things.

(e)throgh the grace of God in Chrift ourLord, & throgh his pro- mife.
Ecclef.18.

Let vs therfore , much , and
many tymes cofider this diuine *Iudg*-
mēt, that fo we may draw a holy *Feare*
from thence, and grow therin, and
conferue our felues therby, in a vertuous life, fo long as we fhall contynue in this pilgrimage; fo doth Saint
Peter aduife vs faying , *If you call him*
Father, as indeed he is (who is alfo our
God, and our Lord, and who as a moft
righteous Iudge, *fhall* iudge, *& reward*
euery one according to his workes) moft
iuft and reafonable it is, that during all
the tyme of our being in pilgrimage in
this world (as perfons who are banifhed
from the houfe of our Father) we should
liue in fuch feare, as becommeth his chil-
dren .

1. Pet. 1.

I 4   CHAP.

CHAP. XII.

*How it is very neceſſary, & ful of profit
that a Chriſtian doe exerciſe himſelfe
in this holy Feare; and accompany it
with the exerciſe of diuine loue.*

(a) A
doubt cō-
cerning
the exer-
ciſe of the
actes of
Feare and
Loue,
cleerely
ſolued.

BVT to this, one (a) may ſay, by
way of queſtion; Since the act, &
exerciſe of the *Loue* of God, is more
excellent, and acceptable then that
of *Feare*, why is it not better to exerciſe our ſelues alwaies in the *loue*
of God, and in the conſideration of
his benefits and mercies, and of his
goodnes, and *Loue*, and the reſt of
his deuine perfections, which may
induce vs to *loue*, then to be conſide-
ring his diuine *Iudgment* and the paines of Hell, which oblige vs to *feare*?

(b) The
firſt an-
ſwere.

To (b) this I ſay, firſt, That the act &
exerciſe of *loue*, is more exc llentand
acceptable to God, then any other act
of

of vertue, when that *loue* of God, is cleane and pure from faults, & from selfe loue. But (c) if a person shal only giue himselfe to the exercise of diuine *loue* (for as much as *oue* doth cause a kind of security and comfort to the soule) a man may grow from thence, many tymes, to be slacke in vertue, & forward to commit faults, and come to be remisse in doing of pennance, and mortifications, and admit of certaine delicacies, and so increase in selfe loue. And he may also come to presume vpon himselfe; conceauing that he doth greatly loue God; and by that very meanes, he goes disposing himselfe, to loose the same loue of God, by cōmitting veniall sinnes, & by increasing in them; he arriueth also to fall at last, into mortall sinne, wherby he doth wholy loose *loue* and grace. But in the meane tyme, this negligence which grew to end in mortall sinne, doth not

(c) Take heed thou walke not in the way of spirit without aduice.

I 5 grow

grow from that very *loue* of God,
which of it felfe is all good, and per-
fwadeth vs alfo to all good ; but(d)
it groweth from the infirmity of mã,
and from his bad inclination, and fo
it is wholly the fault of man; who, as
he vfeth many other things ill, fo alfo
he vfeth ill, the *loue* of God.

*(d) So
weake is
man that
he may
well be
fufpected
euen whẽ
he mea
neth beft.*

It is therfore both very profitable, and very fit, & euen neceſſary,
that the good Chriſtian, do ioyne
the holy Feare of God, to the *loue* of
him; and that as he is to exercife himfelfe, in fome confiderations which
may moue him to *loue* God, ſo alfo
he may exercifehimfelf in fome other,
which may moue him to *feare* him.

And although it be true, that at
the firſt when a man is but begin'ing
to ſerue God, it is more neceſſary that
he beſtowe himfelfe more vpon the
confideration of *feare*, then that of
loue; yet is it alfo very conuenient,
euen for them, who haue beene long
in

in his seruice, and are very well ad-
uaunced therin; that although their
cheife practice, may be in the exercises of the *loue* of God, yet, that many
tymes, also, they do intertaine themselues in the thoughtes of his diuine
Feare; and vpon those considerations
which may help them to it. And (e)
thus, accompaning this holy *Feare*,
with the *loue* of God, the inconue-
nience, and daunger, & losse wherof we haue spoken, wil cease; which
yet will be sure to grow through the
frailty of man, if he shall onely imploy himselfe in the exercises, and
considerations of *loue*. For this *Feare*,
when it is ioyned with *loue*, keepeth
a man from being negligent in Gods
seruice; and it leaues no place for any
faults to be comitted against God,
how veniall and light soeuer they be;
and it keepes him from giuing ouer
his penances and mortifications, or
from vsing tepidity therein. Nay it
cau-

(e) The
remedy of
this dan-
ger.

cauſeth him to contynue them with
care, leaſt els he ſhould indeed grow
tepide; & it teacheth him to humble
and deſpiſe himſelfe, giuing no place
to pride, but fearing ſtill his owne
frailty, and the *Iudgement* of God. Al
this is wrought by this holy *feare*; &
the ſame is witneſſed by *Eccleſiaſticus*
who ſaith, *The feare of God, driues ſin
away from the ſoule*. It driues it away
by penance, after it is committed, &
it driues it away, by caution and re-
ſiſtence of temptation, before it is cōmitted. And in another place, he
ſaith, *He that feareth God, is negligent
in nothing; but feare makes him carefull,
and watchfull, towards euery thing that
is good*. For this, did the Apoſtle *S.
Paul*, when he was perſwading
Chriſtians to procure the purity and
ſanctity of their ſoules by efficacious,
ſecure, & certaine means, aduiſe thē
to help themſelues heerein, with the
holy *feare* of God; ſaying, *Let vs
cleanſe*

Eccleſ. 1.

cleanse our selues from all vncleanes both 2. Cor. 7.
of flesh and spirit . That is to say , from
all sinne; as well that which may be committed by these exteriour powers of our
body , togeather with the consent of the
mind , as that other which is committed
by the onely consent of the mind without
the body . And let vs perfect our sancti-
fication, which is that purity & sanctity
which we receiued , either in baptisme ,
or by penance . Let vs go conseruing &
increasing it with good workes, and
by the exercise of vertue , and by
continual reuewing our watchfulnes
and care, in flying al that is offensiue
to God . And let vs do all this, with
a feare of his diuine Maiesty . And S. D. Thom.
Thomas giuing a reason, why the A- in 2. Cor. c.
postle saith not , that we should doe it 7.
with the loue , but with the feare, deliuereth these words : The Apostle
saith not , with charity, but with feare
of God; To teach vs that the affection of
loue, which we are to carry towards God,
is

is to be accompanyed by a solicitude, and reuerentiall feare. For this loue, causeth security, wherby many tymes a man groweth carelesse and negligent in the seruice of God; but he who accompaineth that affect of loue with feare, is watchfull in the seruice of God, and runs diligently towards it, and flyes speedily frō any offence of him. This is deliuered by S. *Thomas*. And for this reason it wilbe fit, many tymes, to vse the cōsiderations of the diuine *Iudgement*, from whence this holy & chast *feare* may be fetcht. And so we may comply with that, which the holy Apostle aduiseth vs saying: *Worke your saluation with feare, and trembling.* Which is as much as to say, *With an interiour feare to offend God, which may be so great, as that it may appeare by your exteriour vigilancy and care to performe your workes, whereby you may obtayne that true and euerlasting saluation.* S. *Bernard* (f) left this truth, confirmed both

(f) A sweet & secure guide for vs to follow.

both by his doctrine, and example, *Bernar. in* in these words: *Happy is that soule wher-* *Cant. ser. 7* *in Christ our Lord hath set the print of* *his two feet ; and wherin he hath left the* *markes and footesteps of them both, which* *are the feare of his diuine Iudgment, and* *the hope of his diuine Mercy. For the* *consideration of the diuine Iudgment a-* *lone, breeds disconfidence and despayre;* *and the memory and consideration of his* *mercy alone, doth occasion a sly deceipt of* *a mans selfe. & ingendreth a very dan-* *gerous kind of security. And so haue I* *experimented in my selfe. For the benig-* *nity of God sometymes hath graunted to* *me (miserable creature) that I might sit* *downe at the feet of Iesus Christ my Sa-* *uiour, and that I might with entier de-* *uotion, imbrace the one foot of feare; &* *at other tymes, the other foot of confi-* *dence, and of loue. And if at any tyme* *it hapned to me, that, being forgetfull for* *his mercy, I detayned my selfe long in the* *consideration and apprehension of the di-*
uine

uine Iudgment, I grow all dismayd, &
distempered with an incredible kind of
feare; and a miserable confusion; and all
trembling, I would be crying out with
the Psalmist, O Lord, who shalbe able to
conceaue or comprehend the power of thy
wrath! And who, through the feare he
hath, shalbe able to measure out the greatnes, and mightines of that indignation, which thou wilt execute against sinners in the other life! And (s) if, on the
other side giuing ouer the consideration,
and exercise of this feare, I detayned
my selfe long in the consideration and
meditation of the mercy of God, I should
be grown to fall into such a deale of carelesse negligence, that euen then already,
my prayer would become more remisse &
my selfe more sloathfull towards a good
workes, and I should be more disposed towards laughter, and such idle intertay-
nements; more free and liberall in my
speach, and more vnsetled both in my
inward & outward man. Being therefore

Psal. 8↑.

(g) See &
imitate
the great
humility
of this
excellent
Saint, and
learne
heereby
to know
thy selfe.

fore taught by experience, which hath bin
a faythfull Maister to me, I will sing to
thee, O Lord, not only Iudgement, nor
only Mercy, but Mercy & Iudgment
both togeather; and both these meanes
of iustification will I exercise, and vse as
long as the tyme of Pilgrimage, in this
banishment of myne shall last, and till I
arriue to be possessed of that most happy
State, wherein all misery, and all cause of
compunction and feare, shall cease, and
all my glory shall b. to prayse thee for all
eternity.

This saying is of S. *Bernard*,
wherin by the testimony of what he
experienced in himselfe, he confir-
meth that, which the holy Scripture
and the doctrine of the Saints doe
teach, concerning the necessity,
wherein all the seruants of God are,
(towards the keping of themselues
still his seruants) to ioyne holy *feare*
with *loue*, and the considerations of
the diuine *Iudgement*, & the punish-

K   ments

ments inflicted by his Iustice, with
the confiderations of the mercy of
God; and of the fauours & benefits,
which he cōmunicateth with a moſt
liberall hand, to ſuch as keepe his
Law.

CHAP. XIII.

*Of how great value, and merit,
this holy Feare is.*

THIS is the firſt way of anſw-
ring that which was demaunded.
The (a) ſecond is, that when we
ſpeakeof *ſeruile feare*, & of accompaning the ſame with the *loue* of God,
it is true, that the exercife of *loue* is
much more excellēt thē that of *feare*.
For as we haue ſaid, feruile feare,
which hath the eye vpon puniſhment
is imperfect, and but of beginners, &
it is found euen in them who are not
yet in ſtate of grace; nor can it be
merito-

(a)The
ſecond an-
ſwere of
the for-
mer obie-
ction.

meritorious , nor wholly acceptable
to our Lord God . But speaking of *filiallfeare* , wherby a man *feareth* and
flyeth from sinne, because it is the of-
fense of God ; and of that *reuerenciall*
feare, wherby the soule reueareth his
diuine Maiesty; and doth humble her
selfe to him, by doing his diuine wil ;
and comparing this kind of feare
with the *loue* of our Lord God , and
considering that which indeed doth
passe in iust persons ; it is not an exercise lesse excellent , nor lesse pleasing to God , nor lesse meritorious
then is that of *loue* . For (b) this holy
feare springeth out of the true *loue* of
God ; and imbraceth the same *loue* as
the fountaine, & roote from whence
it springs . For from louing of God,
doth grow the feare of offeding him;
and from the loue of vertue, groweth
the feare of loosing it ; & frō the high
estimation which the soule makes
of God, and the fulfilling of his will ,

(b) Filiall
fear riseth
out of
loue.

K 2   doth

doth growe a profound reuerence of God, and the keeping of his law, and the feare of doeing any thing which is contrary to the same. And so the good Christian, whilst he is exercising the chast feare of a sone of God, he doth also exercise the *loue* of God.

So saith *S. Augustine*, The *feare* through which a man loues not vertue, but flyes from the punishment of vice, is a *seruile feare*; and this feare is that, *which shutteth Charity out of doores*, and the same *Charity* which alsoshutteth out thiskind of fear, doth produce and breed that other *chast* feare, through which the soule feares to sinne, though it were neuer to be punished. And this is that holy feare, which iust me do exercise in the consideration of the diuine *Iudgement*; because, as we haue declared, through the great desire which they haue to please God, and to do according to his wil in al things, they dispose themselues

Aug. in psal 118. serm. 25.

felues to confider the diuine *Iudgmet*,
fo to know the better, and as it were
to feele, the greiuoufnes of finne, and
the punifhment, that falls vpon it;
and the much that God abhors it; &
fo to procure a forrow and hatred of
finne, as being an offence of God;
and to feare it much, and to fly from
it with great care, as being contrary
to his diuine will; and fo exercyfing
this *chaft* feare, which is an effect &
fruit of diuine *loue*, he exercifeth loue
with all, which is the caufe of that
feare: for this it is, that we haue faid,
that the iuft man exercifing this *filiall feare*, doth not loofe the leaft
graine of the excellency and merit
of his *loue*; and that the exercife of
filiall feare, is not leffe pious and
acceptable to God, then that of *loue*.
For in fine this is the *feare* of Saints,
to all whome the *Pfalmift* fpeakes by
faying *O all yow Saints feare our Lord*. Pfal. 33.
And this is that *feare*, which hath for

K 3   a rea reward, That it obteyneth of God what it will, as the *Pfalmift* doth alfo witnes, faying, *God will fullfill the will of them that feare him, and will heare their pra ers, granting all which they aske.* To (b) conclude, this is that *feare* which maketh men happy in this life, through the liuely hope, and pledge it giues of glory; in the other life it will giue the poffeffion therof. For a truth it is, deliuered by the holy Ghoft, *Bleffed is the man who alwaies liues in the holy feare of God.*

Pfal .140.

(b) True hope ri- feth out of filiall Feare.

Prou. 28.

CHAP.

CHAP. XIIII.

Of the fauours which Christ our Lord
will do to the good at the day of Iud-
gement ; and of the Ioy which they
shall conceaue , by seeing the signes ,
which precede that Iudgment ; and
by beholding the glory of the Crosse ,
which shall go before Christ our Lord.

GREAT are the benefits which
we find in that diuine *Iudgment* ,
& the fruits which we gather thence
by our considering that which Christ
our Lord will shew vpon the wicked.
For , as we haue declared , it doth
cleerly difcouer the greiuoufnes of
finne , and how mightily it is abhorred by our Lord God , and it moueth
vs to a hatred, and a feare therof. But
yet greater are the bleffings which
we find in the *Iudgement* of God ; and
the profit which we reap from thece,
by

by considering that which Christ our
Lord will then do for his seruants ; &
the fauours which he will impart, and
the felicity which he will communicate. For in this , doth he discouer his
goodnes , and the much that he loueth such as are good ; and the estimation which he makes of vertue ; &
he awaketh and prouoketh vs much
to loue him, and he doth animate and
incourage vs much , to labour hard
in his seruice, and that for the pleasing
of him , and complying with his holy will , we must imploy our selues
in all kind of vertue. Let vs therfore
go declaring the fauors which Christ
our Lord will impart to the good , in
this his *Iudgment* ; to the end that we
may gather this fruite from thence.

A great (a) benefit and fauour
shall it be for the good, that those
very signes which are to precede the
diuine *Iugdment* , as namely the dar-
kening of the Sunne, the Moone, &
Starres

(a) How
differētly
the same
things do
worke v-
pon the
good and
the bad.

Starres, the swelling vp of the Sea,
the opening of the earth, withal the
rest, which are to strike such excessiue horrour into the wicked; and
will cause in them such an extreme
affliction and dismay, so far, as that
they shall goe like persons euen distracted and mad with griefe, & shal
euen be dryed vp and withered, thorough the deadly paine and sorrow,
which they shal receaue, as our Lord
himselfe declareth, saying : *Men shall*
whither with the feare they wilbe in of Luc. 21.
those miseryes which they expect, and of
which, those signes are the forerunners :
That these very signes, I say, shal giue to those iust men, the seruants of
God whome they shall find aliue,
great strength & courage great confidence and security in God ; & shall
cause them great alacrity and comfort, and they shall go all refresh't,
and fully at ease, as being animated
with a new spirit of hope and ioy.

(b) The great rea sons, which good men haue to be glad of death, and the day of Iudgment

For (b) iust men, who cordially doe loue Almighty God, do much desire to leaue the miserable estate of this life, where God is so many wayes offended; and when themselues cannot forbeare to fal into some defects; which although they be light & veniall, yet for as much as they goe against the will of God, they feele thē much, and much paine by them; & where they also find, that they haue many impedimentes to keepe them from communicating with God, & from louing him, and tasting him as they desire: These persons do extremely couet the state of immortality & glory, where they shall most perfectly, both in body and soule, enioy the fauours and benedictions of God as the Apostle declareth (c) saying: *We know that all creatures*, that is to say, *all the whole machine of the world* (*which conteyns all the sensible creaturs*) *is groaning vnder the weight, and mu-*

(c) The sense is of the B .Apostle, and it is opened and explained by our Authour. Rom. 8.

tabi-

tability, and corruption, which it is subiect to.

And as a woman who being in labour of her child, doth expect to bring
him forth; so doth it remaine with a kind
of wearines, and griefe, from the very
first beginning of the world, till this instant; desiring & hoping to see it selffree
from this corruption and mutability; &
to be all renewed, according to the imitation, and resemblance of that glorious liberty of the sonnes of God. And we the
disciples & seruants of Christ our Lord,
who haue receaued the chiefe, and first
fruits & gifts of the holy Ghost, dee sigh,
& groan withal the affectiō of our harts,
towards the perfect & complete adoptiō
of the sonnes of God; which is the glory,
not only of our soules, but euen of our
bodyes also, whereby the whole man shall
be deliuered from all mortality, and corruption, and from all euill inclination &
concupiscence; and shall perfectly enioy,
both in body and soule the redemption,
                                    which

Which was wrought by Christ our Lord.
This is of the Apostle . And for as
much as this desire is of iust persons ,
and that, in it selfe, it is so very internall, and so vehement ; when they
shall see the signes of the diuine *Iud-*
gement, they shal know that the tyme
is then close at hand ; wherein that
desire of theirs is to be satisfyed , and
when they are to be possessed of that
happy state , and wherein they are
to be free both in body and soule frō
all corruption and misery both of sin
and pennance . And they shallbe ful
of glory in their soules ; and their bodyes, being adorned with the glorious stole of immortality, are to enioy
God eternally in his kingdome.

(d) The
ioy which
the elect
will haue
to see thē-
selues so
neere the
end of
their
hope.

Now (d) by this so certaine, &
secure hope, that God wilbe so gracious to them, as to graunt that they
may possesse, & enioy that immense
good, which they so mightily desire,
and to which , then , they shall be
brought

brought so neere, they will reioyce,
and be reuiued in a wonderfull manner ; and giue strange thankes to
God, for hauing brought them to see
that day, and for hauing continued
them in his seruice ; and vouchsafed
to giue them such tokens & pledges
of his glory . All this did Christ our
Lord vnfold , in the Ghospell . For
hauing reckoned vp the signs which
are to appeare before his comming
to *Iudgement*, and the feare and sorrow wherewith they shallbe receaued by the wicked ; turning then his
discourse to his disciples (and in their
persons to all such as would be their
imitatours, and were to be aliue at
that tyme) he sayth , after this manner: *When these thinges shall arriue ,*
which are to precede my comming , do
you lift vp your heads. Be not disquieted,
be not dismayd , giue no place to sorrow ,
none to feare, or to distrust, as the louers
of the world will do, who will go with
the

the head all hanging downe like men afflicted and dismayd But haue you great
confidence, conceaue great courage, be
cheerefull and reioyce, and with this confidence and ioy lift vp your harts & your
face, to God, for now your redemption
draweth neere. The tyme approacheth,
and so doth that most happy state and
complete redemption, which now within, Passion and Death I am about to gain
for you, and that is, both security from
all kind of misery, and immortall glory
both to body and soule.

Another great fauour to the
iust, willbe, to see, appearing in the
ayre (and that high vp neer heauen,
and before the person of Christ our
Lord) the signe, and standard of the
most holy (e) Crosse, not made of
wood, or mettall, but of other most
glorious matter, and more brightly
shining, & incomparably with more
beauty, then the sunne; and in proportion so very large, that being
plac't

(e)Happy
soules,
which
heere
are deuo-
ted to the
Crosse of
Christ
our Lord

plac't on high, it may be seene ouer
the whole earth, by all the inhabitãts
thereof. For a matter and motiue it
is of incomparable comfort & ioy,
for them to see in such high honour
and glory, that Crosse, which they
adored, as the Image of Christ, and
which they loued, by enduring and (f) A pro-
suffering affronts and paynes for his found, &
sake. When (f) a worldly man doth conside-
hate any thing, or any person, and ration.
seeth it or him aduanced to honour,
it puts him to payne. Wicked men, in
this life, did abhorre the Crosse of
Christ, becaufe they did extremely
loue the pleasures and delicacyes, &
transitory honours of this world, &
they detested to suffer paine & sham
in the vertue, and for the loue of Phl. 3.
Christ our Lord. So doth S. *Paul* expresse it saying : *There are many who*
liue and conuerse among you (of whome I
haue aduertised you many tymes, & now
againe I repeate it with griefe & forrow
of

of my har.) *who are the enemies of the Croffe of Chrift, fince they giue themfelues to delights and delicacyes, and to ambition and pride, which the Croffe of Chrift doth condemne; and they flye from penance, and mortification, and abftinence, and from the exercifes of humility, to which the Croffe of Chrift doth perfwade and teach.* When therefore thefe men fhall fee, in that diuine Iudgment that the Croffe of Chrift is fo highly honoured, and made fo glorious, which they with their workes did fo abhorre, it fhall replenifh them with paine and griefe. For thereby they fhall more cleerely fee their errour, and the eternall condemnation, which is prepared for them. For that, is to be the end of fuch men, as the fame Apoftle declareth faying: *VVhofe end, is death, and the deftruction of their foules.*

(g) The fame confideration continued.

On (g) the contrary fide, whofoeuer he be that doth greatly loue a-

ny

any thing or perſon, he reioyceth & taketh comfort to ſee that it is honored & eſteemed by others. And now for as much as the ſeruantes of God do cordialy loue the Croſſe of Chriſt which is, To mortify theſelues with thinges of difficulty to fleſh and bloud; and to ſuffer paines, and tribulations, and affronts for his loue, and in the imitation of his Paſſion. For as S. Paul ſayth: *They who are of Chriſt, and who are liuely members of him, and who haue his ſpirit and who are gouerned by him, doe crucify their fleſh, and chaſtiſe it with penances, and by willingly imbracing thoſe affronts & paynes, which God preſents. And by afflicting their fleſh, in this manner, they doe withall, deſtroy and kill the vices, and ill deſires which ſprout from thence.* Now when the ſeruants of God, ſhal ſee that Croſſe, (h) which they loued ſo much, and wherein they did ſo greatly reioyce, become exalted,

Galat. 5.

(h) And haue we not reaſon to loue it, ſince it was the inſtrumēt of our redemption.

L   and

and so glorious, and so highly honoured by Almighty God; and so re-
ueared by the whole world, they shal
receaue thereby, excessiue ioy, and
consolation; to see how well they
chanced in following the Crosse of
Christ our Lord; and they shall hold
it as an expresse signe of the glory,
which God will giue to them. For, a
truth of God it is, which ispronoun-
ced by his Apostle: *That whatsoeuer*
tribulation or paine or trouble is suffered
inthis life for the loue of God (which how
long soeuer it lasts is butmomentary, since
it liues no longer then we liue) & which
how grieuous soeuer it may seeme, yet to
the soules that loue God, and are assisted
by his holy grace, is light and easy)
doth worke in vs, and that as a merito-
rious cause, a weight of most soueraigne
glory, ouerflowing beyond all measure,
and exceeding all that which we can so
much as euen imagine: & this is not to
be of temporall glory, but a glory which
shall neuer end.   CHAP.

CHAP. XV.

Of the fauour which Chriſt our Lord wil
do his ſeruants, at the day of Iudge-
ment, by ſeparating them from the
wicked.

ANOTHER benefit & fauour,
and that a great one, will Chriſt
our Lord, do to his ſeruants in the
day of *Iudgment*, and that will be to
ſeparate them from the company of
the wicked. This was ſignified by
Chriſt our Lord, who ſaid: *When the*
ſonne of man ſhall come to iudge, he ſhall
ſit vpon the throne of his Maieſty, &
all the nations of the earth ſhalbe aſ-
ſembled before him; and, as the ſhep-
heard deuides the ſheepe from the
Goates, ſo ſhall he deuide the good
and bad from one another. The good
he calleth *ſheep*, for the innocency,
ſimplicity, meeknes, & fruitefulnes
in good works wherwith they aboūd

Matt. 25.

L 2   and

and the wicked he calleth *Goates*, for
their barrennes in doing any thing
that is good; and for the ill odour of
their vices, and the impetuousnes of
their passions, to which they are subiect. Three things there are, which
do principally afflict and torment the
good, when they are in company of
the bad. First, they see before their
eyes, many and great offences committed against God, and they are
not able to preuent them. This
(a) is a greiuous torment; and the
more they loue God, & the fulfilling
of his lawe, so much greater is the
griefe which they conceaue, by seeing him offended, and it despised.
This did *S. Peter* explicate, when he
said of *Lot*, *That he was a iust man &*
as such he could not indure to see sins cō-
mitted, and yet he dwelt among such
men, as tormented his very soule, by their
sins.

(a) He that
finds not
this griefe
in his hart
is not so
much in
loue with
God, as he
perhaps
conceaues
2. Pet. 2.

  Another thing which afflicteth
                              good

good men, when they liue and conuerse with such as are wicked, is the
danger (b) wherin they are, of loosing the vertue which they haue. For
as the example of the good, doth induce men to the loue of vertue, so
doth the example of the wicked to
the loue of vice. For this cause, did
the Apostle say to the *Corinthiãs* who
were men of vertue: *Do not suffer your
selues to be deceiued; depart from the cõ
pany and communication of the wicked;
for euill wordes do preiudice and corrupt
good workes, and so make men bad of
good.* For as much therfore as (d)
good men do vnderstand their owne
frailty; they do greately apprehend
their spirituall hurt; therfore do they
feele great paine, by running hazard
of falling into such a thing as sinne,
which they do so much abhorre.

 The third thing which afflicteth
good men, who finde themselues in
the company of wilfull sinners, is

(b) Thou little knowest, the extrem danger into which ill company doth cast thee. 1. Cor. 15.

(d) The more vertuous mē are, the lesse they presume vpon thēselues.

feare to be punished ioyntly with
them. For although, in this life, God
doth not punish the soule of one, for

(e) The
iudgmēts
of God,
are some
tymes se-
cret, but
they are
euer iust.

Iosu. 7.

the sins of another; yet (e) it happe-
neth, that for as much as concerneth
temporall things, God sendeth punishment sometymes to some who are
good, for the sins of other with whõe
they liue. As he did, to the Children
of Israell, who for the sins of Acham
(who tooke some parte of the enemies spoyles against the commaund-
ment of God) retyred his hand of
succour from them all, and discontin-
ued the strength, which he had giuen them; and so they were subdued
and slaine by their enemies. And
God declared, that he sent that puni-
shmēt for the sinne of Acham, saying;
The children of israel, shall not be able to
resist their enemyes, but they shall flye
from before their face; because they are
polluted, by his sinnes, who tooke that,
which was solemnely forbidden. I will
no

*no more declare my selfe in fauour of
you, till you punish him.* And so *A-
cham* being punished, God returned againe to shew them fauour.
Now this course of Gods punishing,
in temporall things some one, for the
sins of another, may be taken by Almighty God (without the least iniustice to any one, because he is the
absolute Lord of all things, and he
doth whatsoeuer he doth vpon perfect reason) *to declare,* as S. Austine
sheweth, *what a wicked thing sinne is,
and how profoundly it is hated by him.*
And this is to be vnderstood, when
the good, who liue amongst the wicked, do not yet participate with them
in their sins; for when they do parta-
ke or consent therin, and doe (f) not
reprehend or correct them, as they
ought, then God doth not onely
rechastise them in temporall things, as
of the body, or goods, but also in
those other which concerne the soule;

*Augu. in
Iosue q. 4.
D. Thom.
2. 2. q. 108.
art. 4.*

(f) It is no
smal sinne
for a man
not to re-
prehend
sinne in
due tyme
& place.

and

and that not onely in this life, but in
that of the other also, according to
the quality of the fault.

Thefe are the things which put
good men in paine, when they are in
cōpany of the wicked. And fo it wil
be a moſt fingular benefit, and of fupreme confolation and ioy, for the
good to fee themfelues feparated, &
that for euer, from the fociety of the
wicked. And to knowe foe cleerly,
that then no longer they fhall be able
to fee with their eyes, nor to heare
wi h their eares, in thofe eternall habitations of theyrs, any thing at all
which may be of the leaft offence to
G d. But that whatfoeuer they fhall
either heare, or fee, is to be nothing
els, but the praifing and glorifying of
his diuine Maiefty with fupreme per-
feſtion. And to knowe, that then
they fhall not be able to haue fo much
as any occafion, or daunger of it, nor
that there fhall be any one, in heauen,
who

who may giue them example of sinne
by deed , or perswade them to it by
word . For all they whom there they
are to haue for companions, & that
for euer , are to be Saints; and so truly Saints, that they shall neuer cease,
not so much as for one little , single
moment from louing God, with the
very highest top of all perfection , &
from doing the holy will of God in
all thinges , with vnspeakable comfort and ioy . And yet further to
know that then they are free for e-
uer, from all kind of punishment; &
from all danger to suffer any . For as
for any sinnes of their owne , they
cannot be punished for any such, because they can commit none ; and as
for the sinnes of others, they cannot
be punished for them , because they
haue not, nor cannot haue the com
pany of any such as can sinne. But
on (ʒ) the other side they are to haue
an augmentation of glory , for the

(g) How
euery one
of the E-
lect will
ioy in the
glory of
each o-
ther.

L 5   most

moſt holy ſociety which they ſhall
enioy of the Bleſſed, through whoſe
glory their glory alſo ſhall increaſe.
For the immenſe ardour of loue,
wherewith they will be carryed to
God, will be the cauſe why they ſhal
take particuler guſt, in that loue,
wherwith euery one of thoſe bleſſed
ſoules, ſhall glorify, & loue Almighty God. And ſo alſo the ſupreme loue
which euery one of the ſame bleſſed
ſoules ſhall beare ech other, wil mak
thē receaue particuler ioy, by euery
one in particuler. O moſt bleſſed
creatures, who are to liue in ſuch a
ſociety; and who are to enioy ſuch a
communication of felicity for all e-
ternity. If it be a great benediction
to enioy the ſociety of good men,
heere on earth; what kind of bleſſed-
nes will it be to enioy the company
of bleſſed ſoules? If it be a matter of
much profit and comfort to participate in the communication of the
guiſts

guifts of grace ; what kind of profit,
what kind of comfort will it be, to
haue communication with so many
Saints both men and Angells, in the
guifts of glory ? O with how much
reason is it sayd : *Blessed are they, O
Lord, who dwell in thy house; they shall* Psal. 23 ◦
*prayse thee there, through the eternity
of all eternityes , Amen.*

CHAP. XVI.

*Of the fauour, which Christ our Lord
imparteth to his seruants at the day
of* Iudgment *, by giuing them his
benediction, and communicating his
kingdome to them.*

THIS benefit and fauour, is followed by another, which yet is
greater . For the good, being once
separated from the wicked, & being
plac't vpon the right hand of Christ
our Lord ; this celestiall King shall
cast

caſt towards them his moſt gracious
countenance, being all full of ſuauity, and delight. And paſſing his ſentence of fauour on them, he will ſay,
Come yee bleſſed of my Father. The benediction of God is the good guift
of God ; and ſo, to be bleſſed by him,
is to be filled withal thoſe good gifts
and graces, which God communi-
cates to his ſeruants. That is, withal
thoſe principall benefits, which the
Saints haue heere on earth (when
once they are made pure and cleane
from all imperfections) and withall
thoſe others alſo, which the Angells
doe poſſeſſe in heauen ; &, which is
more, with all thoſe goods & graces
which the King of heauen himſelfe,
doth poſſeſſe and enioy. For, as S.
Iohn affirmeth, *When he ſhall appeare,*
we ſhallbe made like to Ieſus Chriſt our
Lord, participating of his power, of
his beauty, of his wiſedome, of his good-
nes, of his ioy, of his glory.

1. *Ioan.* 3.

He

He (a) calleth them *Blessed of his* (a) How
Father, to declare the fountayne, & grace and
first offspring, from whence all the glory
benefits of grace and glory spring, proceed
and this is the eternall Father; and from God
besides, because all that which the Fa- the Father
ther operateth, is also the worke of and how
God the Sonne as he is God; as also it also from
is the worke of God the holy Ghost. the other
For the Diuinity, the Goodnes, and persons of
the Power, is the very same in all the the most
three Persons; and to attribute them B. Trini-
all to the Father (as to the first Au- ty.
thour of all that is good) is to offer
them also to the Sonne, as he is God;
and it is also to offer them to the holy Ghost, who is one God, with the
Father, and the Sonne. O happy
men, who are to receaue such a benediction ! A benediction, giuen by
Christ our Lord, in the face of heauen and earth, & of all the creaturs !
A benediction authorized by all the
most Blessed Trinity, as the Authour
and

and fountaine of the same! A benediction which comprehendes all the
chiefe guifts of grace, & al the guifts
of glory! A benediction full of benefits, vnspeakable, most high, and truly heauenly, which containe all the
most chiefe and choice part of heauen! A Benediction of eternall benefit! A Benediction irreuocable,
which can neuer be changed, as long
as God shallbe God! O how highly
is this benediction to be esteemed! O
how much is it to be desired, & procured, which maketh men so truely
happy, as our Lord himselfe declareth saying: *Come and possesse the kingdome, which is prepared for you from the
beginning of the world.*

(b) The *Kingdoms* (b) *& dominions you had*
great dif- *on earth, but temporall kingdoms & do-*
ferences *minions they were & of little value &*
which are
betweene *minions they were & of little value &*
an earthly *cōfort; or rather ful of miseries: & what-*
& a hea- *soeuer they were, they are now growne*
uenly *to an end. Laying aside those miserable*
kingdom. *king-*

kingdomes which already are ended, come
and possesse another kingdome, which is
celestiall & full of incomparable happines;
a kingdome of infinite value; a kingdome
which eternally shall contynue. And
although euery one of you is to be a king of
this kingdome, and is to raigne and possesse the same; yet the kingdom is still but
one. For all of you are to be subiect and
obedient (but it is to be with supreme
loue) to this Soueraigne King, in whose
company you are to raigne. And because all of you are to be of one hart and
of one will, vnited by most perfect loue,
in such sort that the blessings belonging to
any one inparticuler to be of you all (so
farre forth as to reioyce therin) and they
of you all to be of euery one (to reioyce
with them, to whome in particuler they
belonge) this kingdome is also to be but
one. Yet still, though this kingdome be
but one, you shall all be kings, and you all
shallraigne. For the kingdome is infinite
in the greatnes of the felicity, which is
                                    possest

*possest therin; and it is infinite also, in
the contynuance, since it is eternall. And
to the end that you may discerne the altitude of this kingdome, and the great
affection wherwith it is giuen you, Behould, it hath bene prepared for you since
the beginning of the world.*

(c)Of our
election
to the
kingdom
of heauen
and the
prepara-
tion,
which is
made for
vs toward
the same.

    The election (c) of the inha-
bitants of this kingdome was made
before the world was created; for
they were chosen and predestinated
from all eternity to raigne therin.
But the preparing of those things
which concerne this kingdome, and
the putting of those meanes in practice, which had relation to the obteyning therof, did begin at the beginning of the world. From that tyme,
were framed those most sumptuous
pallaces, those most beautifull habitations, and those most glorious
seats and thrones, where the inhabitants of this kingdom were to liue &
raigne. Then were created and were
                    made

made happy thofe firſt Cittizeus of
this kingdom, which are the Angels,
who were to keepe men company
therin , and to augument the glory
which men were to poſſeſſe in this
kingdome. And fo alſo from the firſt
beginingof the world,ther were gifts
of graces which came to be communicated to men,wherby they were to
obteyne this kingdome.And for God
to create man,and withal to communicate iuſtice & grace to him,wherby
he might procure this kingdome, all
that was done at once ; & from that
tyme, to this, nothing hath beene
done, but to diſpofe and help men ,
& giue them meanes that they might
come to poſſeſſe and perfectly intoy
this kingdome,in glory both of body
and foule. This is that moſt bleſſed
fentence , which Chriſt our Lord
will giue in fauour of his feruants; &
that being done , he will inſtantly
rayſe them vp togeather with him-
M felfe

felfe, and will inueſt them with the
moſt glorious poſſeſſion of his celeſtiall kingdome.

CHAP. XVII.

Of the felicity which Chriſt our Lord
will communicate to his ſeruants,
in the kingdome of heauen.

(a) A moſt
excellent
moſt
ſweet,
moſt pro-
found, &
yet moſt
plaine deſ-
cription
of the
ioyes of
heauen,
through-
out this
whole
Chapter.
(b) The
place of
the king-
dome of
glory.

LET (a) vs yet more particulerly cõtemplate the Maieſty of this
kingdome, which Chriſt our Lord
imparteth to his ſeruants; and of that
felicity which is poſſeſt therein; to
the end that we may gather that
fruit, which it is fit for vs to feed v-
pon; which is nothing els, but the
diſpoſing of our ſelues to the obtayning of this kingdome, by an imitation of the vertues of Chriſt our
Lord. And (b) firſt, the ſcituation
and place of this kingdome, is that
ſupreme heauen, which for the glorious

rious brightnes and splendor which
is found therein, is called Empyreal.
The altitude and capacity, and beauty & admirable designe, the grace
and suauity of this place though it be
such, as no tongue of flesh and bloud
can declare; yet to giue vs to vnderstand, some part of that which there
is found, by a comparison of those
thinges which heere we know, S.
Iohn describes it in the *Reuelations*
after this manner. He was carryed
in spirit, to a mountaine which was
great and very high; and he saw that
holy *Hierusalem* the celestiall Citty,
full of the clarity of God; all built of
perfect, pure and most resplendent
gould, like cleane, pure glasse. It had
a wall about it of Iaspar, both very
thicke, and very high, the foundati-
ons wherof, were adorned with pre.
tious stone. In this wal, were twelue
gates, and euery one of them, was
made of a most pretious pearle and

Apoc.21.
& 22.

that

that pearle alone, did make the gate. This Citty had within a very spacious open place, all paued with gold, most pure & most resplendent, & in the midst of that place, there was a riuer of infinite sweetnes. A Temple also there was, to adorne this Citty; and a light to illuminate it; and this Temple and Light was God himself, and therfore it must needs be farre from hauing any necessity of any other Temple or Light.

(c) We who are sensible creatures, as well as spirituall, must be raised towards spirituall things by such as are sensible; and therefore the vse of ceremonyes, and Images, is very necessary.

By these wordes S. Iohn describeth the scituation of the Kingdome of heauen, and the habitation of the Saints. And although it be true, that there are not there, any of those mettalls of gold or siluer, or any of these pretious stones of earth (for all these thinges are poore and base, and of no valew) yet (c) he deliuereth himselfe thus, that by those thinges which are the most pretious and beautifull of the earth, the soule

may

may rise to consider the greatnes &
beauty of heauenly thinges, vnderstanding euer, that those, are incomparably better then these. And as the
whole globe of the heauens, is so far
exceeding the earth in greatnes, that
the whole earth is but as a point, or
in effect as nothing, in comparison
of the heauens; so is it in all the rest
as well as in greatnes. And all the
brightnes, and beauty, and sweetnes of thinges of this world, being
compared with those of heauen, are
as if they had not, so much as the least
being at all. So that the aduantage
which the habitation of heauen doth
carry beyond this of the earth is such
that it exceedeth all comparison. For
in fine such it is, as is fit to be carryed
by the house of the Creatour in respect of a creatures house; and by the
Citty of God, in respect of the Citty
of men; and by that sphere of felicity and eternall ioy, in respect of this

M 3   Center

Center of miseryes, and this valley
of teares.

(d) Mans
supreme
happynes
consisteth
in the vi
sion of
God.

Apoc. 22

The (d) chiefe felicity which
is enioyed in this soueraigne Citty
by cleare vision, is God himselfe.
His seruantes, sayth *S. Iohn*, in this
Citty of God shal see his face. What
vnspeakable happines, what Abisse,
what immense kind of sea of all felicity, will it be to looke the Diuinity
of God in the face, without the in-
terposition or interpretation of any
creature? To (e) see that diuine essence, in three persons; and three diuine persons in one, and the selfe
same essence; to see the power of the
Father, the wisedome of the Sonne,
& the goodnes of the holy Ghost? To
see how the Father, from all eternity, engenders the Sonne, communicating to him his diuinity; and how
the Father and the Sonne, as one &
the same eternall spring or roote, do
by spiration, giue proceeding to the
holy

(e) A most
sweet ex-
plication
of the
most bles-
sed Trini-
ty.

holy Ghoſt, and communicate their
diuine eſſence to him? To ſee how
all the perfection of God, is in euery
one of the three diuine perſons; and
how al the pertectiō, that any one of
the diuin perſons hath, the very ſame
is poſſeſſed by either of the other diuine perſons. What kind of incomparable ioy wil that be, ſo cleerely to
behould an infinite Good, which is
all amiable, all ful of infinite beauty,
of ſuauity, and of delight. And not
only to ſee it, in ſome manner, which
might be leſſe excellent, but to behould it with the eyes of an incor-
ruptible ſoule, and they moſt brightly clarifyed by the light of glory; &
euerlaſtingly to loue it, without cea-
ſing, & that with a moſt perfect loue,
and to poſſeſſe it with a perpetuity
of ſecurity.

  After (f) the rate of the *knowledge* of any thinge, growes the *loue*
to be; and after the rate of the *loue*

(f) Of
know-
ledge,
Loue and
Ioy, and
how they
grow out
of one an-
other.

is the *ioy* for that which is so much beloued; and that *knowledge* which the Saints haue of God, being the greatest which can possibly be had (since it is the cleare sight of God the *loue* must also be so great, as that greater cannot be conceaued.

The (g) soule is moued to loue a thing, which it knowes, because it is good, because it is beautifull, because it is profitable, because it is delightfull, because it concernes the soule, and is, after a sort, belonging to it. And so much more as that thing is good, more beautifull, more profitable, more delightfull, more concerning it, and more belonging to it, so much more doth the soule (if it *know* that thing well, and be hindered by no impediment at all) delight in it, and *loue* it, with a more intense, and perfect loue. Well then, since all these reasons, and tytles, & motiues of loue, are found to be in God, with infinite

(g) The motiues of loue.

infinite perfection (and the foule
cleerly feeing God, and meeting with
no impediment which may hinder
loue) with what *loue* fo intenfe, and fo
immenfe, will it be fure to loue him?

By (h) feeing that he is *infinite*
goodnes, there is ingédred in the foule,
a moft copious riuer of *loue*; By feeing
that he is *infinite beauty*, there is produced in it, another moft abundant
riuer of *loue* ; By feeing how full of
aduantage it hath bene, and is, and
euer will be to the foule; and that in
fome forte it is euen infinite, there
flowes from the foule another riuer
of *loue*, fo wide, and deepe, as that
it hath neither bottom nor brim. By
feeing that it is an *infinite delight*, and
fweetenes, and that it concernes the
foule fo much, and that fhe doth fo
dearly truly belong vnto it; and that
it is her creator, her father, her God;
and that all her being depends vpon
it; there is alfo created in the foule an-

M 5   other

(h) The
riuers of
ioy which
ouerflow
a foule
which is
in glory,

other moſt copious and moſt abundant riuer of *loue* ; and all theſe riuers
of *loue*, meeting then in one, the ſoule
of euery Saint in heauen growes to
haue in it an vnbridled boundles Sea
of loue.

(i) Be ſtill
attentiue.

He that *(* i *) loues* a thing, doth
wiſh it well; & if he may *ſee* the good
he wiſhes , it giues him *ioy* ; and the
more he *loues*, and the more he *deſires*,
and the greater that the good is , ſo
much the greater is the *ioy* .Now the,
ſince the Saints in heauen do loue
God , with a whole boundleſſe Sea of
loue; and ſeeing that he poſſeſſeth all
the good which they can wiſh (as
namely that he is God himſelfe) and
that , together with God , he is infinitely happy ; who can ſay what delight,who can ſay what ioy they ſhall
receiue ; ſince it is bound to be great
according to the rate of their loue.
Infallibly they ſhall poſſeſſe a whole
immenſe Sea of diuine *ioy* ; an immenſe

menfe Sea fhall they poffeffe, of celeftiall and fupreme delights. This is
that delight and ioy, which the foule
receiues from God himfelfe, being an
infinit good; when once she is poffeft
of a cleare vifion of him, and that by
loue. O (k) *ioy*, which ouercomeft all (k) Infinit
ioy! O *ioy*, which imbraceft all our ioy.
good! O *ioy*, without lymit! O eternall *ioy*! O *ioy* which art the euer running fountaine of al *ioyes*! O *ioy* which
knoweft how to fatiffy all the defirs,
and canft fill vp all the hollowes and Matt. 25.
empty places of the foule; and doft
poffeffe whatfoeuer we fhall euer be
able to think! To this *ioy* doth Chrift (l) The
niuite al his faithfull feruants, & this vnfpeak-
doth he giue them, in reward of their able ioy,
vertue, faying, *Reioyce O thou good &* which
faithfull feruant, enter into the ioy of thy they fhall
Lord. haue by
seeing the
Another (l) felicity which the the moft
bleffed foules fhall haue, is to behold glorious
the moft glorious humáity of Chrift our Lord.

         our

our Lord; and to enioye it, and to see him (euen as he is man) in so excessiue Greatnes, and Maiesty, and glory. And to see him withal so amiable, and so affable, & so deerly sweet, towards all those happy soules; and to see that that Lord, who is man as they are, and who with his passion and death did for the loue he bare them, redeeme them from eternall damnation; the same man, I say, is the infinite and eternall God. O how will they *loue* that most sacred humanity, which loued them so much, & which did and suffered so great things for them? O how will they reioyce to see that humäity so mightily sublymed, and vnited by an incomprehensible manner, to the person of the Word? O how wil they glory in his felicity? O what delight & sweetnes wil they receiue, from such a sight and from such a loue? For as the prophet saith *Isa. 33. They shall see the king in his beauty.*

Another

Another (m) supreme felicity for thole happy foules, fhalbe to fee the loue which God carries towards them; and wherwith the eternall father, did, from all *Eternity* loue, and choofe them, & did, in *Tyme* beftow his Sonne vpon them; and deliuer him ouer to death for them; and to fee that this loue, in it felfe, is infinite, and the very fame wherewith God loues himfelfe. The (n) feruant of a King, will much efteeme, that the king do him fauour, beftowing fome important place vpon him in his houfe, with good prouifion belonging to it. But much more will he efteeme it, and much more contentment & cōfort will he receiue, to fee himfelfe beloued, by that king; and that he is a fauorite of his. And thogh he haue but fome coniectures of this loue, and that it may eafely be cooled and changed into a difaffection; yet doth he neuertheles efteem it more, then

(m) It wil be an ineftimable ioy to fee how infinitly God loueth them.

(n) This truth is prouedby a fit comparifon.

then all the other fauours which the
king doth him . For by louing him ,
he giueth him his hart , which is incomparably more , then if he gaue
him a part of his fortune . What then
will a Saint in glory feele in himselfe
when he shal see, that he is so beloued
by God ; and although the benefits
which God hath done him are very
great , yet the loue he beares him is
much greater ; and although they are
most precious benefits which there
he is enioying , by the guyft of God ,
yet much more pretious is the loue .
For this *loue* is the root & fountaine
of all the benefites , and guiftes , and
graces which he hath comunicated ;
nay this *loue* , is euen very God himselfe . Now then to knowe this loue
of God , not by coniecture , but by
seeing it expresly in God , with as
great clarity as that wherewith he
seeth God himselfe ; and still to see
with the same clarity that this *loue*
cannot

cannot be loft, no nor changed, but that for euer it fhall remaine inuariable, with the felfe fame permanency wher with the truth of God himfelfe fhal remain, of which truth it is fayd *that it shall remaine for euer*; O how highly wil the *Bleſſed* efteeme & value this *loue* of God! O how imcomparable ioy will they receiue to fee théfelues fo beloued by God!

Pſal. 118,

When *loue* is great, it hath this property & power, that by the band of the fame *loue*, it makes (o) him that loues, become the fame thing with him that is beloued, and that he lodgeth his whole hart in him ; & that with the chaynes of loue he becomes imprifoned, and euen captiued by him, who is beloued, & that he depend wholy vpon him ; willing that which he wills, and communicating to him all his goods. Now then, fince the Bleſſed foules, knowing that this is the property of intenfe

(o) Of the vnion, of feuerall things which is made by loue.

tenfe loue, and feeing themfelues fo
beloued by God with this loue which
hath no meafure, nor had no beginning, nor will hauè end; what kind
of immenfe, incomparable ioy, wil
this be to them? Without all queſtion
except the ioy which they ſhall haue
in the felicity of God, whome they
loue more then themfelues, this o-
ther is their greateſt ioy, to fee themfelues fo beloued by him, who is omnipotent, and who is infinite beauty
and glory, and the infinite fountaine
of all Good. Of this *Loue* God himfelfe giueth teſtimony, ſaying by the
Prophet *Hieremy* : *With eternall loue
I haue loued thee ; and therefore did I
in tyme ſhew mercy to thee, and I called, and drew thee to my friendſhip and
glory.*

Hier. 13.

CHAP.

CHAP. XVIII.

Of other benefits which Christ our Lord comunicateth to his seruantes, in his heauenly kingdome ; and of the fruit of gratitude , which we must gather from the Consideration of this reward .

BESIDES these benefits which are the chiefe , there are others yet , which are enioyed by happy soules in the kingdome of heauen , which are also of inualuable value , and of incomparable ioy . One of them is , to be in cōpany of the Blessed ; where there is such a multitude of (a) Angelicall spirits , distinguished into nine Quires , as that they are in greater number , then all the men , which haue beene , which are, and which shall euer be ; yea more , then all the corporeall creatures of

the

(a) The incomprehensible number of the Angels.

N

the whole world put togeather. And
where there are so many Patriarkes,
and Prophets, and Apostles, and A-
postolicall men, and Martyrs, and
Confessours, and Virgins; and so
many others, who by pennance haue
made their way to heauen, & whom

Apoc. 7. S. *Iohn* (who saw them in a *Reuelation*) sayth, to be so many, as that they
cannot be numbred. And (p) all of

(b) The them, are the sonnes of God, and
dignity & *Grandes* in the Court of God; and
excellen-
cy of Kings in the kingdome of heauen;
those ce-
lestiall in- and all of them, most perfect in ver-
habitants. tue, and most sanctifyedly wise, and
most beautifull, and full of immense
glory; and all of them, so well content, and at ease, that they desire nothing but what they haue, because

(c) What they haue as much, as possibly they
a noble
conuersa- can desire. And (c) notwithstanding
tion will that they are so very high in dignity,
this be? and glory, yet withall, euery one of
them is most profoundly humble;
all

all affable , and milde , and of moft
fweet condition . And being fo innumerable as they are , they yet doe
all, know one another much better,
and in a more intrinfecall manner,
then a man on earth can euer arriue
to know himfelfe . And they all do
treate, and communicate with one
another ; and they loue one another
with fuch a loue, as doth incomparably exceede , the loue which any
Mother can beare to a child . For
in them all, there is but one affection
and will, which is that of God , by
the vnion, and conformity of wi'l ,
which euery one hath with his ; and
the felicity of all , euery one eftee-
meth as his owne ; and the glory of
euery onein particuler, is held as proper to euery one . And (d) fo, euery
one of the Bleffed hath as many particuler ioyes, as there are Angels, &
Saints in heauen . For euery one of
them reioyceth at the others good, as

(d) Euery
one of
them hath
exceffiue
ioy in the
glory of
any other.

at his owne ; and he enioyeth the ioy
of another, as his owne ioy ; and so
much more will one happy soule be
glad of the glory of any other , as he
shall see God to be more glorifyed in
that other .

(e) The
inestima-
ble ioy
which e-
uery of
the Blessed
haue in
behoul-
ding , and
treating
with the
all imma-
culate
Mother of
God.

But amongst all the (e) *Blessed*,
whether they be Angells, or meere
men and women, the creature, who
doth more enoble, and engrandize ,
and delight , and make happy that
most glorious court of heauen , is the
most sacred *Virgin Mary* , that Lady,
that Queene, that most deerly diuinely sweet enamoured mother of thé
all. For she is the true & naturall mother of him who created them all, &
who redeemed them all , and who
indued them all with that beatitude .
They all are great , they all are most
sublimely happy ; but this Lady , is
more great, more happy, and more
glorious , then they all together. All
of them do ardétly loue one another,
and

and they all conuerse, and behould
ech other with admirable sweetenes;
and they are all a cause of excessiue
ioy and glory to one another. But (f)
this soueraign Queene loues them al,
and euery one of them as her deerest
Children, and as her brethren and
companions, and as the louing members of *Iesus Christ* our Lord, who is
her naturall sonne. And she behoulds
them all, with most gratious, & most
amorous eyes; and she treates & com-
municates with them all, with a most
incomparable sweetenes; and by
that presence, and communication of
hers, she causeth in euery one of them
farre more ioy, and farre more glory,
then any other creature doth.

(f) And woe will be to thē, who do not loue & honour and admire, and serue this soueraign Queene.

    This blessed life, and this com-
pany of the *blessed* is described by the
Prophet *Isay*, speaking partly of the
militant Church, but principally of
the *triumphāt*, which is that celestial
Hierusalem, in these wordes: *There*

Isa. 60.

        shall

shall neuer be in thee, O thou Soueraigne
Citty, and thou land of the liuing, any
sinne or punishement; nor any newes, or
noyse therof. Insteed of paine, thou shalt
haue perfect & eternal health; & insteed
of sinne, thou shalt haue the continuall
& euerlasting exercise of the loue of God.
Our Lord God shall be all in all to thee;
thy Sunne, and thy Moone, and thy
light and thy glory, and all thy good.
And all the elect are to make vppe, in
thee, a people, and a most glorious and
blessed common wealth; to the end that all
together, may eternally enioy the inheritance of those celestiall benedictions.
And let vs see (since there are to be
so many inhabitants in that soueraigne Citty, and since euery iust person
is to be a Cittizen therof) if there may
there be found, any one who is weake
or impotent, or who is subiect to the
least disgust. The Prophet doth instantly proceed, and say, *The least of
them al shalbe so full of power, as that he*
                                    may

may stand for a thowsand, of the stron-
gest men; and the little one shall stand
for a mighty Army. That is to say,
euery one of the *Blessed* shall participate so much of God, and shall finde
God to be so truely his, as that whatsoeuer he haue a mind to do, for
that he shall haue sufficient power.
And whatsoeuer felicity he shall desire, the same he shall possesse, for in
God he can do all, and he hath all.

These (g) benefits which we
haue heere recounted, & other which
be like to these, are possessed and
enioyed in that celestiall kingdome
which Christ our Lord, who is the
iudge both of the quicke and dead,
will impart to the iust, in reward of
their good life. And now let vs reach
towards the fruit which we must procure to gather, from the infallible
knowledge of this truth. Whereof
(h) the first is this : A very great
estimation, and profound internall

(g) The fruites which grow from the consideration of the glory of heauen.

(h) Great estimatiō of the be-nefits; & great thansgi-uing to the bene-factour.

N 4   grati.

gratitude for this mercy, & vnfpea-
ble grace of God; that we being fo
poore creatures, fo weake, fo ignorant, and who, by our owne fault,
made our felues fo miferable, fo bafe,
fo vnworthy of all good, and who fo
well deferued the vttermoft of all
paine, God would yet make choyce
of vs, from all eternity; and firft create vs, and after that finne was committed, redeeme vs; to the end that
we might obteine that moft fublyme,
and fupernaturall end of beatitude;
which confifteth in feeing God, and
in enioying God, and in obteyning
and poffeffing that by grace, which
God himfelfe doth poffeffe by nature, which is to loue & enioy himfelfe. Againe, that he hath created,
and ordayned, and called, and iufti-
fied vs, for the enabling vs to a dignity fo fublime, as it is to be Kings
of heauen; and to haue feates, and
thrones in that heauen which is called

led Empyreall, & that for euer. And
there to posesse the incomprehensible and eternall felicity of glory ; &
in this glory , to be companions of
the Angells, yea and of God himselfe
who is the Lord of the Angels . This
I say, is a grace , and mercy , which
we are to ponder, and most profoundly to esteeme in the very rootes of
our harts ; and to be gratefull to God
for it, withal the powers of our soule;
and with our tongue to blesse and
prayse him for it, with *S. Peter* saying;
Blessed and prayed be our God, and the
naturall fauour of *Iesus Christ* our
Lord , who through his great and
most aboundant mercy, hath engen-
dred vs anew (who were borne in
sinne , and were the Children of
wrath, by our descent from *Adam*) by
liuely *Fayth*, and by the *Sacraments* ;
making vs , by this spirituall generation to become the sonnes of God
himselfe, and giuing vs a certaine &

N 5   true

true hope of the true life, which is that bleſſed and euerlaſting end. And this he wrought in vs, by the *Reſurre-ĉion* of Chriſt our Sauiour. For by his *Reſurreĉion*, he procured that the world ſhould beleeue in him, and ſhould obey his ghoſpell; and by me-anes of this faith, and obedience, the fruit of his life and paſſion might be communicated to it ; and by this li-uely hope, he firſt enabled vs to ex-peĉ, and afterward to obteine, the inheritáce, which is due to the Sonns of God.

The (i) ſecond thinge which

(i) An in-fatiable thirſt after the ioyes of hea-uen.

we are to draw from hence, is a very great, and liuely, and efficatious de-ſire of this kingdome of heauen; and that once we may arriue to poſſeſſe and enioye that celeſtiall happines. A man deſires, euen by the very ap-petit of nature, to be free from the afflićion of paine, & other corporal miſeries; but this deſire cannot be

ful-

fulfilled in this life. For all this life is full of affliction and sicknes, & paines of body, and sadnes and griefe of mind; and difficulties, and troubles, and contradictions, by his kinsmen & friends, and of persecution by iniustice, and oppressions of enemies; and of contrary and ill encounters in point of fortune; and of temptations of deuils, and of the world; and of their lawes and rights; and of our owne corrupt nature, and al our euill inclinations. *A man*, saith *Iob*, *liues but a little tyme, and that little, is full of many miseries*. In heauen it is, where a man may haue this desire satisfied, because there, as *S. Iohn* saith, *God will wipe away the teares from his frends eyes, & there shall be no death, nor lamentation, nor any sad note, nor griefe*. For all this, had an end, in this life; and therfore it is necessary for a man to labour, with desire of the kingdome of heauen, where onely

Apoc. 21.

ly

ly this defire can be accomplifhed .

A man (k) defires , by the appetite

(k) The iuſt reaſõ of this thirſt, drawne from the ſinnes wherwith the world abounds.

of grace, to ſee himſelfe free from the ſins of his ſoule , which induce him to do ill . In this life , this delight cannot be accomplifhed ; becauſe all this life is full of innumerable ſinns ; and wherſoeuer thou goeſt , thou ſhal ſee ſinne, and plenty of wickednes. And althogh, in many places it aboundeth more , or leſſe , then in other ; yet for the moſt part , euery one of them is corrupted & defild with diuers kinds of vices ; yea and euen the moſt iuſt and holy men, haue ſome veniall ſins, of which they cãnot free themſelues; and the ſame men run hazard to fail into other which are greater . For as

ſ. Ioan . 1. *S . Iohn* ſayth , *If we ſhall ſay that we* *haue no ſinne, we deceiue our ſelues ther-* *in , and we ſpeake not truth* . In heauen it is, where this deſire is fulfilled; for there , is neither fault, nether can there be any . For as the ſame Apo-

ſtle

ſtle ſaith, *Into that celeſtiall Hieruſalem nothing can enter, which is ſpotted*. And ^{Apoc. 21.} therfore it is neceſſary, and moſt profitable, for a man to aſpire to that habitatiõ of heauen, where his deſire may be ſatisfied.

CHAP. XIX.

How all the things of this life which are good, and which giue delight, doe induce vs to a deſire of the kingdome of heauen.

(a) We haue reaſon to thirſt after the kingdom of heauen through the conſideration of earthly pleaſures, which are miſerable things, & yet they make a ſhift to pleaſe vs.

NOT (ᵃ) onely do the euills of ſinne, and puniſhment (wherof this life of ours is full) incline vs to deſire the kingdome of heauẽ, which is free from al thoſe inconueniences; but ſo alſo do all good things, which giue vs in this life any contentment, or guſt either corporall or ſpirituall, perſwade and moue vs to the ſame. For they all diſcouer to vs, the immenſi-

menſity of that celeſtiall happines ;
and the greatnes of the appetite of
our ſoule , which cannot be ſatiſfied,
and put in quiet , by any thing ,
which is leſſe then that . For a man
who , by his ſenſes , taketh experience of the ſauour of his meat , and
drinke , and of the ſweetenes of muſicke , and of the contentment which
he hath in ſeeing thoſe things which
are artificiall , gallant , and full of
beauty ; by the light of reaſon , and of
faith , will grow to make this conſideration. If a creature (b)ſo baſe and
of ſo ſmall importance , as a bird , a
liquor of milke, or wine, or any other
thing that concernes our food, being
toucht but by the courſe pallate of
a man, do yet cauſe delight and guſt;
and ſuch guſt, as that for it, ſome
men do expoſe themſelues to much
trouble and coſt, yea and euen to the
very perdition of their ſoules ; what
ſauour, and what ioy ſhall it giue the
　　　　　　　　　　　　ſoule

(b) A
moſt cer-
tavne
truth, and
which en-
treth
ſweetly
into the
ſoule .

foule, to be moſt profoundly inter-
nally with all the powers and forces
therof, vnited with God, and to taſt
God, he being that infinit good, and
that infinit ſweetnes and ioy; yea &
the infinit fountaine of all ioy and
ſweetnes. And with the ſame ſoule,
to ſwallow downe huge draughtes
of that riuer of delights, which is in
the houſe of God; and which, in
ſubſtance, is in euen God himſelfe,
and the infinit and inexhauſted ſea,
of all chaſt and pure delights.

   If to ſee with theſe corporall
eyes of ours, the deſigne, the beauty,
and the grace of creatures (which
yet are but compounded of earth, &
water, and the other elements; and
framed by the will of man, out of
mettall, and wood, and other mate-
rialls of this world) do cauſe ſuch
contentment, and ioy, in the hart
of man, by the ſight therof, that for
this ſight, they endure, and ſuffer
                              much;

much ; and make long iourneys , and
much expence ; what comfort, and
ioy ſhall it be , for the cleere eyes of
the ſoule (being ſtrengthned by ſupernaturall force and light) to behould that beauty of the Angels, and
bleſſed ſpirits ; yea and the beauty of
God himſelfe.

If to heare with our corporall
eares, that Muſicke which is made by
the voyce of a man , and of other
inſtrumẽts of Muſicke, doth impart
ſuch ſweetnes , as that a man will
remaine many houres as if his ſoule
were euen ſuſpended ; and he is content to looſe both his food and reſt ,
for this earthly guſt ; what ſweetnes
will it be , for thoſe inhabitants of
heauen , with the eares of their ſoule,
to heare thoſe conforts & melodious
ſonges , wherwith all the Quires of
the Angells do praiſe and glorify Almighty God. And to heare that moſt
gratious voyce , wherwith the ſame
God

God doth comfort , and recreate all those blessed soules,& discouereth to them his Loue , togeather with the secrets of his very hart . And to heare also euē with the ears of their bodies, the sound of that praise,and thanksgiuing , wherwith all those men who are to be made happy after their Resurrection , shall glorify Almighty God , & giue ioy to the whole court of heauen.

　　A man(c) who considereth and pondereth by these, and such other discourses both of reason , and faith, the greatenes of these celestiall blessings , and who findeth , that neither the naturall appetite of reason , and much lesse the supernaturall , which he hath , being caused in him by grace , is satisfied or contented, or quieted by al the benefits , and gusts, and delights of the earth, but that euen whilst he hath them he becometh more hungry , more discontent ,and

　more

(c) We haue reason to aspire to eternall glory , since nothing of this life can quēch our thirst

more vnquiet then he was before ; &
that onely he can be satisfied by the
delights and gusts, which are in heauen , will be induced , vpon this
motiue , to desire the happines of
heauen with a most vehement ardour
of minde . And he is animated and
encouraged to begge it of God , and
to sigh and grone for it continually;
Psal. 41. and he sayth with *Dauid: As the Hart*
with being chased and tired, and hauing
deadly thirst, desires the waters and goes
panting vp and downe in search therof; so
my soule being ouerwrought by the mise-
ries of this life, desireth thee o my God &
hath a mighty thirst, and an vnsatiable
appetit towards thee who art the foun-
taine of the liuing water both of grace &
glory, which can only satiffie and appease
my whole appetit. How longe o Lord am I
to liue in this place of banishment! When
wil it be granted me that being freed
from the miseries of this exile, I may
present my selfe before thee , and
behould

behould thee face to face, and enioy
thy prefence, in the fociety of thofe
happy foules! And as longe as this
fentence of banifhement lies vpon
me, & that the fight of thy Diuinity
is deferred, I take contentment in
nothing, but fpending of fighes and
fhedding of teares, day and night,
throgh the exceffiue defire that I haue
to be with thee; and by thefe teares
my foule is comforted & mantained.
Thus did *Dauid*, and all thofe holy
Patriarcks and Prophets, and great
feruants of God of the *old Teftament*
afpire, figh and groane, with vehement defire of this celeftiall beatitude. And much more, and with more
reafon, did the Saints of the *newe*
Teftament performe the fame, and
fo fhould all true Chriftians do. Firft
becaufe till the paffion of Chrift our
Lord was paft, the Saints, how fully
foeuer they were purged from all
finne and paine, went not yet to hea-

O 2   uen,

uen, but to the *Lymbus* of the holy
Fathers, where they ſtaid frō entring
into heauē, till the redemption of the
world were accompliſhed by Chriſt
our Lord . But ſince his death , all
they , who are puꝛified, either in this
life , or in the other , do inſtantly riſe
vp, to the poſſeſſiō of euerlaſting beatitude . And ſecondly now in tyme
of the *lawe of grace* , the guifts of the
holy Ghoſt are more aboundantly
communicated to the faithfull; & ſo
they receiue more conſolations , and
ſpirituall ioy , and haue more guſt , &
feeling , and experience of celeſtiall
graces ; and do more perfectly vnderſtand the height , the value , and
the maieſty therof, and conſequently
they deſire them more , & with more
ardour of affectiō then did the Saints
of the *old Teſtament* . It doth alſo increaſe this deſire in the tyme of the
lawe of grace, to knowe that heauen is
full of bleſſed creatures , who are of
the

the race of mankinde , and who are
expecting vs there ; and do greatly
desire our Society . For by the entry
which any one of the *elect* doth make
into heauen , the glory of God is
increased ; who is far more beloued
and praised , and glorified by the iust
in heauen , then on earth ; and so also
doth the accidentall ioy , and glory of
euery one of the *elect* increase , vpon
the arriuall of any other . But much
more then they altogether , doth (d)
Christ our Lord (who redeemed , &
saued vs by his death) desire to haue
vs there with him . Both because he
loueth vs much more then they all are
able to do , as also for that by the entry of the elect into heauen , and by
the possession which the is giuen the
of that kingdome , the whole fruit of
his passion , and death is gathered ; &
all that is perfected and established ,
which he did and suffred for vs heere;
that so he might make vs completely

(d) This
reason
would ex-
tremely
oblige vs,
though
ther were
no other.

O 3   happy

happy, & be like to himſelfe in glory;
& be partakers of his heauenly kingdome; and in fine, to make vs ſuch,
as that togeather with him, we may
perfectly prayſe, and glorify, and enioy his eternall Father . For theſe
reaſons doth he much deſire to ſee vs
in heauen; and when that deſire of
his is ſatisfyed by the aſcent which
any of the elect maketh thither; that
moſt ſacred ſoule of our Lord doth
receaue a new delight, & ioy, which
belongeth to his accidentall glory.
For as that kind of glory may increaſe in any of thoſe other Bleſſed
Spirits, ſo may it alſo do, in the moſt
glorious Humanity of Chriſt our
Lord.

CHAP.

CHAP. XX.

*Hŏw from this knowledge, concerning
the Kingdome of Heauen, which
Christ our Lord will giue his seruãts,
we are to gather a resolute purpose
to fly from sinne, and to fullfill the
Commandments of God, & to despise
the commodityes of this life.*

THE (a) third, and the principall
vse which we are to make, of this
our knowledge, and estimation, and
desire of heauenly beatitude, is a stout
and resolute minde, and a stiffe and
effectuall purpose, to put in executiõ,
all those meanes, which ar either necessary, or but euen conuenient, for
the obteyning of this kingdome of
heauen. Now, for the entring into
heauen, it is necessary to cast sinne
away. For Sinne giues impediment
to al approach thither; and they who

(a) The
considera-
tion of e-
ternall
glory
must a-
wake vs
to hate &
fly from
sinne.

O 4   haue

haue the soule loaden with any one
mortall sinne, cannot enter into the
kingdome of heauen. Let vs therfore
clense our soules from former sinne,
by penance; and let vs resist all temptations (least els we may returne to
fall againe) accordiug to the aduice
of the Apostle, who saith, *Houlding*
fast those promises of God, which are so
great, and so certaine, and do concerne
those sublyme guifts of grace and glory,
let vs, my brethren much beloued, clense
our selues from all spot of sinne; whether
it be interiour, or exteriour. He saith,
from all sinne, because it will behooue
vs to be clensed from al; and we must
fly with diligence from all. From
mortall sins, because they are against
Charity, & do separate vs from God;
and from *veniall sins,* because they are
contrary to the will of God, and they
weaken the soule; and dispose it to
commit mortall sinne, & consequent.
ly to forfaite the kingdome of heauen.

uen. So alſo, for entring into heauen,
it is neceſſary to do good works, &
ſuch as are acceptable to God ; as
Chriſt our Lord affirmeth, ſaying, *Matt. 19*
If thou wilt enter into that eternall life,
which is true life , keepe the commaund-
ments . Complying (b) therefore (b) It
with this obligation , let vs per- muſt ſtir
forme holy workes, wherby we may vs vp to
fulfill the commaundement of God; & ſe of
and let vs put in execution the all vertue.
vertues of Humility , Chaſtity ,
Mercy , Iuſtice , Temperance , Forti-
tude , Religion , and Charity ; by
which if they be wrought in ſtate of
grace, and do growe out of Charity,
they will make vs worthy of eternall
life.

Beſides , (c) for the obteyning (c) It ex-
of this kingdome of heauen, it is ne- horteth vs
ceſſary that we continue in the good to perſe-
begun , till we end in doeing well, uerance.
as our Lord did teach vs ſaying, *He Matt. 24.*
that conty ueth to the end, ſhall be ſa-
O 5 *ued*

ued . Let vs therfore perſeuere in good life ; and although the deuills comber vs with their temptations , & though men do perſecute vs with their iniuries , and though our Lord God do trye vs by many tribulatiõs, let vs not turne backe , nor be diſmaied, nor ſuffer our ſelues to fall downe , to inordinate ſorrow, nor impatience, nor diſconfidence ; but let vs continually make our recourſe to God ; and praying to him with humility , let vs beg ſtrengh at his hands , wherwith to ſuffer, and conſtancy that we may perſeuere, & confidence that we may not diſpaire. So doth the *Apoſtle* aduiſe the *Galathians* ſaying : *We who are liuing well, and do exerciſe our ſelues in good workes, let vs not faint , nor giue ouer , no nor growe ſlacke in the good courſe begunne but let vs contynue , and grow therin, with great conſtancy . For in due tyme we ſhall gather the fruit , if we doe not faint.*

Galat. 6.

faint . That is to fay , we fhall eat the fruit of glory , which fhall haue no end .

Moreouer (d) for the arriuing to enioy celeftial beatitude, we muft defpife the goodes, and pleafures of this world. And it is neceffary that we place not our hartes or endes in them ; nor that we feeke for comfort in them, as Chrift our Lord did fignify to vs by faying , *Woe be to you, who are the louers of riches, and who haue placed your comfort, in the comodityes of this life* . For this reafon it will be neceffary, in moft particuler manner, to contemne all the commodit008 tyes of this life ; namely riches , honours, and pleafures, as poore things tranfitory, and bafe ; for by defpifing them we fhall not place our end, nor feeke for comfort in them .

This is therefore that fruit, which we are to gather from the knowledge, and defire of celeftiall

be.

(d) We muft not thinke of finding our heauen in this life , if we meane to haue it in the next .

Luc. 6.

beatitude . For knowing the greatnes , and beauty, and valew of heauenly things, we grow quickly, and
clearely, to see the vilenes, & poor-
nes of such as be earthly; and by desiring and tasting eternall things, we
grow instantly to loose the loue, and
tast of all thinges transitory . And
thus shall we perfectly accomplish
that which the Apostle asketh at the
Colos. 3 . hands of all the faythfull , saying : *If*
you be raysed vp with Christ , seeke the
things that are aboue . That is (ᵉ) to
(e) A place say , *Since you are risen vp in soule to a*
of S. Paul *spirituall life of grace , with hope to be*
excellent- *raysed vp , in due tyme , to an immortall*
ly ponde- *and glorious life both in body and soule ,*
red . *(in imitation of Christ our Lord, who*
rose vp from the dead to an immortal and
glorious life) seek you with your thoghts,
with your desirs, with your good works ,
and with continuall prayer , the kingdom
of heauen . And since Christ our Lord
who is your head , is seated at the right
hand

hand of his Father, possessing and enioying euen as man, the greatest anthori-
ty and the greatest felicity of glory which
he did euer communicate in Tyme, or will
euer communicate for all Eternity, you
that are members of his, take gust and
sauour in heauenly thinges; and place not
your delight, and loue vpon those of the
earth, but desire those others so from the
hart, and with so great purity of life,
that you may, euen by experience, find
the gust and most pure sauour of them;
& addresse your life, in order to this end
of eterna'l glory, which you loue, and for
which you hope.

This efficacious purpose, &
determinate resolution to cleanse the
soule from all vice, to imploy it with
perseuerance in good workes; and
cordially to despise earthly thinges,
is the vse which we are to make, of
the knowledg and desire of celestiall
beatitude, as hath beene sayd. And
it is most iust, & due, that so we do,
and

and that, for the going through with this enterprize which we are to make, vpon heauen, we be content to vndertake all labour, and to encounter with any difficulty . All the things (f) of this life, which are of any valew , & are able to giue but the least cōtentment, do cost some trouble, and in all them some difficulty is to be endured. The husband-mā, for gathering in of a little corne, doth manure, and plough the ground before he sowes; and after he hath sowed, and that the blade is vp , and the corne is growne, is fayne first to cleanse it, and then to sheere it, with much labour . The Sheepheard for the breeding of his poore flocke, doth content himselfe to endure the heats, and coldes, and raines, and windes, and night-watches . All Marchants and Factors, and all the Maryners & conductors who are of seruice to thē in their negotiations, do , for the getting

(f) A plaine demonstration , and I am in good hope, that it will conuince.

ting

ting of a little money, paffe through intollerable troubles, both by Sea & Land ; and do expofe themfelues to great danger of death. All kind of tradefmen, for the getting of a poore liuing, do labour and fweat both day and night, in their feuerall occupations . The fouldier, for his miferable pay, and for a little fume of honour, is fubiect to extreme inconueniences, and runs hazard of his life, at euery moment. The feruants and Courtiers of great Princes, for the obtayning of fauour, which yet doe paffe, and change like any wind, depriue themfelues of their owne guft, and deny their owne will, and are hanging day and night, vpon that of others ; and for the giuing of contentment to their Lords, they take an aboundance of difcontentment & difguft to themfelues . They who are enamoured of this world, the couetous, for money ; the intemperate,

for

for curious fare ; the dishonest , for that filthy pleasure ; the proud , for that vaine delight in honour , and commaund ; and all of them in fine, for the poore comodities of this life, do suffer greiuous paines , and endure excessiue torments , and sicknesses , and other afflictions , which vpon these occasious they incurre; as themselues do confesse when the punishment of God shall haue laid their errour before their face . And then they will say , *We went astray* Sap . 5. *from the way of truth and were estranged from that diuine light ; and did ouerworke and tyre our selues in the way of sinne , and vice, and there we endured many difficulties .*

If then the men of this world , for the obteyning of most base and transitory riches , and of certaine pleasures , which are vaine and pernicious , both to body and soule; & for the giuing of contentment to mor-

mortall creatures; & for the yeilding
of obedience, to thofe infernall Diuels, who perfwade them to the loue
of earthly things, doe ingulfe themfelues into fuch a fea of troubles, and
breake through fuch a world of difficultyes; what, in the name of God,
will it not be fit for Chriftians and
the feruants of Chrift to do, for the
being faythfull; and loyall, to that
diuine Maiefty; and for the exact
complying, with that obedience, &
loue, which they owe him, both as
to a father, and as to a Lord; and for
the obtayning of the kingdome of
heauen, & the poffeffing of thofe immortall riches of the houfe of God; &
the honour & glory of being the fons
of God; and confequently the ioynt
heyres with Chrift our Lord, of his
patrimony Royall, and of his euerlafting entaile; and for the inioying,
and that for euer, of thofe incomprehenfible delights of his beatitude?

P   Cer-

Certainly, it is moſt iuſt, it is moſt due, that they ſhould vndergo any trouble and ouercome any difficulty, and expoſe themſelues to any temporall hazard, how greatſoeuer. For as the Apoſtle ſayth, by way of confirming this truth: *All* (g) *men who ſtriue, and fight with others, in the place deputed to that end (as the vſe of the Romains was to do in their entertainements and feaſts) do for the ouercomming of their oppoſites, abſtaine from all thoſe thinges of guſt, which may be of any impediment to them in their combat, as namely from delicate meates, from wine, from women, and the like, which are wont to make men dull, and weake; and they feed vpon groſſe meats, they obſerue the rules of continency and temperance, and they prepare and accuſtome themſelues before hand, to labour. And all this they do, to obtayne the reward of winning a corruptible crowne, which might perhaps be ſome Iewell, or ſome*

ſuite

(g) This truth confirmed by S. Paul, moſt diuinely, & excellently pondered by our Author 1. Cor. 9.

suite of clothes , or some garland of bayes
or flowres, or some vaine applause , and
flying prayse of men . What then are we
Christians obliged to do . in this spiritual
contention . and strife which we are ma-
king against sinne , for the obtayning of
that crowne of immortality , and glory ;
& of that celestiall kingdome? It is moſt
certain , that if for the giuing of contentment to Almighty God , and for
the obtayning of that eternall and
immenſe beatitude, it were neceſſary
to ſuffer all thoſe pains put togeather
which al the men of the world, from
the beginning of it to the end, will
haue beene to ſuffer ; and which all
the holy Martyrs haue endured ; it
were all reaſon, that we ſhould willingly be content to endure them all.
And if it were neceſſary, not only to
ſuffer all the paines of this life, but to
endure (yea and that for many ages)
all the torments of hell , yea and of
many hells ; it (h) were moſt iuſt, &

(h) The
ioyes of
heauen
are more
to be deſi-
red , then
euen the
paines of
hell to be
auoyded,

P 2   fiſ

fit to endure them all, for the obtayning of the kingdome of heauen afterward. For greater is the good of the glory of heauen, then the euill of the paines of hell. And how much then more iust, and more conuenient will it be, to suffer the payne and difficulty which belongs to vertue, and which accompanyeth the fullfilling of Gods commandments. Which (i) difficultyes besides that they are short (for as much as at the most, they last no longer then this life) they are with all both light and sweet. For the loue of God, and the heauenly consolations which he communicateth to his seruants, doth make them sweet; and the helps and succours of grace which otherwise he giues thē, make them light. So doe iust persons find this to be by experience, as the Apostle confesseth, saying: *After the rate of the tribulations and afflictions, which we suffer for Christ our Lord, and where-*

(i) How the difficultyes of vertue grow delightfull through the goodnes of God, besides that all temporal labour is light, since it is so short.

2. Cor, 1.

whereby we go in imitation of him, so do the consolations which are given by Almighy God, through the vertue and merit of our B Sauiour, increase and copiously abound in vs.

If (k) then the labours & troubles of this life, be, on the one side, so momentany and so short; and on the other so sweet and light; and the reward of glory, and of that celestial kingdome, so eternal, and immense; and that as our good workes doe grow to be increased, so also doth the reward of glory go increasing; in such sort, as that to euery of our good workes, yea (l) and to euery one of our desires, and euen to euery moment of a life which is lead in state of grace, there is a distinct degree of glory which correspondeth: what man is that, who will not labour for the leading of a vertuous life? Who will not be diligent, in making resistance to all temptations

(k) Consider seriously of the conclusion of this discourse.

(l) O infinite bounty ofGod! And are we then in ourwits when we be either sinnefull, or euen but slouthfull in Gods seruice.

what-

whatfoeuer ? Who will not fuffer a-
ny iniury, or paine , for liuing well;
And who will not refolue with
ftrength and courage , to perfeuere
in that good caufe which he hath begun ? Let vs all both heare, and with
great fidelity, obey the voyce of that
Prophet who fayth : *You who are the*
people of God, do you encourage, and ani-
mate your felues to ferue him, and to con-
tinue in that feruice of his without dif-
may ; for , in fine , your labours fhall e
anfwered with a great reward .

2. Paral.
25.

CHAP. XXI.

How we are much to animate our felues,
to the exercife of good workes ; confi-
dering the great eftimation which
Chrift our Lord doth make of them at
the day of Iudgement ; and the re-
ward which he alfo imparteth to thē.

THERE is alfo another particular confideration , belonging to
this

this diuine *Iudgment*, and to the reward of good workes , which doth
greately moue the soule, to labour
hard in the seruice of God. And this
is, the *Reason*, and *Tytle* which Christ
our Lord alledgeth, in giuing his benediction, and reward to the iust,
when he saith; *Come yee blessed of my* Matt. 25.
Father possesse the kingdom which is pre-
pared for you. *For I was hungry, and*
you gaue me to eat, I was thirsty and you
gaue me to drinke; I was a stranger, &
you receiued me into your howse; I was
sicke, and in prison, and you came to
visit me. For(a) by these words Christ
our Lord doth mightily discouer (a) The
the estimation, and price which he great va-
hath stamped vpon good workes , our Lord
which are done in grace ; and the doth
great fauour and honor which they make, e-
receiue in his diuine presence ; the our least
much that they please him, and the good
immense glory wherwith he rewar- workes.
deth them; since so meane workes, &

so very easy to be wrought, as it is to giue a peece of bread to a poore hūgry body; or a cup of water to a thirsty; or a shirt to couer the naked; or a nights lodging to a stranger; or a visit to an imprisoned or sick person; though it be but to comfort him with good words (for we see he doth not say, *I was sicke and you cured me; or I was imprisoned and you freed me*; but such easy workes, as are those other, and which put vs to so little cost and trouble;) that excellent Maiesty of his, is pleased to publish & proclaime in that great Theater, vpon the day of *Iudgement*; in the presence of the whole world, and he setteth out and praiseth them which his owne sacred mouth; & he sublymes then so high, as to take them for seruices and deare fauours imparted to his owne persō, which giue him great contentment & gust. And so much (b) account he makes therof, as to esteeme them for

merits

(b) That which maketh a good worke meritorious, is the flowing of it, from the grace of God in Christ our Lord, and the being seconded by his promise of a reward, which promise makes the reward due.

merits which are worthy of eternall life; and he receaues them as a price of the kingdome of heauen; And he esteemeth them for meritorious; & that, not only, all together, but euery one of them a part; and a part he takes euery one of them for the price of glory, and of that kingdome which hath no end.

But (e) now, if Christ our Lord, who so highely esteemes, and vouchsafes the fauour of so great reward, to so light and easy workes as those, what will he do, to such workes of mercy as are great & hard; and which grow out of much Charity? As when a man doth giue all his goods, or a great part therof to the poore; or lodge Pilgrims for a long tyme; and serue them, and prouide them of all things necessary; & depriue himselfe of clothes to cloth the poore naked Christian; and to serue sicke persons day and night;

(e) What will not our Lord do to ve, for greater works since he doth so much for the lesse.

P 5   and

and that in the cafe of troublefome
and contagious difeafes , as when
they may be ftrucké with tne plague;
and to drawe with much trouble of
perfon and charge of purfe , fuch as
are prifoners , or Capriues , out of
their chaines : How much , I fay ,
will Chrift our Lord efteeme fuch
works as thefe , which coft much labour and money ; and for the performing whereof a man endures much
incommodity , and imbraceth many
paineful things , and wraftling with
ftore of difficulties ; and mortifies
himfelfe much , to comfort others ;
& renounces his owne will in many
things , that fo others may be comforted and releeued ? There can no
doubt be made , but that much more
he will efteeme them, and will afford
them the fauour in that day of Iudgement of a reward fo much higher,
as the works are more excellent, &
more acceptable in his eyes , for being

ing growne vp out of greater Charity.

And if the Corporall works
of mercy, which are exercised vpon
the bodyes of men, which must quickly dy; and for the maintenance and
preseruation of this corporall life,
which is soone to haue an end, be so
much esteemed, and fauoured, and
so highly rewarded by Christ our
Lord; what will he be sure to do to
the workes of spirituall mercy, wherby immortall soules are succoured, &
redrest; and wherby they, being deliuered from the death of sinne, and
euerlasting paine, there is imparted
to them saluation, and a life of euerlasting glory? A plaine (d) case it is,
that, the worke of mercy, wherby a
soule is assisted, is more excellét, then
that other wherby a body is releeued;
& that these works of piety, wherby
the spirituall and eternall life is holpen, is of much more valew, and

(d) How
much
therefore
are we
bound to
such as do
assist our
soules,
though it
be with
hazard of
theirliues.

merit

merit, then that other, wherby that
corporall and fraile life is succoured.

D. Thom.
cont. Gen.
l. 4. cap. 55.
For as much, as according to S. *Tho-*
*mas, Amongst all those things which are
created, no one is greater, then the saluation of a reasonable soule, which consisteth in the enioying of God*: So also
there is no other greater almes, then
that, wherby this saluation, and this
life of grace and glory is procured; &
consequently a much greater benefit
doth he impart to another, who re-
medieth the necessityes of his soule,
then if he had giuen him a great sume
of money. And since they who giue
a little bread to the hungry, and a
little water to the thirsty; and they
who retyre a Pilgrime to their house,
and apparel a naked person, with a
peece of cloth; and visit a man who is
in prison or sicke, giuing him a little
temporall comfort, be so esteemed
and honoured by Almighty God, in
the presence both of heauen & earth,

in

in that terrible tribunall of his *Iudg-ment*; and are so enobled, and sublymed with the Crowne of celestiall glory, and with the dignity of the euerlasting kingdome ; what will Christ do, that most iust and righteous Iudge, and that most liberal God with them who dispense the bread of heauenly doctrine to such as haue need, and are hungry after it ; and who powre out the drink of spiritual comfort, and ease, to such as are afflicted, and deiected, that so they may beare their miseryes with patience ; & who cloath their soules with vertues and celestiall guifts, who are naked & depriued of al spiritual graces, and who cure, and recouer, out of their miserable infirmityes, and who draw and deliuer out of that horrible captiuity, them who are sicke of sinne, and are taken prisoners, and made slaues by Sathan. Most certain it is, that although all they who ex-

preffe

preſſe mercy towards their neighbours, ſhallbe eſteemed & honored
in that Tribunal; & ſhalbe ſublimed
with glory and royall dignity, yet
theſe others who haue imparted it towards the ſoules of mē, ſhalbe much
more eſteemed and honoured, by
Chriſt our Lord, and his Angels, &
ſhalbe raiſed to greater glory,& more
aduaūced in the kingdom of heauen.

It is alſo to be conſidered, that
although theſe works of mercy, whether they be corporall, or ſpirituall,
and which reſpect the ſpirituall or
corporall good of our neighbour, are
excellent and of great value,and merit, as we haue already ſayd; yet the
interiour, and exteriour workes of
Fayth, Hope, Charity,and Religion,
which haue (e) imediate relation to
Almighty God, and to the worſhip
& ſeruice which is due to him as our
God, and our Creatour,are more excellent, and of greater value, & merit,

(e) How
highly
gratefull
thoſe acts
of vertue
are,
which do
immedia-
tly reſpect
Almighty
God.

rit, then the workes of mercy, which
ayme but at the côfort of our neighbours . And so much more as any
vertue doth draw neere, & approach
to God , so much more is the vertue
more excellent . Now the vertues ,
which are called Theological, which
are *Fayth, Hope,* & *Charity* , do looke
vp, and serue & immediatly honour
Almighty God , belieuing his truth,
and louing his goodnes , and hoping
in his mercy . And the vertue of Religion, doth respect, and exercise the
worship , and veneration , which is
due to God, as being soueraigne Authour and Lord of all thinges . And
these vertues being more excellent,
then that of *Mercy* towardes our
Neighbour , it is cleare, that those
faythfull Christians, who with firme
and liuely fayth , haue beleeued in
Christ our Lord, and who confessed
his fayth, in the face of Tyrants ; &
who placed all their confidence , &
loue

in Chrift, fearching, with care, after
his glory; and refigning themfelues
entirely to his moft holy will; and
honoring him, & reuering him with
true worfhip, & with pure prayers,
and with an exact performance of
their promifes, and the vowes which
they make to his diuine Maiefty; certaine I fay it is, that in the day of his
diuine *Iudgment*, they fhall be more
efteemed, and honoured by Chrift,
for hauing done and fuffered thefe
thinges, then either they, or any o-
thers fhallbe; for any other inferiour
works which they may haue wroght
towardes their Neighbours. And
therefore, the reward of glory being
fo illuftrious and fo high, which for
the workes of fpirituall and corporall mercy they fhall receaue; & con-
fidering that yet, the reward which
thefe others fhall obtayne, is to be
much more eninent and great; and
fince, notwithftading that the kingdome

dome which is to be giuen in reward
of thefe workes of mercy, is celeftiall
& eternall; yet for thefe acts of *faith*,
and *Charity*, and *Religion*, a greater,
and a better portion fhall be allotted,
and fet out in the fame kingdome;
let vs be moft diligent in the leading
of a good life;in côferuing our foules
pure and cleane; in exercyfing our
felues in the acquifitiô of vertue. And
let vs be full of feruour towards the
works of mercy, whether they be fpirituall or corporall, euery one according to his Tallent.

    O happy (f) and for euer moft
happy they, who fhall thus imploy
themfelues: *Happy*, becaufe they were
elected from all *eternity*, by almighty
God; *Happy* becaufe they were called in *Tyme* to his faith, and Religion,
and were inftructed therin; *Happy*,
becaufe they did correfpond to that
vocation of God, and did begin to
lead a good life; *Happy*, becaufe they

(f) Con-
clufion.

        Q   did

did contynue therin ; *Happy* , becaufe if they fell, they quickly rofe againe, by penance, and were conftant therin ; And *Happy* beyond all *happies* , becaufe, when our Lord came to call them to accompt , at the houre of their death, he found them imployed in a good life , and watchfull in the exercife of good workes , expecting the tyme of his comming, to receaue the reward of their labours , at his mercifull, and moft liberall handes . For it is fayd , by no leffe then Truth it felfe , *Happy is that feruant , whome his Lord , when he commeth , shall find watching , and imployed in the difcharge of his duety , with fidelity and prudence , and complying with his obligations , whether they be common to all Chriftians , or particulerly belonging to his ftate . I tell you as an vndoubted truth, that to fuch a feruant as this, his Lord shall deliuer vp the poffeffion of all his goods .* That is , Chrift our moft
merci-

Luc. 12.

mercifull Lord, and our God, will rayfe him vp from the bleffinges of grace in this life, to the bleffinges of glory in the next; and from the ba-fenes of this earth, to raigne eter-nally, together with himfelfe, in heauen. Amen.

Q 2 THE

THE
CONCLVSION

TO THE READER.

MAKE accompt, good Reader, that this difcourfe is a Letter, & this which now thou art reading, is the Poftfcript of it. Thou haft feene the torments of Hell, and the ioyes which are imparted to the elect in heauen. Thou haft feene that if thou dye in mortall finne, thou wilt for euer be chayned in thofe torments; & for euer be depriued of thofe ioyes.

Q 3   Take

Take heed therefore of all sinne; and especially take heed of the sinne either of *Schisme* or *Heresy*, which are of the greatest that can be comitted. The nature of *Heresy*, consisteth in this, That a man will make election of some one doctrine, or more, which is contrary to the beleefe of that true Church, which is celebrated in the *Creed* of the first Councell of *Nice*; to be *One*, to be *Holy*, to be *Catholike*, & to be *Apostolike*. Be sure thou be of that one true *Church*, which soeuer that be (for thogh my self be resolued, yet I will not heere handle that question, by way of Controuersy;) but there is but one wherin a Christian can be saued, one in the faith which it professeth, howsoeuer it may be accounted many, in respect of the infinite persons which it conteyneth, and consequently of the particular Churches which it imbraceth. The nature (a) therfore of *heresy*, doth not consist

(a) Wherin the nature of heresy, doth indeed consist.

confift in the multitude or quality
of the Articles of Religion , which
are held , in difference from the do-
trine and direction of the holy Catholike Church ; but it confifteth
properly, in the pride and prefump-
tion of that hart , which dares pre-
ferre a priuate opinion , of any one,
or feuerall Countries , or any interpretation of holy Scripture (which
interpretation , is alfo no more then *(b)* **For he**
a(b) meere opinion) before the Iud- will make
gement of that *Church* , which is , & tur affirm
is ftill to be inftructed and taught by and deny
the holy Ghoft . And this finne , is of will.
fo high a nature , as that vnleffe it be
remoued by pennance , the man in
whome it liues, fhall (c) dye a double *(c)* No
death, and neuer behould the face of heretike
God; howfoeuer he may , otherwife, without
feeme to be a perfon of moft holy life, ce can be
& fo ful of Charity, as to fell his ftate, faued,
and giue it all to the poore; and of fo
valiant and Chriftian a hart, as,
Q 4   amongft

amongſt Infidels, to ſuffer death, &
torments for the name of Chriſt. For
to proue that euen this will not ſerue
the turne of an Heretike towards ſaluation, ſee heere the authority of the
greateſt Fathers of the church cōcerning this point. Who(d) (beſids, that
in the way of practice, the Church of
their tyme, did cōdemne many men
for *Hereſy*, who held, though it were
but one point of doctrine, in contra-
riety to the Catholike Church (and
ſomtymes of ſome ſuch doctrine, as
in it ſelfe, did not ſeeme to be of moſt
importance) they do alſo declare,
and that in moſt cleere and conſtant
words, in what certainty of damnation they are, who dy in any Hereſy
at all. *Whoſoeuer*, ſaith S. Cyprian *&
what kinde of perſon ſoeuer, a man be,
a(*e*) Chriſtian he is not, vnles he be in the
Church of Chriſt*. And againe: *He belongs not to the reward of Chriſt, who
forſakes the Church of Chriſt; ſuch a one*

(d) The
practiſe
of the pri-
mitiue
Church
in this
point.
See *S.
Aug. ad
Quod-vult
Deum*, &
the Cata-
logues of
*S. Irenæ-
us*, and *S,
Epiphani-
us*.
*D. Cypr.
epiſt. in
Anton.*
(e) No he-
retike is a
Chriſtian
any more
then only
in name.
*Idem de v-
nit. Eccleſ.*

ịị

*is an alien, he is a prophane perfon, he is
an enemy.* And to this effect, he also
fayth, if such an one should euen giue
his life for the confeffion of the name
of Chrift, he should yet (by the Iudgement of this holy Father) be condemned to the flames of Hell for his
Herefy, and not be receiued to the
ioyes of heauen for his conftancy; &
he expreffeth himfelf in thefe words,
*Non effet illi corona fidei, fed pæna per-
fidiæ.* S. *Hierome,* in like manner, fpeaking of the Church of *Rome* affirmeth
it to be, *The true houfe of Chrift ; and* D. *Hier.*
that whofoeuer eateth the lambe, out of epift. ad
that houfe, is a prophane perfon, and that Dam. l. 2.
vnles he be found, in that Arke of Noe,
he shallbe ouerwhelmed, and perish in
the floud.

S. *Auguftine* doth alfo abound D. *Aug.*
euery where, in the profeffion of this tom. 7. fu-
truth. *A man,* fayth he *cannot obtaine* ter geft.
faluation, but in the Catholike Church: vlt. med.
he may haue all except faluation ; he may

Q 5   *haue*

haue honour, he may haue the sacramēts,
he may sing Alleluia, he may answere A-
men, he may belieue the Ghospell, he may
be baptized in the name of the Father, &
of the Sonne, and of the holy Ghost, but
no where can he haue saluatiō, but in the
Catholike Church. No man cometh, saith
he, to saluation, and life eternall, but he
that hath Christ for his head; and no
man can haue Christ for his head, who
is not in his body, which is the Church.
Heretikes by belieuing falsely of God, do
violate the faith; and Schismatikes by
their wicked dissentions, flye of from fra-
ternall charity, although they belieue as
we do. And therefore neither doth the
Heretike belonge to the catholike Church
because he belieueth not God; nor the
Schismatike, because he loueth not his
Neighbour.

*Let (*f*) vs suppose that a man were*
chast, and contynent; not couetous, no
worshiper of Idolls, but full of hospitali-
ty; no enemy to any man, nor contenti-
ous,

D. Augu.
tom. 7. de
vnit. Eccl.
vlt. med.

Idem. tom.
3. de fide
& symb.
(f) The
schismatik
hath no
Charity,
and the
Heretike
hath nei-
ther Cha-
rity, nor
Fayth.
Idem. tom
7. de Bapt.
cont. Don.
l. 4. c. 18.

ous, *but patient & quiet*; *not emulating
or enuying any body, but sober and fru-
gall; but yet withall, that he were an heretike, and there can no doubt be made,
but* (g) *that for this only,* That he is an
Heretike, he shall not possesse the
kingdome of heauen.

(g) **No**
Heretike
can be la-
ued,
though he
be neuer
so virtu-
ous other-
wise.
Idem. tom.
4. *l.* 1. *de*
serm. Do.
*in monte
c.* 9.
(h) **No**
heretike,
or schis-
matike
can be a
Martyr.
Tom 1. *de*
*fide ad Pe-
trum. c.* 39.
(i) Some
doubt,
whether
this book
be of S.
Auguftin,
or of S.
Fulgenti-
us, who

It is not sayd alone, Bleſſed are
they who ſuffer perſecution, *but theſe
words are added,* for iuſtice ſake. *Now
where* (h) *true Fayth is not, there can
be no luſtice,becauſe the luſt man liues
in Fayth. Neither yet let Schiſmatikes
promiſe themſelues any thing thereby,be-
cauſe where there is no* Charity, *neither
can there be any* luſtice. *For Charity towards ones Neighbour, doth worke no
euill; which Charity if they did peſſeſſe,
they would not teare the body of Chriſt,
which is his Church.*

Belieue (i) *moſt firmely, and haue
no manner of doubt, but that euery Heretike and Schiſmatike, though baptized
in the name of the Father, and of the
Sonne,*

lliued within 40. yeares after S. Auguſtine.

Sonne, and of the holy Ghost, if he returne not to the Catholike Church, how great (k) *Almes soeuer he distribute*, *yea and though he shed his bloud for the name of Christ, he can by no meanes be saued. For neither Baptisme, nor most liberall almes, nor death endured for the name of Christ, can auaile any man to saluation, who holdeth not fast the vnity of the* Catholike Church; *and so long as any* (l) *hereticall, or schismaticall iniquity (which leadeth men to destruction) remayneth in him.*

(k) Euen the giuing al in alms and suffering death for the name of Christ, wil not deliuer an heretique from damnation.

(l) How small soeuer that be.

These are they, amongst many others, whome God hath giuen to his Church, as lightes whereby all good Christians may be guided towardes their saluation; and take heed thou be not so miserable, as to follow any *ignis fatuus*, insteed of them; for thy error in this life, will import thee no lesse then thy eternall damnation in the next.

FAVLTS

F A V L T S

escaped in the Printing.

Page	Line	Fault	Correction.
10.	10.	intention	attention
20.	*vlt*	fo	of
35.	1.	interiourly	exteriourly
36.	12.	he is to make	*deleatur* he
49.	16	vnanfwerable	vnanfwerably
50.	3.	to friend	to that friend
55.	13.	and for zeale	and zeale of
63.	1.	whither	wither
65.	7.	for thus	for this
78.	13.	infinity	infinite
79.	13.	guifts	gufts
81.	14.	Sathan that	*deleatur* that
90.	16.	is infinite	is an infinite
101.	10.	is hauing	is their hauing
Ibid	11.	then being	their being
110.	7.	by all	by ill
113.	17.	my pennance	*deleatur* my which

Page	Line	Fault	Correction.
118.	8.	which	with
122.	18.	ſtrike inro him	ſtrike him into
143.	22.	for his mercy	of his mercy
154.	5.	when themſelues	where themſelues
174.	6.	containe	containes
175.	16.	to be of	are to be of
187.	17.	niuite	inuite
201.	15.	fauour	father
216.	1.	the ſoule	their ſoule
223.	14.	yet doe	yet doth
230.	5.	cauſe	courſe
232.	19.	them	them

FINIS.

JOHN HEIGHAM
The Gagge of the Reformed Gospell
1623

THE
GAGGE
OF THE REFORMED
GOSPELL.

BRIEFLY
Difcouering the errors of
our time.

WITH
The Refutation by expreffe textes
of their owne approoued
Englifh Bible.

THE SECOND EDITION;
Augmented thoroughout the whole, by the
Author of the firft.

By thine owne mouth I iudge thee, naugh =
tie feruant. Luc. 19. 22.
With permiffion. Anno 126̧.

TO THE CATHOLIQVE

READER, HEALTH AND
encouragement in his
holy Faith.

Vrteous Reader, before thou peruse this litle Treatise, haue (I pray thee) so much patience, as to permit me to giue thee myne aduise , concerning some certaine points , very necessar e for thee, the better to serue thy selfe therof with fruit and profit.

1. The first point is, that in the inscription therof, it doth not tell thee, out of which English Bible, the alleadged passages are extracted , for as much as this were meerely in vaine, sith England hath brought forth within these few yeares past, a great number of seue-

A 2   *rall*

rall forts of Bibles, far different one from another; So that our aduersaries (to Whom I Wish from my very hart, as I doe to thee, that this little booke may prooue profitable) haue not all one fort of Bible. NotWithstanding knoW for certaine, that they are faithfully taken forth of the Bible in quarto, printed at London by Thomas Barker, anno 1615. But if any one shall sheW vnto thee some other Bible, Wherin they are not so Written, Worde for Worde as here they are, yet rest assured, and out of dout, that thou shalt finde them Written as they ar here alleadged, in this edition of Robert Barkers.

2. The second point is, that thou admire the splendor of the truth, the Which is such and so passing bright, that notWithstanding they haue endeauoured to obscure the same. by so many varieties of translations, and by such a number of grosse corruptions and falsifications. yet neuertheles their condemnation is so exprisly set doWne in their

oWne

owne Bible, and is so cleare to all the
world, that nothing more is needfull
hereto, but that thou know to reade,
and haue thine eyes in thy head to behould the same, at the opening of this
their booke. This can not choose but
be, an exceeding comfort vnto a Catholique, concerning the vprightnes of
his cause, to offer to be tried, and to
confound them by their owne Bible, the
translation wherof, doth in a number
of places, and particularly of those that
are most in question, swarue and differ notoriously from the authenticall
Latin, and that to the incredible
disparagement, darkning and obs-
curing of the Catholique cause. Neuer did, nor neuer dare our aduersaries, offer themselues, to giue the like
aduantage vnto vs, as to stand to be
tried, by our translation, and
that in fiftie and od maine points of
controuersie.

3. The third point is, that when
thou shalt vrge or alleadge any passage,
in fauor of thine owne faith, if anie
A 3

one returne ther change, be it ether in
vsing recrimination and blaming of the
Roman Church, or be it in alleadging
some obscure textes and ill vnderstood,
to counterpoint those alleadged by thee;
Shew then the partie amiably, that this
is not to proceed in due order, nor dea-
les not with thee as he ought, in oppo-
sing a passage darke and obscure, to
confound a passage that is most cleare.
For example, when we set before their
eies these few wordes (much more clea-
rer then the Sunne it self at noone day)
Take eate, this is my body, this
is my blood which shal be shed. &c.
Marc. 14. 25. they suppose to haue
found forth an important place, yea
and to haue giuen vnto vs a great
ouerthrowe, if they presently reply,
that our Sauiour saith in S. Iohn 6.
63. The flesh profiteth nothing,
the wordes that I speake vnto you,
they are spirit, and they are life; a
passage far more obscure, then that
which is in question, & which affirmeth nothing lesse, then that which
they

they pretend to prooue thereby; for how absurd were it to say, that the flesh of Christ profiteth nothing? And if (as they themselues say) we must interpret one passage by another, then doutles, it is better to explicate an obscure passage, by one that is cleare, then one that is cleare, by a passage obscure: and that one text giue place to many, rather then many to giue place to one, or to fewer.

4. *The* fourth point is, *that if they reiect some of the passages which thou producest, pretending it to be Apocripha; know that to preuent this obiection, no such scriptures as they call Apocripha are here produced, but allwayes there goe accompanied with them, others also that are canonicall by their owne confession: and so far forth as Apocripha, shall and doe agree with Canonicall, they themselues by their owne rule, are bound to receiue them. W*hich *will also fully stop the Reformers mouthes, in their common pretence of conferences of places; for*

A 4   *rare-*

rarely hast thou lesse, then three or four
seuerall passages cited at large (besides
references) for the proofe of euerie se-
uerall point; All the pack of them put
together, being neuer able in their de-
fence to doe the like, that is, to produce
so many in number, so expresse & cleare,
and for so great a quantitie of con-
trouersies, as are here disputed and cou-
ched in so litle a roome.

5. The fift point is, *that if they*
shall contend with thee, not about the
wordes themselues, as being cleare,
but about the sence and meaning of
them; for such places, I say, as may be
subiect to this cauill, thou shalt forth-
with haue recourse and fly to that,
which the scriptures call, the Rule of
faith, *to wit, to the euer constant and*
vniforme iudgement of the Church and
Fathers, who in euery age since Christ
our Lord vnto this present, haue vn-
derstood the point in question, in the
selfe same sence that Catholiques doe,
an example wherof thou maist lay be-
fore him, or them, out of that learned
trea-

treatife, intituled The Summarie of Controuerfies, *debating the queftion of the bleffed Sacrament* : which ha-uing done, then bid thine aduerfarie to doe the like, and thou wilt inftantly yeld vnto him (a thinge which he can neuer doe in his defence.*) Which being fo, what man of reafon will reiect this Rule, *grounded fo clearly in holy fcrip-ture, to prefer the priuat interpreta-tion of fome fillie Cobler, before Saint Chrifoftome, of a Baker, before S. Ba-fill, of fome Tinkar before Tertullian, or of any Nouellist whatfoeuer, before the iudgement of the Church , and the whole ftreame of the holie Fathers?* This point therfore being fo important, *shall be the very firft, which I wil for-tifie and proue by the word of God in this prefent Treatife , I meane this* Rule , *and therfore in no wife for-get , allwayes to rap thine aduerfa-ries with this* Rule *, as often as they shall proue vntruly , and thou shalt be fure to get the victorie, although there be thoufandes of them aga.nft*

A 5   *thee*

thee alone.

The sixt and last point is, *that I here protest in the presence of God (whom I call vpon in this behalfe, and pray thee also to call vpon, for the salvation and reduction of all those that goe a stray) that it is not in the power of all our aduersaries that are in England, to finde in their owne Bible, one only expresse text, I say one only, I say in their owne Bible, by the which they can possibly proue, one only point of their false doctrine, without their vsuall art of adding, diminishing, or changing it by interpretation: which yet should be to alter the text, and to employ mans wisdome, insteed of the pure word, a thinge by their owne confession, flatly forbidden them: they protesting, that the word of God, doth in such sort containe all that which is necessarie to saluation, that it is not lawfull for men, nor yet for Angells, to adde, diminish, or alter ought therof; and command their followers and adherents, vtterly to renounce all anti-*

tiquitie, customes, multitude, human wisdome, iudgement, decrees, edicts, counsailes, visions, and miracles them-selues: defending obstinatly (but with-out foundation) that the scripture con-taines all that is necessarie for the ser-uice of God, and our saluation. Far-well, my deare Reader, seing I haue now said vnto thee, all that which I desired.

A 6   THE

THE
GAGGE OF THE
REFORMED GOSPEL.

BRIEFLY
Difcouering the errours of our time.

WITH
The Refutation, by expreffe textes, of
their owne approued English
Bible.

They mayntaine in the firft place.

I.

*That there is not in the Church, one,
and that an infallible Rule, for
vnderftanding the holie fcriptures,
and conferuing of vnitie in matters
of faith.*

Ontrary to the expreffe
wordes of their owne Bi-
ble, Rom. 12. 16. *Hauing
then giftes, differing according to the
grace*

grace that is giuen to vs, whether pro-
phecie (that is interpreta ion) *let vs*
prophecie (that is interpret) *accor-*
ding to the proportion , or Rule , of
faith. Whence we gather, that prophecie according to the Rule of
faith , is one of the giftes which
God bestoweth on his Church.
Therfore there is in the Church,
one, and that an infallible Rule for
vnderstanding the holy scriptures.

Philippians 3. 16. *Neuertheles,*
wherto we haue attained, let vs walke
by the same Rule, let vs minde the same
thinge. Loe how plainly the Apostle speaketh in this second place, of
a certaine Rule to be walked by:
clearly presupposing , that in matters of faith , we can neuer be of
the same minde , vnles we walke
by the same *Rule,* Therfore &c.

Gal. 6. 16. And *as many as walke*
according to this Rule, peace be on the,
and merce. And 2. Cor. 10 15. *Hauing*
hope when your faith is increased, that
we shall be enlarged by you, according

to our Rule, abundantly, to preach the gospell in the regions beyond you, and not to boast in another mans line. Loe here againe, because that euery man is to direct and order his beleefe, according to the doctrine of the Church, therfore it is called by S. Paul, both the *Rule,* and *Line* of our holy faith. Therfore &c.

1. *Cor.* 11.16. *But if any man seems to be contentious , we haue no such custome, nor the Church of God.* Loe how S. Paul still pleadeth the *Rule* and *Custome* of the Church, against the contentious : which if it could then, by the sole prescription of twentie or thirtie yeares, and by the authoritie of so few pastors, stop the mouthes of new sect-masters, what ought not the custome of sixteene hundred yeares, and the decrees of so many hundred pastors giyne, of reasonable , modest and humble men? Therfore &c.

And here I would haue it to be noted, that this Analogie, or *Rule of faith,*

faith, (besides the titles already re-cited) the holie scripture in other places, calleth by the name of *forme of doctrine*, as Rom. 6. 17. *A thinge made* readie to our hande, as 2. Cor. 10. 16. the *Depositum*, or Treasure, *committed to the Churches trust*, and euer most carefully to be kept by her, as 1. Tim. 6. 20. And with al in the very selfe same places, alwayes stileth that which is contrary to this R le, by the name of *Disunion, Discord, Disobedience, forsaking, of our first vocation, Diuision, Contention, Prophane and vaine balbinges, Opposition of sciences &c.* Whence plainly appeareth, how great the necessitie is for euery Christian, to keepe this *Rule,* the least breach or crack wherof, doth presently crack his Christia credit wich the Church of God, and with all good Christians.

See more Rom. 6. 17. Gal. 1. 6. Rom. 16. 17. Actes 15. 2. 1. Tim. 6. 20. Rom. 12. 16.

See therfore according to this
very

very Rule, Fathers who affirme the
fame, S. Ireneus l. 4. cap. 45. Tertul. de præfcrip. cap. 19. Vincent.
Lyr.in fuo Commoniorio, faying.
*It is very needfull in regard of fo many
errors proceeding from the misinterpretation of fcriptures, that the line of
prophericall and Apoftolicall expofition, should be directed according to
the Rule,of the Ecclefiaft.call and Catholique fenfe:* h is writeth this moft
worthie witneffe. Tertul. prefcrip.
heref.cap. 15.& ibid. cap. 19. faith.
*We doe not admit our aduerfaries to
difpute out of fcripture, till they can
shew who their anceftors were, & frõ
whom they receiued the fcriptures. For
the orderly courfe of doctrin requires,
that the first queftion be, whofe the
fcriptures are by right, from whom,
and by whom, and to whom, the forme
of Chriftian religion was deliuered.
Otherwife prefcribing againft him as
as a ftranger &c.* Thus he.

Loe how thefe two ancient Fathers, lay hou d of, and vrge thefe
two

two very termes, *Rule*, and *Forme*,
of faith and religion, euen as before
the holy scripture aid, from whence
doutles they tooke the phrase. And
with very great reason, for the
knowledg of Tradition (which is
this Forme or Rule) goes before the
knowlege of the scripture : for the
Rule must be first knowen, before
the thinge Ruled can be assuredly
knowen: as the Carpenter cannot
know certainly, that he hath measured his timber aright, nor the
Taylor, that he hath measured his
cloth aright, except he first assuredly know that his measure be
both true and right: but the Rule
of faith, to wit, the summe of all
those points, that euery Christians
is bound expresly know, as deliuered to them from hande to hande,
is the knowledg of Tradition.
Therfore &c.

II. *That*

I I.

That in matters of faith, we must not
not relie vpon the iudgment of the
Church and of her Pastors,
but only vpon the writ-
ten worde.

Ontrarie to the expresse wordes of their owne Bible. Mat.
23. 2. *The Scribes and the Pharises sit*
in Moyses seat, all therfore whatsoe-
uer they bid you obserue, that obserue
and doe. In which wordes, Christ
not only commädeth vs in matters
of faith, to haue recourse to som-
what else besides the only written
word (to wit, to the pastors of the
Church) but moreouer, biddeth vs
to obey them: and that not only in
some principall matters, but in all
whatsoeuer, without distinction or
limitation. Therfore in matters of
faith, we are not tyed to rely, only
vpon the written word.

Luc.

Luc. 10. 16. He *that heareth you, heareth me, and he that despiseth you, despiseth me: and he that despiseth me, despiseth him that sent me.* Heare againe Chrilt our Lord honoreth, and giueth as much authority to the preachers of the word, as he can poſſibly doe to the word it ſelf, ſaying. *He that heareth you &c.* Therfore.

Mat. 16. 19. *Whatſoeuer thou shalt binde on earth, shall be bound in heauen: Whatſoeuer thou shalt looſe in earth, shal be looſed in heauen.* Where is to be noted, that he doth not ſay, *Whomſoeuer,* but *Whatſoeuer;* giuing vs therby to vnderſtand, that not only the bondes of ſinnes, but as well all other knotts and difficulties in matters of faith, are to be looſed by S. Peter, and by the paſtors that ſucceed him in the Church. Therfore &c.

See more Deut. 17. 8. Aggeus 2. 11. 2. Chron. 19. 8. vnto the end. 2. Theſ. 2. 15.

See

See Fathers that affirme the same.
S. Greg. Naz in orat. excusat. Ter-
tull. l. de prescrip. hæret. S. Cyprian l. 1. epist. 3. S. Aug. l. 1. con.
Crel. cap. 33. & l. cont. epist. fund.
cap. 5. Vincent. Lyr. in suo com-
monit. S. Anselme l. de Incar. cap. 1.
who writing to Pope Vrban, saith
vnto him. *Vnto no other is more right-*
ly referred to be corrected, whatsoeuer
ariseth in the Church against the Ca-
tholique faith. S. August. cont. epist.
fund. cap. 4. the place beginneth.
Quibus ego obtemperaui dicentibus.

I I I.

That the Scriptures are easie to be vn-
derstood, and that therfore none
ought to be restrayned from
reading of them.

Ontrary to the expresse wordes of their owne Bible 2. Pet.
3. 16. where S. Peter speaking of S.
Paules epistles saith . *In which are*
some

fome thinges hard to be vnderſtood,
Which they that are vnlearned and vn-
ſtable wreſt, as they doe alſo the other
ſcriptures, vnto their owne deſtruct.ō.
But all vnlearned Reformers, both
reade, and are allowed to reade
thoſe hard thinges (yea the Reuelations alſo, harder then thoſe)
without reſtraint of man or woma,
which yet they vnderſtand not:
therfore they wreſt them, as alſo
other ſcriptures, to their owne
deſtruction.

Actes 8. 30. *And Phillip ſaid. Vn-*
derſtandeſt thou what thou readeſt?
And he ſaid. How can I, except ſome
man ſhould guide me? Where firſt
may be noted, that this noble
Enuch freely confeſt, he could not
vnderſtand the ſcriptures, without
an interpreter to expound them,
albeit he was a great & ſerious ſtu-
dier of them, and with all a ho'y
and an humble man, as S. Hierom
noteth of him. Epiſt.ad Paulin. de
ſtud.ſcrip, And next that he ſaith,
Except

Except some man guide me : and fled not to his priuat spirit, nor yet to conferring of place with place , as these men doe. Therfore the scriptures are not easie &c.

Luc. 24. 25. Christ called two of his owne Disciples *fooles* , *and beginning at Moyses, and all the Prophets, he expounded vnto them in all the scriptures, the thinges concerning him selfe* . How then are the scriptures so easilie to be vnderstood of the vnlearned, when the Disciples them selues vnderstood them not, till first they were expounded to them?

Reuelations 5. 1. &c. The Angel speaking of *the booke, sealed with seauen seales, wept much , because no man in heaue nor in earth, was able to open the booke, nether to looke theron.* A strange case , to reade in scripture it selfe, that the booke of scripture should be shut with so many seales: but much more strange, that euen in S. Iohn and the Apostles time, none

none could be found , nether in
heauen nor earth, able to open the
same, nor to looke theron , which
euery prentice now a dayes, without any difficultie will vndertake
to doe. Therfore &c.

See more 2.Pet.1.20. Mat.13.11.
& 36. Luc.24.45. 1.Cor. 12.10.Luc
8.10.& 54. Luc. 2. 50. 2. Tim. 3.7.
1.Iohn 4. 6. Iohn 5.35. Psal. 119.18.
& 34. Reue.5. 1. &c.

Our next recourse shal be to our
former Rule, for which see S. Ireneus l. 2. cap. 47. Origen. l. cont.
Celf. S. Amb. epift.44. ad Conftat,
calleth it *a sea, and depth of prophe-
ticall riddles.* S. Hier. in præfat. comment. in Ephes. 5. S. Aug. epift. 119.
cap. 21. faith . *The thinges of holy
scripture that I know not , are many
more then those that I knowe.* S. Greg.
hom. 6. in Ezech. and many other
fathers confesse the fame. S. Denis
Bifhop of Corinth , cited by Eusebius lib. 7. hift. Ecclef. 20. *Of
this booke, this is my opinion , that
the*

the matter thereof is far more profound
then my wit can reach into.

III.

*That Apoſtolicall Traditions, and an-
cient cuſtomes of the Church, (not
found in the Written Word) are not
to be receiued, nor doe oblige vs.*

Contrary to the expreſſe wordes of their owne Bible. 2.
Theſ. 2. 15. *Therfore brethren ſtand
faſt, and hold the Traditions, Which
yee haue bene taught, Whether by Word,
or by our epiſtle.* Hence it is as cleare
as the Sunne that ſhines, that ſome
Traditions were deliuered to the
Theſſalonians by word of mouth,
and thoſe of equall authoritie with
what was written, if not of more,
for the holy Ghoſt doth name them
firſt (as they were indeed the firſt
in being:) yea it is certaine, that
before the new Teſtament was
written, the Apoſtles deliuered all
by

by Tradition and word of mouth.
Therfore Apostolicall Traditions are
to be receiued and doe oblige vs.

2. Thes. 3. 6. *Now I command you
bretheren, in the name of our Lord Ie-
sus-Christ , that yee withdraw your
selues from euery brother that walketh
disorderly , and not after the Tradition
which he receiued of vs.* Lo, He saith
not, *I councell you,* but, *I commaund
you*; But these men reiecting al Traditions, walke disorderly : therfore
they breake the Apostles commandment:
Yea, they *stand* not, but are
fallen: they let goe , what the word
it selfe, doth will them to *hould*: and
therfore in the name of our Lord
Iesus Christ, let all good men withdraw them from them.

1. Cor. 11. 2. *Now I praise you
bretheren, that you remember me in all
thinges, and keepe the Traditions , as I
haue deliuered them vnto you.* But these
reiect al Traditions, therfore needes
must S. Paul speake thus vnto them.
Now (none of my bretheren) I dis-

praife you, for that you forget me in all thinges, and keepe not the Traditions, as I haue deliuered them vnto you.

Laftly, If nothing at all be to be beleeued, but only that which is left vs written , wherein fhould the Church haue exercifed her felfe frō Adam to Moyfes, the fpace of two thoufand fix hundred yeares? Therfore &c.

See more 1. Tim. 6. 3. 20. & 2. Tim. 1. 13. 2. Tim. 2. 2. Iohn. 20. 30. & 21. 25. & 16. 12. 1. Cor. 11. 16. 34. 2. ep. Iohn 12. 3. ep. of. S. Iohn 13. Actes 16. 4. & 15. 28.

See fathers that affirme the fame. S. Ireneus l. 3. c. 4. Origen in cap. 6. ad Rom. S. Damaf. l. 4. c. 17. S. Chrifoft. in 2. Thef. 2. S. Bafil l. de Spiritu fanéto faith. *Some thinges we haue from fcripture , other thinges from the Apoftles , both which haue like force vnto godlines.* S. Chrifoft. hom. 4. in 2. Thef. faith. *It is a Tradition , feeke thou no further.*

V. *That*

V.

That a man by his owne vnderstanding
or priuat spirit, may rightly iudge
and interpret scripture.

COntrary to the expresse wordes of their owne Bible 1.
Cor. 12. 8. &c. *To one is giuen by the*
spirit, the word of wisaome : to ano-
ther the word of knowledg by the same
spirit : to another the working of mira-
cles:to another prophecie: to another
discerning of spirits: to another kindes
of tongues:to another the interpretation
of tongues, diuiding to euery man seue-
rally, as he will . Where the Apoftle
in expresse words,oppofeth & refel-
leth this vnfauory doctrine,teaching
that the gifte of prophecying, or
truly to interpret the holy fcripture,
is not giuen to all the faithfull , but
to fome only in particular: yea he
prefuppofeth that one may haue the
gift, euen to worke miracles, & yet
may want the gift, truly to interpret
the

the word of God. Therfore a man
by his owne priuat spirit cannot &c.

2. Pet. 1.20. *Knowing this first, that
no prophecie of the scripture is of any priuat interpretation, for the prophecie came not in old time* (margent, or at any
time) *by the will of man, but holy men
of God, spake as they were moued by the
holy Ghost.* Loe how clearly the A-
postle taketh this facultie and authoritie, from a priuat and prophane
man, restrayning the same to a companie and societie of men, and those
also of some especiall note for their
sanctitie and holines, assuring vs that
such spake as they were moued by
the holy Ghost. Therfore &c.

1. Iohn. 4. 1. *Beloued, beleeue not
euery spirit, but try the spirits, whether
they are of God.* By which wordes we
are taught, that the spirit of others
are to be examined, whether they
proceed from God or not, but this
caueat cannot be vnderstood of the
spirit of the whole Church, sith then
it would follow, that there should
be

be none left to try the said spirit of
the Church (euery particular man
being included therin.) If then it be
to be ment of priuat men (as needes
it muft) it followeth, that a priuat spirit cannot be this iudge, sith it selfe
is to vndergoe the iudgment and
examination of some other. Therfore &c.

See fathers that affirme the same,
S. Aug. epift. 162. & l. de Baptifmo.
cap. 18. ad Epictetum. S. Bafil. epift.
78. S. Amb. epift. 32. S. Leo epift. 53.
S. Hier. lib. cont. Luciferanos. Vincent Lir. cont. prophan. heref. noui-
tates. And laftly Luther him felfe
faith lib. de poteftate Papæ. *We are
not certaine of any priuat perfon, whether he hath the reuelation of the father
or no, but that the Church hath it, we
ought not to dout.*

V I.

That S. Peters faith hath fayled.

Contrary to the expreſſe wordes
of their owne bible. Luc. 22.
31. *Simon behould Satan hath defired to*

haue

haue you, that he may sift you as wheate:
but I haue praid for thee, that thy faith
fayle not. Loe Satan required to sift
them all, but our Lord here prayed
for Peter only, that his faith principally might not fayle. Therfore S.
Peters faith hath not fayled.

Mat. 16.18. *And I say vnto thee, that*
thou art Peter, and vpon this rock I will
build my church, and the gates of hell
shall not preuayle against it. But had S.
Peters faith fayled, the gates of hell
had preuailed. Therfore &c.

Mat. 23. 2. *The Scribes and the Pha-*
rises sit in Moyses seat, al therfore what-
soeuer they bid you obserue, that obserue
and doe. How could Christ bid the
people of the old law, doe all whatsoeuer he should bid them, by those
that sate in Moyses chaire, if they
could erre? But God hath no lesse
preserued the truth of christian religion, in the chaire of S. Peter, which
is in the new law, answerable to
that of Moyses in the old. Therfore &c.

Iohn

Iohn 11. 49. 51. speaking of Cayphas, saith, *And this he spake not of him selfe, but being high priest that yeare, he prophecied that Iesus should die for that nation.* Loe how in this most wicked time of the sinagogue, at the very dregges, and last cast of that disobedient people, yet speaking forth of that chaire, which Christ had commanded to be heard and obeyed, touching matter of faith, they answer truly, and their bishop prophecieth: therfore S. Peters faith nor chaire hath not fayled.

See Fathers that affirme the same. S. Leo ser. 3. de assump. sua. *The danger was common to all the Apostles, but our Lord tooke speciall care of Peter, that the state of all the rest might be more sure, if the head were inuincible.*

VII.

That the Church can erre, and hath erred.

Contrary to the expresse wordes of their owne Bible. Isay. 49. 21. *As for me, this is my couenant with*

them

them, faith the Lord. My fpirit that is vpon thee, and my wordes which I haue put into thy mouth, shall not depart out of thy mouth, nor out of the mouth of thy feede, nor out of the mouth of thy feedes feede, faith the Lord, from hence forth, and for euer. Therfore the Church cannot erre &c.

Iohn 14. 16. *I will pray the father, and he shall giue you another comforter, that he may abide with you for euer, euen the fpirit of truth.* But the Apoftles them felues aboade not for euer, therfore this is to be vnderftood of the perpetuall aboade of the fpirit of truth with their fucceffors. Therfore &c.

Mat. 18.17. *If he neglect to heare the Church, let him be vnto thee as an heathen man and a publican.* Whence is clearely to be gathered, that the Church in her cenfure cannot erre.

Ifay 9.35. *And a high way shal be there, and a way, and it shall be called the way of holines, the vncleanne shall not paffe ouer it, but it shall be for thofe:the way-*
faring

faring men though fooles, shall not erre therin. How far deceiued then are many simple soules, who doe affirme, that all the whole Church and all holy men that euer haue bene therein for thefe thoufand yeares, (how wife foeuer) haue all erred?

Ephef. 5. 27. *That he might prefent it to him felfe a glorious Church, not hauing fpot or wrincle, or any fuch thinge, but that it should be holy and without blemish.* Note well thefe wordes, *without fpot, wrincle, or any blemish:* Tel me now it is poffible, that reading this, thou caft euer beleeue, that fhe hath taught fuch horrible blafphemies & abhominations as fhe at this day is charged with? Therfore &c.

See more Iohn 16. 13. Ephef. 5. 27. Hay 9. 7. Ezech. 37. 26. Luc. 22. 32. Mat. 23. 3. 1. Pet. 2. 9. Iohn. 17. 17. 1. Cor. 11. 25. Pfal. 101. 23. 29. Ephef. 2. 10. Iohn 10. 16. Acts. 4. 32. Ephef. 4. 5. 11. Luc. 10. 16. Deut. 17. 8. Ieremie 3. 15. Malac. 2. 7. Mat. 16. 18. Acts 15. 28. 2. Cor. 13. 8. 1. Tim. 3. 15.

B 5   See

See Fathers that affirme the fame.
S. Aug. cont. Crefcon. lib. 1. cap. 3.
Alfo vpon the 118. Pfal. the place
beginneth. *Ne auferas de ore meo ver-*
bum veritatis vfquequaque . S. Cypr.
epift. 55. ad Cornel. num. 3. S. Ireneus lib. 3. cap. 4. with manye
others.

VIII.

That the Church hath bene hidden
and inuifible.

C Ontrary to the expreffe wordes
of their owne Bible, Mat. 5. 14.
Yee are the light of the world , a cittie
that is fet on a hill, cannot be hid . Ne-
ther doe men light a candle , and put it
vnder a bushell, but on a candleftick,
and it giueth light to all that are in the
houfe . But the Catholique Church
is fuch a light, fuch a candle , and
fuch a cittie, built vpon Chrift as
vpon a mountaine , therfore hath
not, nor cannot be hidden, nor inuifible.

Mat. 18. 17. *Tell the Church, if he ne-*
glect

glect to heare the Church , let him be
vnto thee as a heathen man . But it
were a very hard cafe to be condemned for a heathen, for ether not telling , or hearing a Church which
hath fo clofely lyen hid, that no man
could heare, fee , feele or vnderftand it, for a thoufand yeare. Therfore &c.

2. Cor. 4. 3. *If our gofpel be hid, it*
is hid to them that are loft . Loe the
cenfure of S. Paul vpon all fuch , as
affirme that the Church, or her gofpell, can be hid.

Ifay 2. 2. *And it shall come to paffe*
in the laft dayes, that the mountaine of
the Lords houfe, shall be eftablished in
the top of the mountaines , and shall be
exalted aboue the hilles, and all nations
shall flow vnto it. In a thoufand places doe the prophecies fpeake of
this kingdome of Chrift as Dan. 7.
14. Mich. 4 7. which fhould be all
in vaine, if this his kingdome could
be inuifible; for a prophecie muft be
of thinges, which may be feene and

B 6　　　　per-

perceiued by our senses; otherwise euery man might be a prophet, and fortell of thinges to come, which if they should not come to passe, he might answere, that they had come to passe in very deed as he had prophecied, but that it was inuisible to the world. Loe the visible absurdities of this inuisible Church.

See more. Psal. 27. 8. Rom. 10. 14. 1. Cor. 11. 19. Psalm. 19. 3. 4. Isay. 60. 20. Acts. 20. 28. Isay. 61. 9.

See Fathers that affirme the same. Origen. hom. 30. in Mat. *The Church is full of light , euen from the east to the west*. S. Chrysostom. hom. 4. in 6. of Isay . *It is easier for the sunne to be extinguished , then the Church to be darkned* . S. Aug. tract. in Ioan, calleth those *blinde, that doe not see so great a mountaine*. S. Cypr. de vnitate ecclesiæ.

IX. *That*

*That the Church was not alwayes to
remaine Catholique or vniuersall, &
that the Church of Rome is not
such a Church.*

COntrary to the expresse wordes
of their owne Bible, Psalm. 2.8.
*Aske of me , and I shall giue thee the
heathen for thine inheritance , and
the vttermost parts of the earth for
thy possession .* And Luc. 1. 33. *He
shall raigne ouer the house of Iacob for
euer , and of his kingdome there shall
no end .* But none of these promises
haue bene so much verefied as they
haue bene in the Church of Rome;
therfore both the Church hath bene
alwayes vniuersall, and Church of
Rome only such a Church.

Colos. 1.3. &c. W e *giue thankes to
God for you &c. since we heard your faith
&c. for the hope which is laid vp for you
heauen , wherof yee heard before in the
word of the truth of the gospell, which
is come vnto you, as it is in al the world,
and bringeth forth fruit, as it doth*
also

*also in you, since the day you heard of it,
and knewe the grace of God in truth.*
But no faith or gospell hath, or is,
so dilated in all the world, nor hath
fructified and growen (for so we
reade) as the faith of the Roman
Church hath done. Therfore &c. but
all this shall appeare much more
plainly by that which followeth.

Rom. 1. 8. *First I thanke my God
thorough Iesus Christ for you all, that
your faith is spoken of thoroughout the
whole world.* Where in expresse tear-
mes, S. Paul calleth the faith of the
whole world (or Catholique faith)
the faith of the Romans, that is to
say, of the Church of Rome. Therfore the Church of Rome, and no
other, is truly and in deed such a
Church.

See more Colof. 1. 23. Gen. 22. 18.
Mat. 24. 46: Acts 1. 8. Dan. 2. 35. Luc.
24. 47. psal. 46. 9. psal. 72. 8. (we 71.)
Marc. 16. 20. Ezech. 13. 3. Mat. 28.
19. Actes 1. 8.

All which places are to be vnderstood,

ftood, not that the whole world
fhould be Catholique at one and the
fame time, but that the whole fhould
be conuerted to Chrift at fundrie times, and that it fhould comprehend
a greater part of the world, then any
fect of hereticks fhould euer doe: and
this is the true fence of being Catholique or vniuerfall.

To follow ftill our former Rule,
fee Fathers that affirme the fame. S.
Cypr. ep. 57. writing to Cornelius
pope of Rome, fayeth. *W* hilft *with*
you there is one minde and one voice, the
whole Church is confeffed the Roman
Church. S. Aug. de vnitat. ecclef. cap.
4. faith. *W* ho *fo diffente from the bo-*
die of Chrift, which is the Church, that
they doe not communicate with all the
whole corps of Chriftendome, certaine it
is, that they are not in the Catholique
Church. S. Hierom in his Apologie
againft Ruffinus, and in other places, faith, that it is all one to fay the
Roman faith, and *the Catholique faith.*
Againe S. Aug. vpon the pfal. 45. 16.
(we

(we 44.) But much more excellent-
lie the same holy Doctor ad Hono-
rat. epist. 161. The place beginneth.
Dignare ergo rescribere nobis. As also
cont. lit. Petil. l.2.cap. 16. The place
beginneth. *Si queras.*

X.

That the Churches vnitie is not ne-cessarie in all pointes of faith.

Ontrary to the expresse wordes
of their owne Bible, Ephes. 4.
5. *One Lord, one Faith, one Baptisme.*
Therfore vnitie is necessarie in all
points of faith. The reason is, the
Church being a congregation of the
faithfull, one faith is necessarie to
make one Church; but our aduersaries differ in matters of faith, therfore they haue not the vnitie requisite to one Church.

Iames 2. 10. *Whosoeuer shall keepe*
the whole law, and yet offend in one
point, he is guiltie of all. And euen so
is it in our faith, for who denieth one
article, denieth all.

Acts

Acts 4.32. *And the multitude of them that beleeued, were of one hart, and of one ſoule.* And againe 2. Cor. 1. 10. *Now I beſeeche you bretheren, by the name of our Lord Ieſus Chriſt, that yee all ſpeake the ſame thinge, and that there be no diuiſions among you, but that yee be perfectly ioyned together in the ſame minde, and in the ſame iudgement.* But our aduerſaries will needes ioyne with vs in vnity of Church (yea and with others alſo) who differ frō them in matters of faith. But this as you ſee, cannot be. Therfore &c.

See more Ierem. 32. 39. Can. 2. 6. pſal. 67. 7. Mat. 12. 25. Marc. 3. 24. Luc. 11. 17. Mat. 18. 19. Epheſ. 2. 14. 15. 16. 8. 21. Epheſ. 5. 27. Phillip. 3. 16. Phillip. 1. 26. 27. Galat. 5. 9. & 1. 8. Coloſ. 3. 15. Iohn 17. 11. 2. Cor. 3. 11. pſal 121. 3.

And now to Rule with our commō Rule, the breakers of vnitie & of Rule. *In cathedra vnitatis, poſuit Deus doctrinam veritatis,* ſaith S. Aug. (cited by the Manuduc. p. 134) In the chaire of of vnitie, God hath placed the doctrine of veritie. And cont. ep. Par. l. 3. cap. 5. The place beginneth. *Qui non vult sedere.* S. Cyprian lib. de vnitate ecclef. num. 3. faith. *This vnitie of the Church, he that holdeth not, doth he thinke he holdeth the faith?* Laftly S. Hillarie lib. ad Conftantium Auguftum, with many more.

X I.

That S. Peter was not ordained by Chrift the Firft, Head, or Chiefe amongft the Apoftles, and that amongft the twelue, none was greater, or leffer then other.

COntrary to the expreffe wordes of their owne Bible. Mat. 10. 2. *Now the names of the twelue Apoftles are thefe. The firft Simon, who is called Peter.* All the Euangelifts doe put bleffed Peter in the firft place, and wicked Iudas in the laft : and wherfore this ? but becaufe the one was Firft in dignitie and worthieft of the reft; and contrariwife, the other laft, worft, and vnworthieft of all his fellowes.

lowes. Againe, why as Peter is called *First*, are not the rest called , *Second, Third &c?* But to shew therby,
that they did not therfore call Peter
First, becaufe he occurred first to be
named, but becaufe he was the First,
both in dignitie & authoritie, whom
therfore they all number First, and
call the *First*.

Mat. 16.18. *And I say also vnto thee,
that thou art Peter, and vpon this rock I
will build my church , and the gates of
hell shal not preuaile against it.* Wordes
clearly infinuating S. Peters supremacie in the Church of God; for according to the Greeke and Syriack
text (as our doctors note) thefe wordes; *Thou art Peter,* found thus. *Thou
art a rock, and vpon this rock I will
build my church .* So that to fay, that
Peter is the rock of the church, is all
one in fenfe, as to call him chiefe or
head of the Church.

Nether without efpeciall myfte-
rie, did our Lord impofe vpon him
this new name, the name of Peter (a
Rock

Rock or Stone) being one of the most
excellent names of Iesus Christ, who
is many times in holy scripture, tear-
med by the name of a Rock, or Stone:
as Psal. 117. 22. Isay 28. 6. Dan. 2. 34.
Mat. 21. 42. Rom. 9. 33. So that this
soueraigne and absolut pastor of the
Church, did communicate this new
name vnto his vicar, to represent
the more liuely, the supreame authoritie, which he would giue vnto
him ouer his troupe.

And note, Christ saith not, *I haue*
built, or, *I doe build*, but, *I will build*;
the Church being built vpon Christ
from his Incarnation: so that these
wordes referred to Christ (as our
Reformers vse to doe) doe not well
agree to build the Church on Christ
as head therof for time to come: but
doe well agree to S. Peter, as head
therof for time to come. Therefore &c.

Mat. 16. 19. *And I will giue vnto*
thee, the keyes of the kingdome of hea-
uen, &c. by these wordes also, no
lesse

lesse then by the former, is clearly
signified S. Peters supremacie ; For
none hath the gouernment or commandement of the keyes of any
towne or cittie, but the Prince or
Gouernor of the same . And that soueraigne power is signified by the
keyes, is likewise proued by that of
our Sauiour Christ . *I haue the keyes
of hell and of death* . *Reuelat.* 1. 18.
Againe. *He that hath the keye o fDauid,
he that openeth, and no man shutteth,
shutteth and no man openeth.*

Now adde to this that hath bene
saide , the correspondence of the
wordes of our Sauiour to S. Peter , with the wordes of S. Peter a-
gaine to him, and how cleare will
this doctrine appeare to all ? For
when our Lord asked his disciples.
Mat. 16. 15. *Whom say yee that I am?*
he demanded not how they called
his name,which was Iesus (for that
they knew full well before)but what
his qualitie,office, and dignitie was.
And S. Peter answering . *Thou art*
Christ

Chriſt the Sone of the liuing God. Chriſt
tould him not his name (which was
Simon) but gaue him another name,
and ſuch an one, as likewiſe ſignified
the office, qualitie and dignitie that
he beſtowed vpon him, ſaying. Thou
art *Cephas* or *Petrus*, that is to ſay, a
Rock or Peter. Therfore &c.

1. *Cor.* 3. 4. 22. *One ſaith* I *am of*
Paul, I *am of Apollo,* I *of Cephas,* I *of*
Chriſt . Loe how from thoſe he
would haue eſteemed leſſer, he aſ-
cendeth to thoſe whom he would
haue eſſeemed greater, and placeth
Peter next to Chriſt. Therfore &c.

Luc. 22. 31. *And the Lord ſaid, Si-*
mon, &c. when thou art conuerted
ſtrengthen (we reade, *confirme*) *thy bre-*
theren. Now what other thinge is it
for Peter, to ſtrengthen or confirme
his brethren, but to practiſe and exerciſe his greatnes ouer them ? for
he that doth ſtrengthen or confirme
others, is the greater : and they who
are ſtrengthned or confirmed, are
made therby inferiors to him, who
                                    doth

doth ſtrengthen or confirme them.

Luc. 22. 26. *He that is greateſt a-*
mongſt you, let him be as the younger, &
he that is chiefe, as he that doth ſerue.
Where the wordes, *is greateſt*, *is*
chiefe, doe euidently ſhew, that a-
mongſt the twelue, one was greater
then another, and was ſo accounted
euen by Chriſt him ſelfe.

Iohn 21. 15. *Ieſus ſaid to Simon Pe-*
ter : Simon loueſt thou me more then
theſe ? Feede my lambes, *feeede my*
sheepe. (Where the Greeke hath in the
ſecōd place for *feede, gouerne* or *rule.*)
Hence it followeth, that ether the
Apoſtles were not cenſured to be in
the flock of Chriſt, or elſe they were
ſubiect to S. Peter as to their head,
when Chriſt commanded him to
feede or gouerne, not only his lambes (to wit, the lay people) but his
ſheepe alſo, to wit, the Apoſtles and
paſtors them ſelues: for beſides lambes and ſheepe , there is nothing in
the Church of God : Againe, if S.
Peter loued our Lord more then all
his

his fellowes did, it followeth necef-
farily, that he receiued more power
to feede then all his fellowes did;
For it cannot be conceiued that he
is willed to loue, more then to feede:
but he loueth more thē others, therfore he is willed to feede more then
the others; and confequently, is head
of the others.

Mat. 12. 25. 26. *Euery kingdome di-*
uided againſt it ſelfe, is brought to de-
ſolation &c. And if Satan caſt out Sa-
tan. Sathan therfore hath a kingdome, wherof he is the chiefe kinge.
If then there be, not only a viſible
head of the Church triumphant in
heauen, but alſo a viſible head euen
in hell, why not a viſible head alſo
in earth? Therfore &c. But here I
craue pardon, for hauing far excee-
ded my pretended breuitie, though
as much no more might be ſaid,
ether vpon this, or vpon any other
point, as hath bene of this.

See more pſal. 18. 43. pſal. 45.
16. (we, 46.) Marc. 2. 16. Actes 1. 3.
Luc.

Luc. 1. 33. 2. Cor. 11. 5.

See fathers that affirme the same.
Theophilact in 22. Luc. calleth Peter, Prince of the Disciples. Eusebius
in Chron; First bishop of Christians.
S. Cyril of Hier. cat. 2. Prince, and
most excellent of all the Apostles. S.
Chrysost. Hom. 55. in Mat. Pastor
and head of the church. Euthym. in
cap. vlt. Ioan, Master of the whole
world. S. Leo epist. 89. Head and
chiefe of the Apostles.

XII.

That a woman may be head or supreame
gouernesse of the Church in all cau-
ses, as Queene Elizabeth
lately was.

COntrary to the expresse wordes
of their owne Bible. 1. Tim. 2.
11. *Let the woman learne in silence, with*
all subiection. But I suffer not a woman
to teache, nor to vsurpe authoritie ouer
the man. Therfor a woman cannot
be head or supreame &c.

1. Cor. 14. 34. *Let women hould*
their peace in the Churches, for it is not

C   *per-*

permitted them to speake, but to be sub-
iect, as also the law saith. Therfore &c.

I produce no fathers for disproofe of this point, for neuer was any woman so presumptuous in our forefathers dayes, but will content my selfe to refute this folly, with an euident and conuincing reason, the which is this.

Whatsoeuer power an inferior minister of the Church hath, that the head of the same Church hath (at the least) if not much more. But euerye inferior minister of their Church, hath power to Baptise, to giue the Communion, to marrie, to burie, and to preache in pulpit: therfore the Queene could Baptise, giue the Communion, marrie, burie, and preach in pulpit. And who now is so simple as sees not the ridiculous sequel of this doctrine? for the which notwithstanding, hundreds of ours haue bene hanged, cut vp, and quartered aliue, as most wicked traitors.

But that no secular Kinge can be
this

this head, an infinitie of Fathers doe
affirme. S. Iohn Damafcen . fer. 1.
The place beginneth . *Tibi ô Rex.*
And againe. *Non assentior.* I confent
not that the *Church of God, be gouerned
by kinges .* Theodoret. hift. ecclef. l.
4. c. 28. recounteth of one Eulogius
that he anfwered to an officer of the
Emperor Valens (telling him the
Emperor would haue it fo)with this
prettie quippe, faying . What, was
he made a Bifhop , that day that he
was crowned Emperor ? The place
beginneth. *Tum ille.*S. Ignatius epift.
ad Philadelph,willeth all men without exception , euen the Emperor
him felfe, to be obedient to the Bishop: the place beginneth.*Principes o-
bedite Cafari.* S. Chrifoft. hom. 5. de
verbis Ifaiæ , calleth the Bifhop a
prince as well as the Kinge, yea and
that a greater alfo . And hom. 38. in
Mat, 21. The place beginneth. *Quia
in rebus fpiritualibus.*

C 2   XIII.

XIII.

*That Antechrist shall not be a parti-
cular man; and that the Pope
is Antechrist.*

Ontrary to the expresse wordes of their own Bible. 2. Thes.
2. 3. *Let no man deceaue you by anie
meanes, for that day shall not come, except there come a falling away first, and
that man of sinne be reuealed, the sonne
of perdition .* Where these wordes,
man of sinne, and, *sonne of perdition*,
doe plainly prooue, that a succession
of men (as the Popes are) cannot be
this man of sinne: for so S. Peter also should be Antechrist, for he was
Pope, and the very first of all the
Popes. Therfore Antechrist shall be
a particular man &c.

Reuelations 13. 18. *Let him that
hath vnderstanding , count the number
of a man .* Therfore the great Antechrist, that egregious Apostata, or
notable enimie of Iesus Christ, shall
be a particular man.

1. Iohn 2. 22. *Who is a lier, but he
that*

*that denieth that Iesus is Christ? This is
Antechrist, which denieth the Father &
the Sonne.* But the Pope denyeth nether of both; Therfore the Pope is not Antechrist.

Againe in the 2. Thef. before alleadged 2. 4. the fcripture faith, that Antechrist fhal be extolled aboue al that is called God: and verfe 8. that our Lord Iefus fhal kil him with the fpirit of his mouth, at his coming: but none of al thefe agree to the Pope, no more then that our Lord Iefus is come the fecōd time. Therfor &c.

Iohn 5. 43. *I am come in my Fathers
name, and yee receaue me not: if another shall come in his owne name, him
yee will receiue.* He meaneth fpecially the wicked Antechrist: how then can the Pope be he, feeing the Iewes receiue him not?

See more Dan. 7. 7. & cap. 12. 11. Reuel. 13. 17. & cap. 17. 8. 11. Luc. 13. 14. Mat. 24. 15.

To follow our Rule, fee Fathers that affirme the fame. And firft S.

C 3   Chri⸗

Chrisostom and S. Cyril. doe both
thus vnderstand this very place last
alleadged. S. Amb. vpon the 2. Thes.
2. Hierom in ep. ad Algasia quæst. 11.
S. Aug. in 29. tract. in Ioan. S. Ireneus l.5. cont. heres. Valentin. Theodoret. in the epitome of the diuine
decrees cap. de Antichristo.

XIV.

*That no man , nor none but God , can
forgiue or retaine sinnes.*

COntrary to the expresse wordes
of their owne Bible Iohn 20.
21. *As my Father hath sent me, euen so
send I you.* Now Christ was sent by
his Father, not only to teache, preache, administer sacraments , and to
worke miracles, but also to forgiue
sinnes: but the Disciples were sent
with power to teache, preache, administer sacraments , and to worke
miracles: therfore also to forgiue
sinnes.

Ibid. v. 22. 23. *When he had said
this , he breathed on them , and saith
vnto them . Receiue yee the holy Ghost:*
Whose

*whose soeuer sinnes yee remit, they are
remitted vnto them, and whosoeuer sinnes yee retaine, they are retained.* Chrift
hauing firft fhewed his owne com-
miffion , which was to pardon finnes , prefently giueth his Apoftles
power to doe the fame, breathing on
them the holy Ghoft . He therfore
that denieth man to haue this power,
ether denyeth that the holy Ghoft
can forgiue finne, or that Chrift gaue
not his Difciples the holy Ghoft to
this end and purpofe : both which
are clearely falfe , and againft the
fcripture. Therfore &c.

Mat. 9. 3. 8. *But when the multitude saw it, they maruelled and glorified God, which had giuen such power
vnto men,* as to forgiue finnes. Which
though they knew to appertaine to
God only by nature , yet they perceiued that it might be done by mãs
miniftrie in earth, to the glorie of
God . Yea thofe , who affirme
God only fo to remitt finnes, that
the minifteriall power therof cannot

be communicated to men, deny the
one part of Christes distinct, or double maner of remittinge sinnes, to
wit, only in heauen, and not in earth.
Therfore &c.

See more Mat. 16. 19. & Mat. 18.
18. 1. Cor. 5. 5. 1. Tim. 1. 20. 2. Cor. 2.
10. 2. Cor. 5. 19. Num. 5. 6.

Alwayes to comply with our
common Rule see, Fathers which affirme the same. S. Aug. tract. 49. in
Ioan. And in his booke of fiftie ho-
milies hom. 9. S. Chrisost. de sacer-
dotio l. 3. S. Amb. l. 3. de pœnitentia . S. Cyrill. l. 12. cap. 50. or 56. in
Ioan saith. *It is not absurd, that they*
should remit mans sinnes, who haue in
them the holie Ghost. S. Basil. l. 5. cont,
Euuomius proueth the holy Ghost
to be God (which that detestable
heretique did deny) because he for-
giueth sinnes by the Apostles. S. Ireneus l. 5. cap. 13. S. Greg. hom. 6. in
Euang.

XV.

XV.

That we ought not to confesse our sinnes,
to any man, but to God only.

Ontrary to the expresse wordes
of their owne Bible, Mat. 3.5. 6.
Then went out to him (to wit, to Iohn)
all Hierusalem, and were baptised of him
in Iordan, confessing their sinnes. Not
by acknowledging them selues in
generall to be sinners, but euery man
to vtter and tell his particular sinnes. Therfore we may confesse our
sinnes, not only to God, but also
to man.

Actes 19. 18. *And many that belee-*
ued, came and confessed and shewed
their deedes (behould Confession) *Ma-*
nie also of them which vsed curious
artes, brought their bookes together,
and burned them before all men: and
they counted the price of them, and
found it fiue thousand peeces of sil-
uer (behould Satisfaction.) Therfore &c.

Num. 5. 6. *When a man or woman*
shall, commit any sinne &c. then they

shall

shall *confesse their sinne which they haue done.* And that this is not vnderstood to God in heauen, but also to his Priest in earth, the whole chapter, from verse 12. vnto the end, doth clearly testifie. Adde, that he saith not, they shall confesse their *sinnes* (to wit, in generall) but their *sinne*, to wit, in particular. Therfore &c.

See more Marc. 1. 4. Iames. 5. 16. Mat. 18. 18. Mat. 17. 14.

To bring vnruly people to Confession by the helpe of our holesome Rule, see Fathers that affirme the same. S. Ireneus l. 1. cap. 9. Tertulian l. de pœnitentia, where he reprehendeth some, who for human shamfastnes, neglected to goe to Confession. It is written of S. Ambrose, that he himselfe sate in Confession, Amb. ex Paulino. S. Clement S. Peters successor, speakes wonderfull pithylie to this purpose. Epist. ad frat. Dom. But of all others, Origen is most plaine for this point. l. 3. Periorchon: S. Chrisost. l. 3. de sacerd.

&

& hom. 85. in Ioan . S. Aug. cited a litle before and others. S. Amb. orat. in muliere pecatrice, faith . *Confeſſe freely to the prieſt, the hidden ſecrets of thy ſoule.*

XVI.

That Pardons and Indulgences, were not in the Apoſtles times.

COntrary to the expreſſe wordes of their owne Bible. 2. Cor. 2. 10. *To whom yee forgiue any thinge,* I *forgiue alſo: for if I forgiue any thinge, to whom I forgaue it , for your ſake forgaue I it, in the perſon of Chriſt* . The Corinthian aforſaid, was excommunicated, and put to penance by the Apoſtle, as plainly appeareth 1. Cor. 5. 3. and in the 2. Corinthians laſt cited, he giueth order for his pardon. A plaine proofe of the Apoſtles power, there of binding , here of looſing: there of puniſhing , here of pardoning. Therfore pardons were in vſe in the Apoſtles times.

2. Cor, 2. 6. *Sufficient to ſuch a*

C 6 *man,*

man, *is this punishment*. Whence it
is cleare, that it lyeth in the handes of the fpirituall magiftrates,
to meafure the time of fuch punifhment, or penance impofed. Therfore &c.

See more Mat. 18. 18. & Mat. 16. 19

See Fathers that affirme the fame. Tertul. l. ad Mart. cap. 1. 5.
S. Cyp. l. 3. ep. 15. & fermo de lapfis. Concil. Lateran. Can. 62. The
decrees of Innocentius 3. & 4. de
pœnitent. & remif. cap. quod autem. S. Amb. l. 1. de pœnit. cap.
2. the place beginneth, *Dominus par*
ius. S. Aug. ep. 75. ad Auxilium
Epifcop. The place beginneth, *Spi-*
ritalis pœna. S. Chrifoft l. 3. de fa-
cerdot: the place beginneth. *Si rex*
aliquis. Laftly, Pope Vrban the 2.
granted a plenarie Indulgence to
fuch as would goe to the holy
warre.

XVII.

XVII.

That the actions & passions of the Sain-
tes, doe serue for nothing to
the Church.

COntrary to the expresse wordes
of their owne Bible, Colof. 1.
24. *I reioyce in my sufferinges for you,*
and fill vp that which is behinde (we
reade wanting) *of the afflictions of*
Christ in my flesh, for his bodies sake,
which is the Church. Hence hath
the ground bene alwayes taken, of
Indulgences (but much more principally, from the superaboundant
merits of Iesus Christ.) Therfore the
actions and passions of the Saintes,
doe serue for somethinge to the
Church &c.

Phillip. 2. 30. *Because for the*
worke of Christ, he was nigh vnto
death, not regarding his life, to supply
your lack. Therfore &c.

Contrary also to an article of our
Creed, *I beleeue the communion of*
Saintes. But to what purpose beleeue
we this, if their actions and passions,
may

may not be imparted to vs, nor ſerue
to no purpoſe to the Church. Therfore &c.

See more pſal. 119.63. (we 118.) 1.
Cor. 12.12.2. Cor. 11.28.pſal.53. (we
52.) 9.2. Mac.15.16. Mat. 17.3. Luc.9.
30.31. Mat.27.52. Apoc. 5.8. Gen.26.
5.& 48.16. Exod.32.13.Iob.5.1.Hier.
15.1. Iſay.37.35.Marc. 14.36. Luc. 8.
44. Acts 5.15. All theſe paſſages con-
tayning actions or prayers, of the
Church triumphant, for the militant
or patient, or for both, I care not
which they grant, and yet one they
muſt needes confeſſe. Therfore &c.

See Fathers that affirme the ſame,
S. Aug. lib. de cura pro mort. cap. 1.
The place beginneth, *Etſi nuſquam.*
And againe the ſame Saint in the
ſame booke, the place beginneth,
Prouiſus ſepeliendis. S. Maximus ſer.
de ſanctis Octauio, Aduentio, the
place beginneth, *Cuncti martyres.* S.
Bede hiſt. eccleſ. Angliæ l. 3.cap. 19.
the place beginneth, *Furſeus.* S.
Auguſt. in Pſal. 61. the place begin-
neth,

neth, *Vnus enim homo* : as also S. An-
felme vpon the fame.

XVIII.

That no man can doe workes of fupererogation.

Ontrary to the expreffe wordes
of their owne Bible. Mat. 19.
21. *If thou will be perfect, goe and fell
that thou haft, and giue to the poore, and
thou shalt haue treafure in heauen, and
come and follow me.* Hence it plainly
appeareth, that man by the afiftance
of Gods grace, may doe fome thinges councelled, which are of more
perfection then the thinges commã-
ded: and thefe we call workes of
fupererogation.

1. Cor. 7. 25. 38. *Now concerning
virgins, I haue no commandement of
the Lord, yet I giue my iudgment* (we
read councell) *as one that hath obtained mercie of the Lord to be faithful:
he that giueth her in marriage doth wel,
but he that giueth her not in mariage,
doth better.* To doe that which is
councelled is not neceffarie, becaufe
one

one maybe ſaued notwithſtanding,
but he who omitteth what is commanded (vnleſ he doe penance) can
not eſcape eternall paines . Therfore. &c.

Mat. 19. 12. *There be Eunuches
Which haue made them ſelues Eunuches
for the kingdome of heauen, he that is
able to receiue it* (we reade, *take it*) *let
him receiue it.* But this cannot proper-
lie be ſaid of precepts, as S. Aug. noteth vpon this place, ſer. 61. de temp.
for of precepts it is not ſaid ꝗ keepe
them who is able , but abſolutly.
Therfore &c.

See more Luc. 10. 25. 1. Cor. 7. 1.
Reuel. 4. 3. Actes 2. 44. Actes 4. 34.
See Fathers that affirme the ſame.
S. Amb. l. de viduis. Origen in c. 15. ad
Rom. *Thoſe thinges Which Wee doe ouer
and aboue our dutie.* Euſeb 1. Demon-
ſtrat. cap. 8. S. Chryſoſt. hom. 8. de
act. pœnit. *Blame not our Lord , he
commandeth nothing impoſsible, yea ma-
nie doe more then they are commanded.*
S. Greg. Nicen. 15. Moral. cap. 5.
　　　　　　　　　XIX,

XIX.

That by the fall of Adam, we haue all
lost our free will: and that it is not
in our owne power to choose
good, but only euill.

Ontrary to the expresse wordes of their owne Bible 1.
Cor. 37. *He that standeth stedfast in his*
hart, hauing no necessitie, but hath
power ouer his owne will, and hath so
decreed in his hart, that he will keepe
his virgin, doth well. But if a man
haue not freedome of will, as well
to the one, as to the other, why
doth the holy Ghost (Prou. 23. 26.)
require of vs to giue him our hart, if
we cannot consent but vnto euill?
Therlore it is in our power to choose
good, or euill.

Iohn 1. 11. 12. *He came vnto his*
owne, and his owne receiued him not:
but as many as receiued him, to them
gaue he power to become the sonnes of
God. Wordes which plainly imply a
libertie of will; For when he saith
some receiued him, & some not, who
sees

sees not the libertie both of the one,
& of the other: for these would not
receiue him , and these would.
Therfore &c.

Deut. 30. 19. *I call heauen and earth*
to record this day against you , that I
haue set before you life and death, bles-
sing and cursing , therfore choose life,
that both thou and thy seede may liue.
And rightly may we call heauen and
earth to witnes against them , who
commit the same fault touching
grace, which the Turkes doe touching nature ; For the Turkes beleeue that the fire burnes not , nor
water wetts not , but God by the
fire and the water: so they, that a man
desireth no good , nor dooth no
good, but only that God dooth all
by man : but this is false. Therfore. &c.

Luc. 13. 34. *O Hierusalem, Hieru-*
salem &c. how often would I haue ga-
thered thy children together, as a henne
doth gather her brood vnder her winges,
and yee would not. I would, and yee
would

would not; what for Gods fake can
be fpoke more plainly?

See more Luc. 10. 42. Acts 5. 4.
Ad Philemon v.14. 1.Cor.7.37.& 9.
1.14. 2.Cor.9.7. Ofe. 3. 9. Num. 30.
14. Iofua 14.13. 2.Reg.24.12.3.Reg.
3.5. Ecclef. 15. 15. Mat. 19. 17. Iofue
24.15.2. Samuel 12. Pro. 11. 24. Re-
uel.3.20. Ifay 1.19.20.

For further proofe we will fly to
our Rule. Eufeb. Cefar. de prep.
l.1.cap.7.faith, that thofe who hould
this opinion, doe peruert and ouer-
throw, *Vniuerfam vitam humanam, all
the life of man.* And in very deed his
reafon is good, for vpon this confideration of mans free wil, are grounded all politicall lawes, precepts and
prohibitions, paines and rewardes,
which elfe were meerely fuperfluous
and againft reafon. S. Hilarie l. 1. de
Trinitate, faith . *He would not there
should be a necefsitie for men to be the
fonnes of God, but a power.* S. Aug. l.
1. ad Simp. q. 4. faith. *To confent, or
not to confent vnto Gods vocation, lyeth*
                                        in

in a mans owne will. So teacheth S.
Amb. in Luc. cap. 12. S. Chrisost.
hom. 19. in Genes. S. Ireneus l. 4.
cap. 72. S. Cyrill. lib. 4. in Ioan.
cap. 7. We *cannot in any wise deny*
freedome of will in man. And S. Aug.
afore recited saith, lib. 2. cap. 4. de
act. cum Felic. Manich. *How should*
our Sauiour reward euerie one accor-
ding to their workes, if there were no
free will?

XX.

That it is impossible to keepe the Com-
mandements of God, though assisted
with his grace, & the holy Ghost.

Ontrary to the expresse wordes
of their owne bible. Philip. 4.
13. *I can doe all thinges, thorough*
Christ which stregthneth me. Therfore
it is possible to keepe the commandements, or else it is false, that he
could doe all thinges.

Luc. 1. 5. 6. The scripture speaking of Zacharie & Elizabeth, saith.
And they were both righteous before
God, walking in all the commandements
and

and ordinances of the Lord, *blameles.*
Yet they vfuallie fay, that none are fo
righteous as that they can keepe any
of them: but thefe two were fo righteous as they kept all of them : now
whither of thefe wilt thou beleue?

Luc. 11.27. 28. *Bleffed is the wombe*
that bare thee, and the papes which thou
haft fucked . But he faid; Yea rather,
bleffed are they that heare the word of
God, and keepe it. Chrift pronounceth them bleffed, who heare the
word of God and keepe it : but the
commandements are the word of
God (which they affirme no man can
keepe) therfore they affirme that no
man can be bleffed . And like vnto
this is that of Iohn 13.17. Mat. 12.50.
Iohn. 14.23. with an infinit number
of fuch like places, al which this lew-
ed doctrine, doth plainly dally with
all, as it doth with this.

Luc. 11.2. *Thy wil be done as in heaue*
fo in earth. In making this demand,
ether we demād a thinge impoffible,
or the Saints in heauen fulfill not the
will,

will of God in all thinges, or it may be fulfilled alſo by vs on earth (one of the three:) But the two firſt are ful of abſurdities: therfore the later is to be granted.

1. Iohn 5.3. *For this is the loue of God, that we keepe his commandements, and his commãdements are not greeuous.* If the cõmandements were impoſſible, they could binde no man: for it is not to be conceiued how one ſhould ſinne in a thinge, which he could not poſſibly auoide. And Chriſt ſaying to the young man; If thou wilt enter into heauen, keepe the commandements, is as if he had ſaid; If thou wilt enter into heauen, take hould of the Moone betwixt thy teeth.

See more Ezech. 36. 27. Mat. 11. 30. & 19. 17. Eccleſ. 15. 15. Rom. 13. 8. 10. & 7. 3. Ioſua 11. 15. & 22. 5. pſal. 17. 3. Deut. 30. 11. 1. Iohn 2 4. Iob. 27. 6. & 1. 22. Rom. 2. 27. Luc. 10. 28. &c. 15. 7. 3. Reg. 14. 8. & 15. 5. Epheſ. 1. 4. Galat. 5. 14. Gen. 6. 9.

But

But to rectifie them herein by our common Rule, see Origen hom. 9. in Iosue. S. Cyril. l. 4. cont. Iulian. S. Hillar. in psal. 118. S. Hier. l. 3. cont. Pelag. S. Basil, who saith . It is an impious thinge to say, that the commandements of God are impossible.

XXI.

That only faith iustifieth; And that good workes are not absolutely necessary to saluation.

C Ontrary to the expresse wordes of their owne Bible 1. Cor. 13. 2. *And though I haue the gift of prophecie, and vnderstand all mysteries, and all knowledge; and though I haue all faith so that I could remoue mountaines, and haue no charitie, I am nothing.* Therfore faith only doth not iustifie : yea this plainlie proueth, that faith is nothing to saluation , without good workes.

Iames 2.24. *Yee see therfor, how that by workes a man is iustified, and not by faith only.* S. Aug. lib. de fide & operibus

ribus cap. 14. writeth, that this heresie, was an old heresie, euen in the
Apostles times. And in the preface
of his comment. vpon the 32.psal. he
warneth all men, that this deduction
vpon S. Paules speeche, *Abraham was
iustified by faith, therfore workes be not
necessarie to saluation,* is the right way
to hell and damnation. See the Rhe-
Test. vpon this place.

Iac. 2. 14. *What doth it profit my
bretheren, though a man say he hath
faith, and haue not workes? Can faith
saue him?* This proposition (but especially the former) is directly opposite
to that which our aduersaries hould.
Neuer can they pretend, that there
is the like opposition or contradiction, betwixt S. Iames speeches and
S. Pauls : for though S. Paul say,
Man is iustified by faith, yet he neuer
sayeth, by faith only.

Gal. 5. 6. *For in Iesus Christ, nether
circumcision auaileth any thinge, nor vn-
circumcision, but faith which worketh
byloue.* Note well this place; for if
                                        our

our aduersaries, who pretend confe-
rence of places, to be the only rule
to explicate the hard paſſages of holy
ſcripture, had followed but this their
owne Rule, this one text would haue
cleared vnto them all other, wherin
iuſtice and ſaluation might ſeeme to
be attributed to faith alone.

See more Mat. 7. 21. 22. Mat. 5. 21
Mat. 19. 17. & 11. 26. Mat. 12. 33.
Mat. 16. 16. Gal. 3. 12. 1. Tim. 5. 8. 1.
Ioan. 2. 4. 1. Ioan. 3. 22. Rom. 3. 31.
Phillip. 2. 12.

See Fathers that affirme the ſame.
Origen in 5. Rom. S. Hillar. cap. 7.
in Mat. S. Amb. in 4. ad Heb. ſaith.
..ith alone ſufficeth not. S. Aug. de
fide & operibus cap. 15. ſaith. *I ſee
not, why Chriſt ſhould ſay*. If thou
wilt haue life euerlaſting keepe the
commandements, *if without obſer-
uing of them, by only faith, one might
be ſaued.*

D   XXII.

XXII.

That no good workes are me-
ritorious.

COntrary to the expresse wordes of their owne Bible . Mat.
16.27. For the *Sonne of man shall come*
in the glorie of his Father , with his
Angells , and then he shall reward eue-
rie man according to this workes . He
saith not, that he shall reward euery
man according to his mercie, or their
faith, but according to their workes.
So S. Aug. de verbis Apost. ser. 35.
Therfore &c.

Mat. 5. 12. *Reioyce and be glad , for*
great is your reward in heauen . The
word Reward, in latin & greeke, signifieth very wages, and hyre, due for
workes, and so presupposeth a meritorious deed , as the Rhe. Test. noteth vpon this place. Therfore &c.

The like of this place , is that of
S. Mat. 10. 42. *And whosoeuer shall*
giue to drinke, a cup of cold water on-
ly, in the name of a Disciple , verely I
say vnto you, he shall in no wise loose
                                    his

his reward. Therfore.

1.Cor.5.10.For *we must all appeare before the iudgment seate of Christ, that euery one may receiue the thinges in his body*, *according to that he hath done, whether it be good or bad* . Wordes most cleare, that heauen is as wel the reward of good workes , as hell is the ftipend of euill workes, how-foeuer the aduerfaries of good life and workes, doe teache the contrarie.

See more 1. Cor. 9. 17. & 18. 25. Heb. 11. 26. Pfal. 18. 20. 1.Cor. 4.5. & 3. 8. 2. Efdras 15. 19. Apoc. 22. 12. Apoc. 16. 6. Apoc. 3. 4. & 22.12. Rom. 2.6. Ecclef. 12. 2. Colof. 3. 23. Luc.16.9.& 6.38. Gen. 15. 1. Ierem. 31.16. Sap.5.16. 1. Tim. 4.8.2.Thef. 1.6. Rom. 11. 21.

See Fathers that affirme the fame. S. Amb. de apolog. Dauid cap. 6. S. Hier. l.3.cont. Pelag. S. Aug. de fpi-ritu & lit. cap. vlt.

XXIII.

XXIII.

That faith once had, cannot be lost.

COntrary to the expreſſe wordes of their owne Bible. Luc. 8. 13. *They on the rock, are they, which when they heare, receiue the word with ioy, which for a while beleeue, and in time of tentation fall away.* Therfore faith once had, yet afterwards may be loſt.

1. Tim. 1. 18.19. *This charge I commit vnto thee, ſonne Timothie, according to the prophecies which went before on thee, that thou by them, mighteſt warre a good warfare, houlding faith and a good conſcience, which ſome hauing put away, concerning faith, haue made ship-wrack.* Both which places doe plainlie reproue this falſe doctrine, that no man can fall from the faith, which he once truly had.

2. Tim. 16. &c. *Shun prophane and vaine bablinges, for they will increaſe vnto more vngodlines, and their word will eate as doth a canker, of whom is Hymeneus and Philetus, who concerning the*

the truth haue erred, faying, that the refurrection is paft already, and ouer-throw the faith of fome. If faith once had, could not be loft, this faying of the Apoftle fhould be falfe. Ther-fore &c.

See more 1. Tim. 6. 20. Reuela-tions 2. 5. Luc. 19. 24. Mat. 25. 8. &c. Rom. 11. 20.

See Fathers that affirme the fame. S. Auguft. de gratia & lib. arbit. De correp. & gratia & ad articulos falfo impofitas. Concil. Trid. feff. 6. cap. 9. 12. 13.

XXIIII.

That God by his will and ineuitable de-cree, hath ordained from all eter-nitie, who shall be damned, and who faued.

C Ontrary to the expreffe wordes of their owne Bible. 1. Tim. 2. 3. 4. *God our Sauiour, who will haue all men to be faued, and to come to the knowledge of the truth.* Meaning, by his conditionall will, that is to fay, if men wil themfelues, by accepting,

D 3   dooing,

dooing, or hauing done vnto them,
all thinges requisite by Gods law:
for God vseth not his absolute will
or power towards vs in this case.
Therfore he hath not willed, and
ineuitably decreed, any at all to be
damned.

2. Pet. 3. 9. *The Lord is not slack
concerning his promise &c. not willing
that any should perish, but that all
should come to repentance.* Therfore
far off from euer making anie such
decree.

Wisdome 1. 13. *For God made not
death, nether hath he pleasure in the
destruction of the liuing.* The reasons
which conclude this truth, are very
manifest: for we must assure nothing
of those thinges, which depend vpon the only will of God (without
cleare and euident reuelation) but
predestination is such. Therfore.

See more. Ose 13. 9. Ezech. 18.
32. Wis. 11.24. Ioan. 3.16. Rom. 11.
20. 32. Pro.20.9. & 28. 14. Phil.2.12.
1. Cor.4.4. & 9. 27. & 10.12. Eccles.
5. 5.

5. 5. Iob. 9. 21. Ioel 2. 14. Ionas 3. 9.
Acts 8. 20. Ierem. 17. 9. 2. Ioàn 1. 8.

See Fathers that affirme the ſame.
S. Aug. l. 1. ciuit. Tertul. orat. cap. 8.
S. Cyp. l. 4. ep. 2. S. Amb. lib. 2. de
Cain & Abel, will not that we refer
vnto God, the preuarication of Adã,
or the treaſon of Iudas, though he
knew the ſinne before it was committed.

XXV.

That euery one ought infallibly to aſſure
him ſelfe of his ſaluation, and to
beleeue that he is of the num-
ber of the predeſtinat.

Ontrary to the expreſſe wordes
of their owne Bible. 1. Cor. 9.
27. *I keepe vnder my body, and bringe*
it into ſubiectiõ, leaſt that by any meanes,
when I haue preached to others, I my
ſelfe ſhould be a caſt-way. A mã would
thinke that S. Paul might be as ſure
and as confident of Gods grace and
ſaluation, as any one of our aduerſaries be, and yet you ſee he durſt
not adhere vnto their preſumptuous

D 4 and

& vnhappie securitie. Therfore &c.

Rom. 11. 20. *Thou standest by faith,
be not high minded, but feare, for if God
spared not the naturall branches , take
heede least he also spare not thee : behould therfore the goodnes and seueritie of God; on them which fell, seueritie;
but towards thee goodnes, if thou continue in his goodnes, otherwise, thou also
shalt be cut off.* Therfore &c.

Philippians 2. 12. *Worke out your
owne saluation , with feare and trembling.* A plaine and forcible place, a-
gainst the vaine securitie of saluatiō.

See more. Pro. 28. 14. Ecclef. 9.
1. 2. 2. Tim. 2. 15. 2. Pet. 1. 10. Toby
12. 2. 13. Pro. 20. 9. Ecclef. 5. 5. Iob. 9.
20. Psal. 18, 13. 1. Cor. 4. 4. Deut. 4.
29. 2. Cor. 10. 18. 1. Pet. 1. 17.

To let nothing slip without our
Rule, see S. Amb. ser. 5. in psal. 118.
S. Basil in constit. monast. cap. 2. S.
Ierom l. 2. aduers. Pelagianos, & l. 3.
in Ierem. cap. 13. S. Chrysost. hom.
87. in Ioan. S. Aug. in Psal. 40. *I know
that the instice of my God remaineth,*
whe-

Whether my iustice remayne or no, I *know not, for the Apostle terrifieth me saying. He that thinketh him selfe to stand, let him take heede least he fall.* S. Bernard. fer. 3. de Aduent. & fer. 1. de Septuagef. Who can fay I am one of the elect? &c To conclude, it is none of the articles of our Creed. Therfore &c.

XXVI.

That euery one hath not his Angell keeper.

C Ontrary to the expreſſe wordes of their own Bible.Mat.18. 10. *Take heede that yee defpice not one of thefe litle ones, for I fay vnto you, that in heauen, their Angells doe all-wayes behould the face of my Father which is in heauen* . Therfore they haue their Angell keeper. A thinge fo plaine, that Caluin dares not to deny it,and yet he will needes doubt of it.l.1.Inft.cap.14.feCt.7.

Pfal 91. (we 90.) 11.12. *He shal giue his Angels charge ouer thee, to keepe thee in all thy wayes, they shall beare thee*
                                    D 5   *vp*

vp in their handes, leaſt thou dashe thy foote againſt a ſtone. This very paſſage S. Cyrill of Alexandria lib. 4. cont. Iulian, applyeth to our Angel keeper. Therfore &c.

Acts 12. 13. &c. Peter knocking at the doore, they ſaid; *It is his Angel.* Loe how apparantly the faith of the primitiue Church appeareth concerning this point.

See more, 1. Cor. 11. 10. Zacharie 3. 10. Luc. 15. 10. Luc. 16. 22. Tob. 5. 15. 20. Tob. 12. 12. Tob. 5. 27. Exod. 23. 23. Ioſue 5. 13. Num. 22. 22. 31. Gen. 24. 40. Dan. 6. 22.

To meaſure this doctrine by our Line or Rule, ſee S. Greg. dial. l. 4. cap. 58. S. Athanaſ. de communi eſſentia. S. Chriſoſt. hom. 3. in ep. ad Coloſ. lib. 6. de ſacerd. Greg. Turonenſ. lib. de gloria mart. S. Aug. ep. ad Probam cap. 9. & epiſt. 69. ad fratres in eremo. lib. 11. cap. 31. ciuit. S. Hiero. vpon theſe wordes, *Their Angels &c.* Mat. 18. 10. teacheth, that it is a great dignitie and maruelous

uelous benefit, that euery one hath from his natiuitie, an Angell for his cuſtodie and patronage.

XXVII.

That the holie Angells pray not for vs, nor knowe the thoughts and deſires of vs on earth.

C Ontrary to the expreſſe wordes of their owne Bible Zacharie 1. 9. 10. 11. 12. *Then the Angell of the Lord answered and ſaid. O Lord of hoſtes, how longe wilt thou not haue mercie on Hieruſalem, and on the citties of Iuda, againſt which thou haſt had indignation, theſe threeſcore and ten yeares?* And what I pray you, is a prayer, if this be not? Therfore the holie Angells pray for vs.

Toby 12. 12. *Now therfore, when thou didſt pray, and Sara thy daughter in law, I did bringe the remembrance of your prayers, before the holy one.* He which pleaſeth to reade the whole chapter, ſhall clearly ſee the manifould benefits beſides this one, which men receiue at the handes of

Angels:

Angels: for which fee the annotations of the Catholique Bible vpon
this place. Therfore &c.

Reuelations 8. 4. *And the smoke of
the incenfes of the prayers of the Saints,
afcended from the hand of the Angell before God.* What can be possibly spoken
more plaine, to proue that Angells
offer vp our prayers before God?
yea this very place is fo vnderstood
by S. Ireneus l. 4. cap. 34. towards the end.

See more Gen. 19. 18. 19. 20. Dan.
3. 15. Dan. 9. 20. Acts 5. 19.

According to our Rule, thefe fathers following affirme the fame. S.
Hillarie in pfal. 129. faith. *The inter-
cession of Angels, Gods nature needeth
not, but our infirmitie doth.* S. Amb.
lib. de viduis. victor Vtic. lib. 3. de
perfecut. Vandal.

XXVIII.

That we may not pray to them.

C Ontrary to the expreffe wordes
of their owne Bible. Gen. 48.
16. *The Angel which redeemed me* (we,
                                    read

read *deliuered) from me all euill , bleſſe the laddes* . But ſome perhappes will here ſay , that this was Chriſt . But this is but a ſorry ſhift, for Chriſt had not then redeemed man, but long af-ter : yea this very paſſage is appro-priated by S. Chriſoſt. to our Angel gardian hom. 3. vpon the 1. of the Coloſ. And by S. Hierom vpon the 66. of Iſay. Alſo S. Baſil. l. 3. cont. Eu-nom, affirmeth that this was ſpoken of a true Angel , and not of Chriſt: which being ſo , who can with rea-ſon ſay, he praied not to him?

Tobie. 5. 16. *And when his ſonne had prepared all thinges for the iorney, his fa-ther ſaid . Goe thou with this man, and God which dwelleth in heauen , proſper your iorney, and the Angell of God keepe you companie*. Loe, both God is here prayed vnto, and his Angell alſo is praied vnto at the ſame preſet, ſaying. God proſper you in your iornie, and the Angel of God keepe you cōpany. Both therfore doe very well cōſiſt to-gether, and be both aggreable to the word of God. Oſee

Oſee 12. 4. *Yea, he had power ouer the Angell, and preuailed, he wept, and made ſupplication vnto him.* Loe, what is plaine, if this be not, for proofe of prayer to the bleſſed Angels?

But ſome perhaps will here ſay; I could be perſwaded to pray to Angells, if I could aſſure my ſelfe that they could heare me, and knew what paſſeth here on earth. Wherto I reply, that we in earth, know that the Angells are in heauen, and often alſo with vs in earth: that they are in full ioy and felicitie: and finally, that they ſee God &c. Now if they know not what we doe in earth (hauing much more perfect knowledge then we haue) we attribute to our ſelues more knowledge in earth, then we doe to them who are in heauen : the which, were blaſphemie to affirme. Therfore we may pray vnto them.

See more, Oſee 12. 4. Song of the three children verſe 36. Pſal. 148. Num. 22. 34. Gen. 19. 18. 19. 29. Pſal. 148. 2.

And

And now to confirme what hath bene said by our Line or Rule. Iob. 19. 21. we reade as followeth . *Haue pittie vpon me , haue pittie vpon me, o yee my friendes for the hande of God hath touched me:* which wordes (as S. Aug. him selfe expoundeth) holy Iob addressed to the Angells. Iob. 5. 1. *Call now &c.* the same. S. Aug. expoundeth of praying to Angels in his annot. vpon Iob.

XXIX.

That the Angells cannot helpe vs.

Contrary to the expresse wordes of their owne Bible. Dan. 10. 13. *Michael one of the chiefe princes came to helpe me.* Which is further verefied Reuel: 12. 7. 10. where the selfe same Angell , with his fellow Angells, fought a battell with the dragon, and with his Angells. Therfore they can helpe vs.

The same chapter, verse 21. *And there is none that houldeth with me in these thinges , but Michael your prince.* Therfore &c.

Acts

Acts 12. from verse 7. to verse 12.
*Now I know of a suretie, that the Lord
hath sent his Angell, and hath deliuered me.* Therfore &c.

See more, Mat. 2. 13. Mat. 4. 6.
Psal. 91. (we 90.) 11. 12. Acts 5. 19.
Acts 27. 23. psal. 104. (we. 103.) 4.
Heb. 1. 7. Luc. 16. 22. Gen. 19. 10. 15.
16. Gen. 2. 117. Isay. 63. 9.

See Fathers that affirme the same.
S. Iustin. Apol. 2. S. Amb. l. de viduis. Victor Vticens. l. 3. de persec.
Vand. S. Aug. de Ciuit. l. 12. cap. 31.
faith. *The holy Angels doe helpe vs without all difficultie, becaufe with their fpirituall motions (pure and free) they labour
or trauel not.* And in pfal. 62. he faith,
The Angells waite vpō vs pilgrimes,
and by the commandment of God,
do helpe vs: the place beginneth, *At-
tendunt nos peregrinos.*

X X X.

*That no Saint deceased, hath afterwards
appeared to any vpon earth.*

Contrary to the expreffe wordes of their owne Bible, Mat.
17. 3.

17. 3. *And behould there appeared vnto them, Moyses and Elias talkinge with them.* Therfore Saints deceased, haue afterwards appeared to fome in earth.

Mat. 27. 52. *And the graues were opened, and many bodies of Saints which flept, arofe; and came out of the graues after his refurrection, and went into the holy cittie, and appeared vnto many.* Therfore &c.

2. Mac. 15. 12. Onias the high prieft after he was dead, appeared to Iudas Machabeus being aliue. The like did Samuel vnto Saul. What fhall we fay then to thofe, that will deny a truth fo cleare? for fome fuch my felfe haue met with.

See more Luc. 16. 27. 28. Ioan. 11. 44. Luc. 7. 15. & 23. Mat. 9. 25. Marc. 5. 42.

Conforme to our Rule, fee S. Bed. l. 5. cap. 13. hiftorie of England. S. Gregorie in his booke of Moralls, in fundry places.

XXXI.

XXXI.

That the Saints deceafed, know not
what paffeth here in earth.

Ontrary to the expreffe wordes
of their owne Bible Luc. 16.
29. Where Abraham knewe, that
there were Moyfes and the prophets
bookes here in earth, which he him
felfe had neuer feene when he was
aliue: as S. Aug. witneffeth *l. de cura*
pro mortuis. cap. 14. Therfore the
Saints deceafed, know what paffeth
here in earth.

Iohn 5. 45. *Doe not thinke that I*
will accuse you to the Father *, there is*
one that accufeth you , euen Moyfes *in*
whom yee truft. But how could Moyfes (dead two thoufand yeares before) accufe thofe that were then liuing, if the Saints deceafed , know
not what paffeth here in earth? Therfore &c.

Like vnto this, is that Reuel. 12.
10. *And I heard a loud voice faying in*
heauen &c. the accuser of our bretheren
is caft downe , which accufed them be-
                                              fore

fore our God day and night . Now the
diuells cannot accuse men day and
night before God, but they must first
know wherof: who then may for
shame deny that to Saints and Angells, which must needes be granted
to the very deuills? Therfore &c.

2. Kinges 6. 12. (we 4. Kinges)
*O kinge, Elisem the prophet, that is in
Israel, telleth the kinge of Israel, the
wordes that thou speakest in thy bed
chamber.* Hence I thus argue; If the
light of prophecie, could extend it
selfe so far, as to make knowen, see,
and vnderstand thinges so secret yea
euen to inward thoughtes: who can
with reason deny, that the light of
glorie can doe the same in the soules
of the blessed?

The like is proued out of many
other places of holy scripture, as 2.
Kinges 5. 26. where the prophet Elizeus, being a far off, saw all that passed betwix Naaman, and Giesi his
seruant. S. Paul was rapt in to the
third heauen, and saw that which
was

was not to be tould to man 1. Cor.
12. S. Stephen saw from earth, Christ
sitting at the right hand of his father,
Acts 7. Diues saw from hell to heauen (as Protestants say) how then say
they, that the Saints cannot know or
see from heauen to earth?

To conclude; without some reci-
procall knowledg, there could be no
communion at all, betwixt the Saints
in heauen, and the faithfull in earth;
which who so denieth, denieth a
part of our common creede: which
yet the continuall passage of soules
thither, doth conuince. Therfore &c.

See more Mat 19. 28. Reuel. 2. 26.
Luc. 22. 30. Acts 5. 3. 1. Kinges 28. 14.
Eccles. 4. 6. 23.

See Fathers that affirme the same.
Eusebius serm. de Annunc. S. Hierom in epitaph. Paulæ. S. Maximus
serm. de S. Agnete.

XXXII.

That they pray not for vs.

COntrary to the expresse wordes
of their owne Bible. Reuelat. 5.
8. *The*

8.*The four and twentie elders fell downe before the Lambe, hauing euery one of them harpes, and golden vialls, ful of o-dors, which are the prayers of Saints.* Loe, how among so many diuine and vnfearchable myfteries fet downe in fcripture without expofition, it plea-fed God, that the Apoftle himfelfe fhould clearly open this point vnto vs, faying: *which* (odors) *are the prayers of Saints*, that fo our aduer-faries may haue no excufe of their er-ror. Therfore they pray for vs.

2. Machabees 15. 14. Then Onias anfwered faying. *This is a louer of the bretheren, who prayeth much for the peo-ple, and for the holie cittie, to wit, Ie-remias the prophet of God.* Ancient O-rigen tom. 18. in Ioan faith. It ap-peareth that Saints departed from this life haue care of the people, as it is written in the acts of the Macha-bes, many yeares after the death of Ieremie. Therfore &c.

Ieremie 15. 1. *Though Moyfes and Samuel ftood before me, yet my minde could*

could not be towards this people. Hence
S. Ierom in his commentaries, and S.
Greg. the 9. of his Morales cap. 12.
doe gather, that Moyſes and Samuel after their death, both could,
and did, ſomtimes pray for the ſame
people: for otherwiſe, it ſhould be
as fooliſh, and abſurd to ſay. *Though
Moyſes and Samuel ſtood before me,* as
if one ſaid; If an Horſe or an Aſſe
ſhould pray. Therfore &c.

Baruch 3. 4. *O Lord almightie, thou
God of Iſrael, heare now the prayers of
the dead Iſraelites* (we reade, *of the
dead of Iſrael.*) And Theodoret para-
praſing vpon the prophet Baruch,
interpreteth this place as Catholiques doe. Therfore the dead of
Iſrael, prayed for the liuing.

Reuel. 2. 2. 26. 27. *And he that ouer-
commeth, and keepeth my workes vnto
the end, to him will I giue power ouer
the nations, and he shall rule them with
a rod of iron.* Sith Ieſus Chriſt therfore imparteth his power vnto them
vpon natiõs, therfore they may with
Ieſus

Iesus Chrift and by Iesus Chrift, pray
for thofe ouer whom they are thus
eftablifhed. So S. Auguft. expoundeth the fame , writing vpon the
2. Pfalme.

To conclude this queftion , we
reade in the 16. of S. Luc. that Diues
in hell, prayed for his brethren that
were in earth; If therfore the Saints
in heauen pray not for vs their bretheren on earth, then let vs fay, that
greater is the charitie of the damned
then of the faued. But this were abfurd to fay. Therfore &c. A conclu-
fion which S. Aug. draweth from
this very place.

See more, Reuelat. 6. 9. Reuelat.
6. 26. 27.

See Fathers that affirme the fame.
S. Aug. ferm. 15. de verbis Apoft. S.
Hillar. in pfalm. 129. S. Damafcen
lib. 4. de fide cap. 16. with many
others.

XXXIII.

XXXIII.

That we ought not to beseeche God, to graunt our prayers in fauor of the Saints or of their merits, nor doe receiue no benefitt by them.

TWo wayes there are, of praying by the mediation of the the blessed Saints. The one, by beseeching God, to grant our desires in fauor of them, and of their merits. The other, by expresly praying thē, to intercede and pray to God for vs: both being impugned by Reformers, we will proue them both out of their owne Bible. The proofe of the first.

Contrary to the expresse wordes of their owne Bible. Exod. 32. 13. *Remember Abraham, Isaac, and Israell thy seruants, to whom thou swarest by thine owne selfe, and saidst vnto them. I will multiplie your seede, as the starres of heauen &c.* And our Lord repented (we reade, *was pacified*) of the euill which he thought to doe vnto his people.

Loe

Loe, how plainly Moyſes prayed to
God, by the mediation of the holie
Patriarches; a forme of praier ſo plea-
ſing to him, as hauing ſaid a litle before, that for their ſinne of idolatrie,
he would conſume them, the memo-
rie of his holy ſeruants being but laid
before him, he preſently pardoned
them . Therfore we may beſeech
God to grant our prayers in fauor of
them. Theodoret queſt. 67. in Exod.
writeth , that Moyſes not thinking
him ſelfe ſufficient , to appeaſe God
by him ſelfe, added the interceſſion
of the holie patriarkes : and the like
doth S. Aug. queſt. 149. in Exod.

2. Chronicles 6.16. *Now therfore,
o Lord God of Iſrael, keepe with thy ſer-
uant Dauid , that which thou haſt promiſed him .* And pſal. 132. (we 131.)
*Lord remember Dauid, and all his afflic-
tions .* Loe againe , the faith of the
ancient Church of God, before the
coming of Ieſus Chriſt, and how
feruent they were in this deuotion,
ſtill alleadging the memories and

E me-

merits of their Saints deceafed, therby to moue Gods mercie towards them. So praied Salomon 2. Chron. 1.9. So praied Ifay 63. 17. So praied Hefter 13. 14. So praied Dauid, 1. Chron. 29. 18. naming Abraham, Ifaac, and Iacob for his intercef-fors. Who euer heard a Proteftant make the like prayer? faying, Lord remember thine owne mother, and all her afflictions, or Peter and Paul and their perfecutions? They defire the Papifts to hould them blameles for feare (for footh) leaft they fhould blafpheme.

Exod. 20. 5. *I the Lord thy God, am a iealous God, vifiting the iniquitie of the fathers, vpon the children, vnto the third and fourth generation of them that hate me, and shewing mercie vnto thoufands, of them that loue me, and keepe my commandements.* Here againe God threatneth to punifh the demerits of wicked mé deceafed, vnto the fourth generation of their children aliue: and to reward the merits of good

men

men deceaſed, vnto the thouſand generation of their children aliue.
Therfore, we aliue at this very day,
receiue benefitte by meanes of our
godly anceſtors, which are deceaſed
ſince a thouſand generations. Thus
much for the proofe of the firſt point,
and now to paſſe vnto the ſecond.

XXXIIII.

That we ought not expreſly to pray to
them, to pray or intercede to
God for vs.

COntrary to the expreſſe wordes
of their owne Bible, Luc. 16.24.
Father Abraham, haue mercie on me
and ſend Lazarus, that he may dip the
tip of his fingar in water, and coole my
tongue, for I am tormented in this flame.
Loe, two Saints are here prayed and
beſought in one verſe, and yet they
vſually bid vs ſhew them, ſo much
as one place in all the Bible for proofe
hereof. Where for Gods ſake, are
their eies?

But they reply that this is a parable: which we deny, offering to be

E 2   tryed

tryed by our common Rule, hauing
on our fide, ten renowmed and ancient fathers, all affirming this to be
a true hiftorie, and not a parable, as
Theophilact, Tertullian, Clemens
of Alexandria, S. Chryfoftome, S.
Ireneus, S. Ambrose, S. Auguftine,
S. Gregorie, Euthymius, and our
owne contryman Venerable Bede.

But granting it to be a parable,
what I pray doth this make, ether
for them, or againft vs? For euery parable, is ether true in it felfe, and in
the perfons named, or at leaft, is, or
may be true in fome other, elfe were
it a flat lye, or at leaft a fiction or a fa-
ble. If they grant this, then are they
gone, and we haue gayned what we
defire.

Where vpon I thus conclude, as
S. Aug. did a litle before vpon the
felfe fame hiftory: If Diues in hel,
prayd to Abraham who (as Reformers fay) was in heauen, why may
not we, who are in earth, pray to
them who are in heauen?

Iob.

Iob.5. 1. Call now, if there be any that will answer thee, and to which of the Saints wilt thou turne? we reade, *and turne to some of the Saints.* Now, if it had not bene the custome in the time of Iob, to inuocate the holy Saints, it had bene friuolous for Eliphas, to haue asked Iob, to which of the Saints he would turne him: no, such an error can not iustly be supposed, in so sensible a man as Eliphas was. Wherto I add, that S. Aug. expoundeth this very place in his annotations vpon Iob, in the same sence that Catholiques doe; yea and long before him the seauenty interpreters.

Contrary to the expresse wordes of their owne Bible, appointed to be publikely read at morning prayer, in the Canticle, *O all yee workes of the Lord, blesse yee the Lord, praise him, and magnifie him for euer*, and with vs is found in the 3. of Daniel, where thus they say. *O Ananias, Azarias, and Misael, blesse yee the Lord, praise him, and magnifie him for euer*. Now,

if

if the vocatiue cafe be knowen by calling or fpeaking to (as euery gramarian wil côfes) ether this is plaine calling vpon, and fpeaking to thefe three Saints, or I will begin my gramar againe. But perhaps they will reply, that in this Canticle of the three children, brute beaftes, and other dead and infenfible thinges, are likewife inuited to prayfe God, or inuoked, as well as the Saints aforenamed: the fcripture faith fo, it muft needes be granted. If therfore beaftes, and other dead and infenfible creatures, may be inuited, or inuoked, to praife God in their kinde, why not Saints alfo in theirs? Or who will fhew him felfe fo fenfles, as to fay, that the liuing Saints(being capable of Inuocation, as hath bene proued, which the others ar not) are no otherwife to be inuited or inuoked, then plants and trees, hilles, and mountaines, and other dead and infenfible thinges? Therfore Saints may be paayed vnto.

See

more 2. Pet. 1. 15. Dan. 3. 28.
Heſter. 13. 14. 1. Chron. 29. 18. Luc.
16. 9. & 15. 10.

See Fathers that affirme the ſame.
Dioniſ. cap. 7. eccleſ. Hier. S. Athanaſius ſerm. de Annunt. S. Baſil orat.
in 44. martyrs. S. Chriſoſt. hom. 66.
ad popul. Finally, S. Hierom prayed
to S. Paula, in epitap. S. Paulæ. S.
Maximus to S. Agnes, ſerm. de S.
Agnete. S. Bernard to our bleſſed
Lady, and the like.

XXXV.

That the bones or Reliques of Saints,
are not to be kept or reſerued: no ver-
tue proceeding from them, after
they be once dead.

COntrary to the expreſſe wordes
of their owne Bible, 2. Kinges
(we 4.) 13. 22. Where it is written,
that the bones of Elizeus, being touched by one that was dead, they did
reuiue him. But this could not be,
had not ſome vertue proceeded from
them: therfore &c.

Acts 15. 14. 15. *And beleeuers were*
E 4   *the*

the more added to the Lord, multitudes,
both of men and women: in so much that
they brought forth the sick into the stree-
tes, and laid them on beds and couches,
that at the least the shadow of Peter pas-
sing by, might overshadow some of them.
It followeth in ours, *and they all*
might be deliuered from their infirmi-
ties : quite left out in the Englifh
Bible. S. Aug. fer. 39. de Sanctis faith.
If the shadow of his body could helpe
then, how much more now, the fulnes
of his power ? Wherin he fuppoleth
two thinges; The one; that the fhadow of his body being here in earth,
did both helpe and heale infirmities
(which the Englifh Bible feaueth
out.) The other, that being in heauen, he can fti'l helpe vs by his power. Therfore &c.

Acts 19. 11. 12. *And God wrought*
speciall miracles by the handes of Paul,
so that from his body were brought vnto
the sick. hand kerchiefes or aprons, and
the diseases departed from them, and the
euill spirits went out of them. S. Chry-
foltome

foſtome tom. 5. cont. Gentiles *quod Chriſtus ſit Deus*, in a whole booke proueth hereby, and by the like virtue of other Saints, and their Reliques, that Chriſt their Lord and maſter is God, whoſe ſeruants ſhadowes and napkins, could doe ſuch wonders. Therfore &c.

See more Exod.13.19.2. Kinges 2. 8. 14. Iohn. 1. 27. Where S. Iohn. had a reuerend eſteeme of the very latchet of our Sauiours ſhoe, as of a Relique he was not worthie to vnbuckle, or touch with his hande : and the woman with the bloody flux, of the hemme of his holy garment.

Se Fathers that affirme the ſame. Euſeb. lib. 7. hiſt. cap. 15. S. Athanaſius in vita S. Antonij. S. Baſil in pſal. 115. S. Chryſoſt. ſerm. de ſanctis Iuuentio & Maximo . Laſtly, S. Ambroſe ſaith ; But if you aske me, what I honor in fleſh diſſolued, I honor in the martyrs fleth, his woundes receiued for Chriſts name

E 5   &c.

&c. I honor his ashes, made holy by
confession of Christ.

XXXVI.

*That creatures cannot be sanctified, or
made more holy, then they are altea-
die of their owne nature.*

COntrary to the expresse wordes
of their owne Bible. 1. Tim. 4.
4. *For euery creature of God, is good,
& nothing to be refused, if it be receiued
with thanksgiuing, for it is sanctified
by the word of God, and prayer.* Yea it
was a common vse in the primitiue
church, to bringe breads to the priests
to be hallowed, auth. op. imp. hom.
14. in Mat. and being blessed, to
send them for sacred tokens from
one Christian to another, as S. Aug.
witnesseth. ep. 31. 34. 35. 36.

Mat. 23. 17. *Yee fooles and blinde,
whither is greater, the gold, or the temple that sanctifieth the gold?* Therfore &c.

Mat. 23. 19. *Yee fooles and blinde,
whither is greater, the gift, or the Altar
that sanctifieth the gift?* Loe how
plainly

plainly our Lord affirmeth in both
thefe places, that the temple fanctifieth the gold, and the Altar the gift:
and generally all creatures, feuered
from comon and profane vfe, to religion and worfhip of God, are therby made facred and holy. Are not
they therfore much to blame, who
keepe fuch a howting at holy water,
holy afhes, & the like? Therfore &c.

See more 2. Kinges (we, 4. 2.) where
the Prophet Elifeus applyed falt, to
the healing and purifying of the waters. Toby 6. 8. where the Angell
Raphaell vfed the liuer of the fifb,
to driue away the diuel. 1. Samuel
(we 1. Kinges) 16. Where Dauids
Harpe and pfalmodie, kept the euil
fpirit away from Saul.

See other Fathers that affirme the
fame, S. Greg. l. 1. dial. cap. 4. S.
Aug. lib. 18. de ciuit. Dei. S. Hierom
in the life of Hilarion, poft medium.
S. Bede lib. 1. cap. 30. hift. Angliæ.

E 6   XXXVII

XXXVII.

That children may be saued by their pa-
rents faith, without the Sacrament
of holie Baptisme.

Contrary to the expresse wordes, both of truth it selfe, and
also of their owne Bible. Iohn 3. 5.
Verely verely I say vnto thee, except a
man be borne of water, and of the spirit,
he cannot enter into the kingdome of
God. Therfore they cannot be saued
without Baptisme.

Titus 3. 5. *Not by workes of righte-*
ousnes which we haue done, but ac-
cording to his mercie he saued vs, by
the washing of regeneration, and re-
newing of the holy Ghost . Therfore &c.

Marc. 16. 16. *He that beleeueth, and*
is baptised, shall be saued : but he
that beleeueth not, shall be dam-
ned . Seing infants therefore cannot beleeue, therfore at the lest they
must be baptised, or cannot be
saued.

But they obiect against vs, that of
S.Paul

S. Paul 1. Cor. 7. 14. That the children of the faithful, are fanctified.
But if they vnderftand by their fanctification , that they are borne
without finne, they doe directly repugne S. Paul, who affirmeth (Ephef.
1.) that we are all borne the fonnes of wrath. Yea S. Paul in the felfe
fame place, faith, that the vnbeleeuing woman, is fanctified by the beleeuing man: and yet I hope they
will not fay, that fhe obtaines therby, the full remiffion of her finne.
Therfore &c.

Gen 17. 14. *The vncircumcifed man-childe , whofe flesh of his foreskine, is not circumcifed, that foule shal be cut off from his people* . But circumcifion , was not more neceffarie to the Ifraelites , then Baptifme to the Chriftians . Therefore &c.

See Fathers that affirme the fame. S. Aug. lib. 1.de peccat.merit.& remiff. cap. 30. & epift. 90. 92. S. Leo epift. 80. ad epifcop. Campaniæ.
S. Ire-

S. Ireneus lib. 3. cap. 19. S. Cyp. lib. 3. ep. 8. ad Fidum.

XXXVIII.

That imposition of handes vpon the peo-
ple (called by Catholiques Confir-
mation) is not necessary, nor
to be vsed.

Contrary to the expresse wordes of their owne Bible, Acts 8. 14. *Peter and Iohn prayed for them, that they might receiue the holy Ghost (for as yet he was fallen vpon none of them, only they were baptized in the name of the Lord Iesus.) Then laid they their handes on them, and they receiued the holy Ghost.* Loe the holy Ghost is giuen in Confirmation, which was not giuen in Baptisme, how then not necessarie, nor to be vsed?

Heb. 6. 1. *Therfore leauing the prin-*
ciples of the doctrine of Christ, let vs goe
on vnto perfection, not laying againe the
foundation of repentance from dead wor-
kes, and of faith towards God, of the
doctrine of Baptisme, and of laying on of
handes. Loe, Confirmation is here
called

called, one of the principles of the
doctrine of Chrift, and a foundation
of repentance, how then not neceffarie nor to be vfed?

See Fathers that affirme the fame.
Tertul. lib. de refurrec. carnis. S. Pa-
cianus lib. de baptifmo. S. Amb. lib.
3. de Sacram. S. Hierom cont. Luci-
fer. Laftly, S. Cyprian lib. 2. epift.
1. fpeakinge both of Baptifme and
Confirmation, faith. Then they may
be fanctified, and be the fonnes of
God, if they be borne in both Sacraments.

XXXIX.

That the bread of the fupper, is but a fi-
gure or remembrance of the body of
Chrift receiued by faith, and
not his true and
very body.

Ontrary both to the expreffe
wordes and truth of their owne
Bible, Luc. 22. 15. *With defire I haue*
defired, to eate this paffeouer with you
before I fuffer. Now to refer thefe
wordes, to a figuratiue eating only
by

by faith, were moſt abſurd, for we
cannot ſay, that Ieſus Chriſt could
receiue or eate him ſelfe in this ſence,
ſith all diuinitie forbids vs, to admit
faith in the Sonne of God; Therfore
that paſche, which he ſo greatly deſired to eate with his Diſciples before he ſuffered, was the paſche of
his owne body.

Luc. 22. 16. *For I ſay vnto you, I will
not any more drinke of the fruite of the
vine, vntill it be fulfilled in the kingdome
of God.* Wordes of wonderfull force,
and which cannot be vnderſtood fi-
guratiuely, no more then the former;
it being a thinge as cleare as the Sunne, that of material bread and drinke,
there is no vſe at all aboue in heauen. Therfore &c.

Iohn. 6. 51. *I am the liuing bread,
which came downe from heauen, if any
man eate of this bread, he shall liue foreuer. And the bread that I wil giue is my
flesh, which I will giue for the life of the
world.* Beza is very angrie, when we
ask him, if the bread that came down
                                    from

from heauen, be liuing, or life giuing?
He willingly gráteth vs the later, but
cannot endure to heare tel of the former, and therfore tranſlateth life-giuing, inſteed of liuing. But this is abſurd, for the Sunne is life-giuing, but
is not liuing: and being granted to be
liuing, what elſe is it then his body?

And note withall, that thus our
Lord ſpake of this bleſſed bread, before he gaue it.

Mat. 26. 26. *Take eate this is my bo-*
die. And Luc. 22. 19. *This is my body,*
which is giuen for you. What I pray
can be ſpoke more plaine? Notwithſtanding, they wil needes ſinge theire
old ſong, that what he gaue, and they
receiued, was nothing elſe but his
bare body. Well, this alſo being granted to them, let vs ſee what they get
therby. That which Chriſt gaue to
eate, was nothing elſe but bare bread:
but that which he gaue to eate, was
that which he would giue for the life
of the world: therfore that which he
gaue for the life of the world, was nothing elſe but bare bread.   Note

Note next , that thus our Lord spake, at the very giuing of it.

1. Cor. 10. 16. *The cup of blessing which we blesse, is it not the communion of the blood of Christ? The bread which we breake , is it not the communion of the body of Christ?* And 1. 11. he addeth. *He that eateth and drinketh vnworthely, eateth and drinketh damnation to him selfe, not discerninge the Lords bodie.* Loe both *before* our Lord gaue it: *at* the very giuing of it: and his owne Disciples *after* he him selfe had giuen it them, and they to others, all of them, call it our Lords body. Poore reformer, whither now is thy figure fled?

Finally, against their true and reall receiuing of Christ by faith ; Ether the soule ascendeth to heauen, there to feede on Christ by faith (which Caluin confesseth:) or Christ descendeth in to earth to feede the same. Not the first , for so the vnglorified soule, should be in two places at once, which they deny to the glorified

rified body of Iesus Chrift. Not the
fecond, for fo Chrift fhould be in
two places at once : whom yet they
fay, that the heauens muft contayne
till the day of iudgment. Acts 3. Therfore &c.

See Fathers that affirme the fame.
S. Ignat. in ep. ad Smyr. S. Iuftin
Apol. 2. ad Antoninum. S. Cyprian
ferm. 4. de lapfis. S. Amb. lib. 4. de
Sacram, faith. It is bread before the
words of the Sacrament , but after
&c. of bread it is made the flefh of
Chrift. S. Remigius faith. The flefh
which the word of God tooke in the
virgins wombe , and the bread confecrated in the Church, are one body.

XL.

That we ought to receiue vnder both
kindes: and that one alone
fufficeth not.

Ontrary to the expreffe wordes
of their owne Bible , Iohn 6.
51. *If any man eate of this bread , he*
shall liue for euer, and the bread which

I

I *will giue, is my flesh*. Loe, euerlasting
life, attributed by our Lord him selfe,
to eating only vnder one kinde.
Therfore one alone doth suffice.

Luc. 24. 30. 8. 35. Christ at Emaus,
communicated his two Disciples vnder one kinde. Both S. Aug. and
Theophilact expound this place of
the B. Sacrament. lib. de consens.
euang. cap. 35. S. Chrysost. hom. 17.
operis imperfecti. S. Thomas of
Aquin cited in the Sauegard, and
many others.

Against that of S. Iohn, *vnles you*
eate the flesh of the Sonne of man, and
drinke his blood, you shall not haue life
in you. The answere hereto, is very
easie, which is, that the coniunction
and, is there taken disiunctiuely insteed of *or*, as is learnedly obserued
by Doctor Kellison, in his Reply to
Sutcliffe pag. 189. Againe, Christ in
those wordes, teacheth vs the precept, and not the maner of the precept; that is to say, he commandeth
vs to receiue his body and his blood,
with-

without determining whither vnder one kinde or vnder both , as the Councell of Trent declareth. For he that said ; *vnles you eate the flesh of the Sonne of man, and drinke his blood, you shall not haue life in you*; hath also said . *If any one eate of this bread , he shall liue foreuer.* He that said; He that eateth my flesh, and drinketh my blood, hath life euerlasting:hath also said; The bread which I will giue, is my flesh for the life of the world. He that said;Who so eateth my flesh, and drinketh my blood, dwelleth in me, and I in him: hath likewise said; He that eateth this bread , shall liue foreuer. Therfore &c.

See more Acts 2. 42. And as for Fathers , they haue before bene al-leadged.

XLI.

That there is not in the Church , a true and proper Sacrifice: and that the Masse is not this Sacrifice.

C Ontrary to the expresse wordes of their owne Bible. Malachie

1. 11.

1. 11. From the rising of the sunne, euen to the going downe of the same, my name shall be great among the Gentils, and in euery place incense shall be offered to my name, and a pure offering. But this sacrifice or pure offering, cannot be vnderstood of Christ vpō the Crosse, which was offered only once, and in one place, and then also not among the Gentils, nor yet can be euer iterated: therfore nether is, nor can be other, then the daylie sacrifice of the Masse.

Psal. 110. (we 109.) 4. *The Lord hath sworne, and will not repent, thou art a priest foreuer, after the order of Melchisedech.* But Melchisedechs sacrifice was made in bread and wine: therfore it must ether be granted, that our Sauiour doth now sacrifice (yea and euer shall) in bread and wine aboue in heauen (which were absurd to say:) or that this is ment of the sacrifice of the Masse, wheron the eternitie of his priesthood doth depend in earth. Nor can this be in a

spi-

spirituall fort only, for that would not make him a prieft of any certaine order. Therfore &c.

Luc. 22. 19. *This is my body, which is giuen for you.* Which wordes doe plainly proue, not only that Chrifts body is truly prefent, but withall fo prefent, as that it is giuen, offered, or facrificed for vs. For Chrift faith not, *which is giuen to you, broken to you, or shed to you,* but, *for you;* Which clearly sheweth it to be a facrifice, it being e-uidét, that on would neuer fay of the Sacrament (in the qualitie of a Sacra-ment) that it is giuen for man, but to man: that is to fay, that a man re-ceiueth it: and contrary wife of a Sa-crifice, that it is offered, not to man, but for man. Therfore &c.

See more Heb. 7. 15. 16. 17. Heb. 8. 1. 3. Heb. 9. 11.

See Fathers that affirme the fame. S. Clement Apoft. conft. lib. 6. cap. 23. calleth it, a reafonable, vnbloody, and myfticall facrifice. S. Aug. a fin-gular, or moft excellent facrifice. lib. 1. cont.

1. cont. aduerſ. leg. & prophet. cap.
18. 19. S. Chryſoſt. hom. in pſal. 95.
The myſticall table, a pure and vnbloody hoſt, a heauenly and moſt re-
uereed ſacrifice. Iſichius in Leuit. cap.
4. ſaith, that Chriſt preuenting his
enimies, firſt ſacrificed him ſelfe in
his myſticall ſupper, and afterwards
on the Croſſe. S. Greg. Niſſen orat.
4. de Reſurrectione, prouing that
our Sauiour gaue his body and blood
in ſacrifice for vs in his laſt ſupper,
ſayeth excellently, that a man cannot eate the ſheepe, vnles the ſlaugh-
ter goe before, and yet auerreth this
to haue bene done by Chriſt in his
laſt ſupper.

XLII.

That ſacramentall vnction, is not to
be vſed to the ſick.

COntrary to the expreſſe wordes
of their owne Bible. Iames 5. 14.
Is any ſick among you? Let him call for
the elders of the Church, and let them
pray ouer him, anointing him with oyle
in the name of the Lord: and the prayer
                                      of

*of faith shall saue the sick, and the Lord
shall raise him vp, and if he haue committed sinnes, they shall be forgiuen him.*
Hardlye is there any Sacrament,
wherof the matter, the minister, and
the effect, are more exprefly speci-
fied in all the scripture, then of this.
The forme is the praier, *Let them pray
ouer him.* The matter, the oyle, *Anointing him with oyle.* The minister, a
Priest or Elder of the Church, *Let him
cal for the Elders of the church.* The pri-
marie effect is, the forgiuenes of sinnes, & the secodary, the easing of the
sick in body, saying. *And the Lord shall
raise him vp, & if he haue comitted sinnes,
they shalbe forgiue him.* Therfore sacra-
métal vnctió, is to be vsed to the sick.

Marc. 6. 13. *And they anointed with
oyle, many that were sick, & healed them.*
Where it is cleare, that the Apostles
them selues, put in practise this holy
vnction; Which Beza cófesseth in his
Annotatiós, saying that it was a Sim-
bole of admirable & supernatural vir-
tu. And had he not reasó so to say? for

F   oyle of

of it felfe, could not be naturally the
Antidote of all difeafes: and albeit it
were, yet the Apoftles were not fent
to practife phifick, but to preache the
gofpell; Yea it were a thinge too ridiculous, to make them Triaclers,
carriars of Drogues, or Paracelfians.
Therfore &c.

Marc. 16. 18. *They shall lay handes
on the fick, and they shall recouer.* But
firft, the Reformers are no Priefts. Se-
condly, they lay not their handes
vpon the fick. Thirdly, they anoint
them not with oyle in the name of
the Lord, as S. Iames willeth : fay
the truth then, and fhame the diuell,
are not they fick in their witts, which
will oppofe fo plaine fcriptures?

See Fathers that affirme the fame
Origen. hom. 2. in Leuit. S. Chrifoft.
lib. 3. de facerd. S. Aug. in Speculo.
& ferm. 215. de temp. Venerable
Bede in 6. Marci. & 5. Iacobi: with
many others.

XLIII.

XLIII.

That no interior grace is giuen by the im-
position of handes, in holy Orders; And
that ordinarie Vocation and Mission
of pastors , is not necessarie in the
Church?

Ontrary to the expresse wordes of their owne Bible, 1. Tim.
4. 14. *Neglect not the gift* (we reade
grace) *that is in thee,* which was giuen
thee by prophecie, with the laying on the
handes of the presbitery. Loe how plaine it is , that holy orders doe giue
grace. Doctor Kellison handling this
question touching the mission of the
Reformers, proueth most learnedly,
as his maner is, that this foundation
being disproued, the whole frame of
their Church and Religion falleth:
yea that they haue nether true faith,
nor worship of God, & his reason is
this. If faith depend of hearing, hearing of preaching, preaching & admi-
nistration of Sacraments, of ministers
and preachers, and preachers & ministers of their mission, where there

is no miſſion (as they haue none)
there can be no true faith, nor lawfull adminiſtration of Sacraments,
and conſequently no religion. Reply
pag. 7. & 44. Therfore vocation is
neceſſarie in the Church.

1. Tim. 1. 6. *Wherfore I put thee in*
remembrance , that thou ſtir vp the gift
of God which is in thee, by the putting on
of my handes. Loe how plaine the holie ſcripture is againſt them; But they
reply, that laying on of handes is not
needfull to them, who haue already
in them the ſpirit of God, and inward anointing of the holy Ghoſt.
To which very queſtion Theodoret
makes anſwer, that God commanded Moyſes (Numb. 27.) to lay his
handes vpon Ioſue, wheras by the
teſtimony of God him ſelfe , Ioſue
had already in him the ſpirit of God.
S. Paul, although he were called immediatly from heauen, yet was after
ſent with laying on of handes. Acts.
13. 3. Therfore &c.

Heb. 5. 4. *And no mã taketh this honor*
ynto

*vnto himselfe, but he that is called of God
as* was *Aarō.* But here our aduersaries
reply againe, that Aarō had no exter-
nal vocatiō. But this is very easily sol-
ued, for Aaron was the first of his order, and therfore could not haue his
calling by successiō. Whose case therfore is far vnlike to our Reformers,
vnles they wil also cōfes that they are
the first of their order : wherin they
shal be easily beleeued. Therfore &c.

See more Acts 13. 2. Tim. 1. 6. 1.
Tim. 5. 22. 2. Tim. 1. 8. Numb. 27. 23.

See Fathers that affirme the same.
S. Aug. lib. 4. quest super Num. S.
Cyprian epist. ad Magnum. Optatus
Meleuir, the place beginneth. *Nequis
miretur.* Tertulian in prescript. The
place beginneth, *Æant origines.*

XLIIII.

*That Priests and other Religious persons
who haue vowed their chastitie vnto
God, may freelie marrie, notwithstanding their vowes.*

C Ontrary to the expresse words of
their own Bible, Deut. 23. 22. Whē

F 3 *thou*

thou shalt vow a vow vnto the Lord thy God, thou shalt not slack to pay it, for the Lord thy God, will surely require it of thee, and it would be sinne in thee: but if thou shalt forbeare to vow, it shall be no sinne in thee. Out of which wordes, two thinges are clearly proued. The one, that it is both lawfull, and laudable to make vowes. The other, that vowes being once made, they doe binde, where otherwise there was no obligation. Therfore such as haue vowed the vow of chastitie, may not, nor ought not afterwards, attempt to marrie; which if they doe, they breake their vow.

1. Tim. 5. 11. 12. *But the younger widdowes refuse, for when they haue begun to wax wanton against Christ, they will marry, hauing damnation, because they haue cast off their first faith.* All the auncient fathers that euer wrote vpon this place, expound the Apostles wordes of the vow of chastitie, or the faith and promise made to Christ, to liue continently; as is

abun-

abundantly proued in the Rhemes
Teftament vpon this place . Therfore &c.

1. Tim. 5. 15. *For fome are already
turned afide after Sathan.* Loe, to
marrie after the vow of chaftitie
once made, is here termed by the
Apoftle him felfe; *turning afide after
Sathan*; And herupon it is, that we
call the Religious, that after marry,
(as Luther, Bucer, Peter Martyr and
the reft of that lafciuious rable) Apo-
ftataes, Gods adulterers, inceftuous,
facrilegious, and like.

See more pfal. 66. 16. Numb. 6. 2.
18. Iofue 2:.26. Ieremie 35, 18. Ecclef.
5. 3. Actes 21. 23.

See Fathers that affirme the fame.
S. Aug. lib. de bono viduit. cap. 9.
S. Athanafius lib. de virginitat. S.
Epiphanius heref. 48. S. Hier. cont.
Iouin. lib. 1. cap. 7. *What is to breake
their firft faith* (faith S. Aug?)*they vowed and performed not.* In pfal 75. I he
place beginneth. *Quid eft, primam fi-
dem &c.*

F 4   XLV.

XLV.

That fasting and abstinence from certaine meates, is not grounded on holy scripture, nor causeth any spirituall good.

Contrary to the expresse wordes of their owne Bible, Ieremy 35. 5. *And I set before the sonnes of the house of the* Rechabits, *pots full of wine, and wine cups, and I said vnto them, drinke yee wine. But they said, we will drink no wine , for* Ionadab *the sunne of* Rechab *our father, commāded vs saying; Yee shall drink no wine, nether yee, nor your sonnes foreuer. Thus haue we obeyed* Ionadab *our father, in al that he hath charged vs.* Therfore fasting is grounded in holie scripture.

Luc. 1. 15. *For he shall be great in the sight of the Lord, and shall drinke nether wine nor strenge drinke.* Loe abstinéce not only foretould, but also prescrided by the Angel; which plainly proueth that it is both a worthie thinge, and also an act of religion in S. Iohn, as it was in the Nazarits, and Rechabits afore-mentioned.

Actes 13. 3. *And when they had fas-*
ted and prayed, and laid their handes on
them, they sent them away. Hence the
Church of God, hath sufficient
ground and warrant, for the vsing
and prescribing of publique fastes.
Which was not fasting from sinne,
as our Reformers pretend (for such
fasting they were bound euer to
keepe:)& that at such time or seafon
as the church pleafed to determine
(as in Lent, or the like)& not when
euery man lift, or the toye takes him,
as Ærius and the like hereticks did
teache, teftified by S. Aug. heref. 53.
Therfore &c.

Mat. 17. 21. *Howbeit, this kind of*
deuill, goeth not out, but by prayer and
fasting. Loe the great force of prayer
and fafting, able to expell the very
deuil. Therfore it caufeth great fpirituall good.

See more. Ioel 2. 12. Mat. 6. 16.
Mat. 9. 15. 29. Toby 12. 8. Luc. 2.
37. Acts 14. 22. 2. Cor. 11. 27. 2. Cor.
6. 5. Numb. 30. 14. 1. Tim. 4. 3.

See

See Fathers that affirme the same,
S. Ignat. ad Phillip. S. Basil orat. de
Ieiunio. S. Chrysost. orat. in sanct.
Lauacrum . & hom. 1. in Gen. S.
Amb. ser. 4. S. Hierom in cap. 18.
Isaij, and many others.

XLVI.

*That Iesus Christ descended not into
hell, nor deliuered thence the soules
of the Fathers.*

COntrary to the expresse wordes of their owne Bible . 1. E-
phes.4.8. *When he ascended vp on high,
he led captiuitie captiue* (margent, *or
a multitude of captiues*) *and gaue gifts
vnto men. Now that he ascended, what
is it, but that he also descended first, into
the lower parts of the earth* . These
freed captiues, cannot be the soules
of the glorified, which no man in his
right witts can call captiues; Nor of
the damned, for so the deuills should
be brought againe into heauen; therfore they were the soules of the Fathers, which Christ deliuered forth
of Limbo.

Actes

Actes 2. 27. *Becauſe thou wilt not
leaue my ſoule in hell, nether wilt thou
ſuffer thine holy one, to ſee corruption.*
Theſe very wordes S. Aug. applieth
to the proofe of a third place , and
addeth. W*ho but an Infidelle, wil deny
Chriſt to haue deſcended into hel.*Epiſt.
99. ad Euodium.

1. Pet. 3. 18. 19. *Being put to death
in the fleſh, but quickned by the ſpirit,
by which alſo he went and preached
vnto the ſpirits in priſon .* To interpret by the word *priſon* , heauen,
there is no ſence, ſith it is called the
ſeate of God, and not the priſon of
God. To vnderſtand it of the wicked, Caluin him ſelfe oppoſeth this
opinion , and maintayneth, that S.
Peter ſpeaketh of the good , which
were knowen from the dayes of
Noe . Add, that this doctrine deſ-
troyeth an article of our Creed, and
maketh the twelue , to be but ele-
uen. Therfore &c.

Heb. 11. 38. 39. 40. *And theſe all
hauing obtained a good teſtimonie, tho-*

rough faith,receiued not the promise (to wit, of heauen) *God hauing prouided some better thinge for vs,that they without vs, should not be made perfect* : to wit, in their perfect and complete glory. Whence it followeth necessarily, that they must needes grant another place, distinct as well frō the heauen of the saued, as from the hell of the damned , wherin these holy soules were cōserued. Therfore &c.

Mat. 12. 40. *For as Ionas was three dayes and three nights in the* Whales *belly, so shall the Sonne of man be three dayes and three nightes , in the hart of the earth.* But how I pray, is this figure fulfilled , if Christ were not as many dayes and nightes in the heart of the earth,as Ionas was, who was not in the whales belly in body only, but also in soule ? Whence it followeth , that ether Christs holye soule,was three dayes, and three nights in the hart of the earth,as wel as his body , or that this place of scripture, is ether false , or vnfulfil-
led.

led. But this were moſt abſurd to
ſay. Therfore &c.

Mat. 27. 52. 53. *And the graues were
opened , and many bodies of Saints
which ſlept, aroſe , and came out of the
graues after his reſurrection , and
went into the holy cittie , and appeared
vnto many.* Vnderſtood by S. Ignatius
biſhop of Antioch , of Limbus Pa-
trum , writing theſe wordes to the
cittizens of Trallis . *Manie aroſe
with our Lord , for the ſcripture ſaith,
that many of the bodies that ſlept , a-
roſe with our Lord . He deſcended a-
lone , but returned with a multitude.*
Therfore &c.

Zacharie 9. 11. *As for thee alſo, by
the blood of thy couenant , I haue ſent*
(we reade, *let*) *forth thy priſoners, out
of the pit, wherin is no water.* Both S.
Hierom and S. Cyril, vnderſtand
this pit, to be ment of Limbus Pa-
trum. And with very great reaſon, for
how abſurd were it to ſay , that the
damned haue their ſhare *in the blood
of the couenant?* Or that they are *let
forth,*

forth, of their infernall pit ? Or that
they may be said to be, *thy prisoners,*
(that is Chrifts) but rather the prifoners of the diuell? Yea, where I
pray (to fpeake properly) hath
Chrift had any prifoners at al(which
he hath let forth) if not out of this
place ? Therfore , ether Chrift let
forth prisoners out of Limbo Pa-
trum, or this place likewife as the
former, is ether falfe, or yet vn-
fulfilled.

r. Samuel 2. 6. Like vnto this place, is that of the Kinges , *The Lord*
killeth, and maketh a liue, he bringeth
downe to the graue (we read, *hell*) *and*
bringeth vp, we reade, *back againe.*
Loe, how plaine and conforme, the
faith of that old church, was and is to
this of ours , *bringeth downe to hell,*
and bringeth backe againe , which
hardly in any cleare fenfe can be a-
uerred, if Limbus Patrū be denyed.
As for the word *graue*, which they
erronioufly haue added, inftead of
hell, to diminifh the force of fo plaine
a place,

a place , bid them but to repeate their Creede, and there to foift in &c ingraft the word *graue* , infteed of *hell,* as here they haue done , and then muft they fay . W*as crucified dead and buried , he defcended into the graue.* And who for Gods fake fees not the groffe abfurditie of this in-grafting ?

See more. Ofee 6.3. Pfal, 16. 10. 2. Pet.3. 19. Zach 9.11. Rom. 10.6. Ecclef. 24. 45. Pfal. 23. 7. Genef. 37. 35.

See Fathers that affirme the fame. S. Hier. in 4. ad Ephef. S. Greg. lib. 13. Moral. cap. 26. S. Aug. in Pfal. 37. v. 1. The place beginneth. *Futu-rum eft enim.*

XLVII.

That there is no purgatorie fire, or other prifon, wherin finnes may be fa-tisfied: for after this life.

COntrary to the expreffe wordes of their owne Bible , 1. Cor. 3: 12. 15. *The fire shall try euery mans worke, of what fort it is. If any mans worke*

worke shal be burnt, he shall suffer losse, but he himselfe shall be saued, yet so as by fire. S. Aug. writing vpon the 37. pfalme, and drawing these very wordes of the Apostle into his discourse, saith. Because it is said, *He him selfe shall be safe,* that fire is contemned. Yea verely, though safe by fire, yet that fire shal be more greuous, then whatsoeuer a man can suffer in this life. Thus he; Therfore there is a purgatorie fire, wherein sinnes may be satisfied for after this life.

Iohn. 11. 22. *But I know, that euen now, whatsoeuer thou wilt aske of God, God will giue it thee.* S. Martha, sister to Marie Magdalen beleeued, that our Lord (whom then she only held for a holie man, but not for the Sonne of God) could obtaine of God, somthinge profitable to her brother Lazarus, who was deceased: For hauing said. *Lord if thou hadst bene here, my brother had not bene dead.* She presently added. *But I knowe, that euen now what-*
soeuer

*soeuer thou wilt aske of God , God
will giue it thee .* Which speeches
she could neuer haue vsed in anie
good sence, if she had not learned
this doctrine of the Sinagogue, who
offered sacrifices, almes and prayers
for the departed : and vnles she had
knowen and beleeued, that the dead
might be holpen by the pietie of the
liuing ; as Cardinall Allen learned
concludeth. Therfore &c.

Actes 2. 14. *Whom God hath raised vp, loosing the sorrowes of hell .* In
which wordes two thinges are to
be noted, which clearly make for the
proofe of Purgatorie. The one, that
in this place , there were certaine
sorrowes and paines , where Christ
was. The other, that some there were
inflicted for sinne , vpon whom he
bestowed that gratious benefit, as to
discharge and loose them of those
paines. For as the Rhemes Testamēt
very well noteth, Christ was not in
paines him selfe , but loosed other
men of their paines.

1. Cor.

1. Cor. 15.29. *Otherwise what shall they doe , that are baptised for the dead?* From this place an euident proofe is drawen, touching the helpe which the soules departed out of this world, may receiue by the Church in earth, and consequently proueth purgatorie: vnderstanding the paines and afflictions which voluntarily we doe inflict vpon our selues , to exempt those that are therein: for to baptise, signifieth to afflict ones selfe, to doe penance, to suffer death &c. as Luc. 12.30. *But I haue a baptisme to be baptised with.* And Marc. 10.38.

Luc. 16. 9. *And I say vnto you, make to your selues friendes of the mamon of vnrighteousnes, that when yee faile, they may receiue you into euerlasting habitations .* S. Ambrose vpon this place, and S. Aug. lib. 21. de Ciuit. cap. 27. say, that it is to receiue succour after death, according as the word *faile,* enforceth. Therfore &c.

Luc. 23. 42. *Lord remember me, when thou comest into thy kingdome.* S. Aug.

Aug. faith in his fift booke againſt
Iulian (about the middeſt) that the
good thiefe in this prayer, preſuppo-
ſed, that (according to the common
opinion) ſoules might be holpen after death. Therfore &c.

2. Mac. 12. 44. 45. *For if he had*
not hoped, that they that were ſlaine,
ſhould haue riſen againe, it had bene ſu-
perfluous and vaine, to pray for the dead.
And a litle after, concludeth ſaying.
It was an holy and good thought. This
place of holy ſcripture, is moſt cleare
for praying for the dead, for had it
not bene, the continuall doctrine
and practiſe of the Church to pray
for the dead, nether could Iudas Machabeus (who was himſelfe a prieſt)
haue euer thought of any ſuch re-
medie, as to gather twelue thouſand
drachmes of ſiluer to ſend to Hieruſalem, to haue prayers made for the
reliefe of the ſoules ſlaine in that
battaile: nether would the multitude
of people haue ether contributed, or
the prieſts of the Temple, receiued
the

the prefent, had they thought (as
thefe men doe) that it had bene fu-
perftition, to pray for the departed,
or no other place had bene, then the
hell of the damned, or the heauen of
the faued. Therfore &c.

See more 2. Tim. 1. 18. 1. Iohn 5. 16.
Ifay. 4. 4. Ifay 9. 18. Acts 2. 24. Mat.
3. 11. Mat. 12. 32. Mat. 5. 2 6. Micheas
7. 8. pfal. 66. 12. Tobie 4. 18. Phil.
2. 10. Zacharie 9. 11.

See Fathers that affirme the fame.
S. Amb. vpon the 1. Cor. 3. & ferm.
20. in pfal. 118. S. Hier. lib. 2. cap.
13. aduerf. Iouin. S. Greg. lib. 4. Dia-
log. cap. 39. Origen hom. 6. in cap.
15. Exod: with many others.

XLVIII.

*That it is not lawfull to make, or
to haue Images.*

Ontrary to the expreffe wor-
C des, of their owne Bible, Exod.
25. 18. *And thou shalt make two Cherubins of gold, of beaten worke shalt thou
make them, in the two endes of the mercie seate.* Thefe grauen Angells, were
Ima-

Images, of the highest order of Angells (one excepted) which is in heauen, and were made with faces of beautifull young men, and commanded to be set vp by God himselfe in the holie of holies: which S. Hierom witnesseth the Iewes to haue worshiped, epist. ad Marcellam: Therfore it is lawfull to make Images.

1. Kinges 6. 35. *And he carued theron, Cherubins, and Palme trees, and open Flowers, and couered them with gold, fitted vpon the carued worke.* Hence is to be gathered, that the precept of not making a grauen Idoll, doth nothing at all concerne Images, that is to say, the true representation of thinges subsisting, but of thinges meerely imaginarie and not subsisting: for as S. Paul saith. 1. Cor. 8. *An Idoll is nothinge*; So that the Idoll, representeth that which is not; the Image, that which is (a remarkable difference.) Therfore &c.

Againe,

Againe, seeing an Idol is that properly, which being nothing (as S. Paul saith) is represented to be somthinge, or that which represents the thinge that is not, if the Reformers beleue the Image of Christ crucified to be an Idoll, they then beleeue, that Christ was neuer crucified : for it followeth necessarily, as thus. The Image of Christ crucified, is an Idoll: therfore Christ was neuer crucified.

Heb. 9. 1. 5. *Then verely the first couenant, had also ordonances of diuine seruice, and a worldly sanctuarye &c. and ouer it, the Cherubins of glorie shadowing the mercie seate.* Loe S. Paul calleth the pictures of the Cherubins which Salomon made, *an ordonance of diuine seruice,* which Reformers call , the making of Idolls : whom shall we now beleeue, whither blessed S. Paul, or a Reformed brother before him? Therfore &c.

To conclude, an Image, is so both of diuine and naturall right, that all vnderstanding, imagination, and sensation,

fation, as well interior, as exterior,
is made by way of Images , called
fpecies fenfibiles & infenfibiles : the
body cannot be in light, without its
fhadow: the Moone and the Starres,
imprint their pictures in the water:
a man cannot looke in a glaffe, without making his picture ; Therefore,
ether God and nature it felfe, doth
breake this commandement, as wel
as wee, or elfe it is abfurd to fay, that
we doe breake it in making of Images. Therfore &c.

See more. 1. Kinges 7. 36. 42. 44.
Num. 21. 8. Mat. 22. 20. Exod. 31. 2.
Exod. 35. 30. where painting and
grauing of pictures , is fo far from
being Idolatrie, that it is proued to
be a fcience diuinely infufed into Be-
feleel by God himfelfe : and fo the
inuention of good Images, came firft
from God.

See Fathers that affirme the fame.
Tert. lib. 2. de Pudicitia. S. Greg.
Naz. ep. 49. ad Olymp. S. Bafil orat
in S. Barlaam. S. Aug. lib. 1. de con-
fenf.

ſenſ. euang. cap. 10. witneſſeth, that in his time, Chriſt was to be ſeene painted in many places, betweene S. Peter and S. Paul.

XLIX.

That it is not lawfull to worship Images, nor to giue any honor, to any dead or inſenſible thinge.

COntrary to the expreſſe wordes of their owne Bible. Exod. 3. 5. *And he ſaid . Draw not nigh hither, put off thy shoes from off thy feete, for the place wheron thou standest, is holie ground.* Loe how cleare a place is here produced againſt Reformers, wherin an inſenſible creature without reaſon, was commanded by God him ſelfe to be honored: for the refrayning to tread vpon it, was the doing of honor to it . Therfore all dead images, repreſenting vnto vs a holy thinge, may be honored.

Pſal. 99. 5. *Adore yee the foote-ſtoole of his feete.* Which place is ſpoken litterally of the Arke of the Teſtamét, according to that 1. Chronicles 28.2.

I had

I had in my hart to build a house of rest, for the Arke of the couenant of the Lord, and for the footstoole of our God. Now the principall reason, why the Arke was worshipped, was in regard of the Images that were set vpon it, which the Iewes did worship, as S. Hierom witnesseth, in his epistle ad Marcellam. Therfore &c.

Philipians 2. 10. *That at the name of Iesus, euery knee should bow, of thinges in heauen, and thinges in earth, and thinges vnder the earth.* Now that is the name of Iesus, which ether is pronounced by anothers mouth, printed in a booke, or painted and grauen in a picture: but at any of these we are commanded to bow the knee: Therfore &c.

Againe, if Images ought not to be worshipped, we may not (whatsoeuer the Apostle saith) bowe our knee at the name of Iesus: seeing wordes (as Aristole saith, and as the truth is) are signes representatiue of the thinges they signifie, & are as the

G pictu-

pictures of the eare, as the others are of the eyes. Therfore &c.

Numb. 21. 8. *And the Lord said vnto Moyses. Make thee a fierie serpent, and set it vp vpon a pole : and it shall come to passe, that euery one that is bit, when he looketh vpon it, shall liue.* Hence are euidently proued diuers thinges , against Reformers. 1. That God commanded the making of this Image. 2. The setting of it vp for a signe. 3. He promised that the lookers theron, should assuredly receiue succour. 4. He warranted the making , the setting vp, the behoulding, and the reuerencing therof, to be exempted from the breach of the first commandement, by working so many, and so manifest miracles, at, and before the presence thereof. Therfore an Image may be made, may be set vp, may be looked on, and be reuerenced, as Doctor Sanders most learnedly concludeth , in his Treatise of Images.

See

See Fathers that affirme the
same. S. Amb. serm. 1. in psal. 118.
S. Aug. lib. 3. de Trinit. S. Greg.
lib. 7. epist. 5. ad Ian. Finally, S.
Basill saith (in Iulian citatus in 7.
sinod.) *I honor the histories of Images,
and doe openly worship them, for this
being deliuered vs from the holy Apostles, is not to be forbidden* . S. Chrisostom in his Masse , turned into
Latin by Erasmus, saith . *The priest
boweth his head, to the Image of Christ.*
S. Damascen lib. 4. cap. 17. saith.
*The worshipping of the Crosse, and of
Images, is a Tradition of the Apostles.*

An obiection.

But before I conclude this present controuersie , I desire to solue
a few obiections , which vsuallie
are brought against the honor of
Images . And first, that of the 2. of
Kinges. (we 4.) 18. where Kinge
Ezechias, broke downe the brasen
Serpent (wherof we last of all made
mention) when it was the cause of
idolatrie.

The

The answer.

This indeed is a common place, from whence our aduersaries collect sundrie false and sophisticall arguments: to wit, from the abuse of any good thinge, to destroy it vtterly; together with the right vse thereof. But by the same argument, they may as well collect, that the Sunne and the Moone should be taken out of the firmament, because they were worshipped by the Gentils as Gods. Likewise that the holie Bible should be burnt, because many an one draweth damnable heresies forth of the same, to his owne perdition. Yea, this sillie argument borrowed from the abuse of thinges, serues passing well more to proue the quite contrarie, for it followes well. Images were sometimes abused, therfore they were good in them selues: for that thinge which is euill by abuse only, must needes be good being vsed well.

The

The 2. Obiection.

You giue that honor to Images,
which is due to God alone, worſhip-
ping, adoring, and creeping to them,
as to God.

The anſwere.

We ſay the contrarie, which thus
we proue. The difference of honor, proceedeth principally from
the minde, and not from the exterior bowing or demeanor of the bodie. For if I fall downe before an I-
mage and kiſſe the ſame, being all
the while of the minde it is no God,
nor reaſonable creature, but only
a remembrance of God, towards
whom I deſire to ſhew myne affection, God knoweth how far off
myne honor is, from that honor
which is due to him alone. As
contrariwiſe, if I lay proſtrat at Chri-
ſtes feete, kiſſed them, knocked my
breaſt, held vp my handes vnto him,
yea calling him the Sonne of God,
yet all this while, thinke him not

to be so in my hart, myne honor tru-
lie should be no honor at all, but a
very contumelie vnto Christ. Adde,
that the wordes which betoken
honor, adoration, worship and the
like, are in a maner confounded in
all languages : but the hart from
whence the honor floweth, knoweth the difference of euery thing. Ex
D. Sanders de imag. pag. 10.

The 3. Obiection.

It is expresly forbidden by God
him selfe, to fall downe before any
Image, or to worship it.

The answere.

Reformers themselues confes to
honor the Sacrament of Christs
supper, which they teache to be, an
Image or representation, of Christs
body and blood. And seeing they
beleeue, no other substance to be
in the Sacrament, besides bread and
wine, nor will not giue the honor of *latria* therunto , hence it
doth follow inuincibly, that they
doe serue or honor some Image:
Now,

Now, as they would not for all this, haue vs to iudge, or call them Idolaters : euen so let it please them (for their owne sakes) to spare vs. For as they doe not stay this honor in the bread and wine, but from thence refer it to Christ him selfe : euen so doe we transfer all our honor from all Images, vnto the first forme or patterne, not suffering our honor to rest or to end, in the Image we honor. Ex eodem pag. 52.

The 4. Obiection.

An Image is a creature, and no God, and to sett vpp a creature to be worshipped, is Idolatrie.

The Answere.

Images are set vp in Churches, not specially to the intent that the people should worship them, but partly to instruct the simple, and partly to stir vp our mindes, to follow the example of those holy men, whose Images we doe behould. So

G 4 that

that the worſhip waich is giuen to
Images, is giuen as it were by a con-
ſequent, and rather becauſe it may
be lawfully giuen, then becauſe it is
principally ſought to be giuen. And
touching the Idolatrie which is ob-
iected, you are to vnderſtand, that
the word is compounded of *Latria*,
and *Idolum*, and is as much to ſay, as,
the giuing of Latria, or of Gods honor, vnto an Idol. But our Images,
are no Idols, nor the honor we giue
them, is not Latria; how then can
it be ſaid, that Images are ſet vp to
be vſed to Idolatrie?

Thus much haue I thought good
to adde in this place, the more to
enlarge this preſent controuerſie,
for that there are many weake and
ſimple ſoules, who ſtumble at the
doctrine of the worſhip of Images,
becauſe indeed they vnderſtand it
not. And hauing proued the wor-
ſhippe of them, I ſhall neede to ſay
nothing in proofe of their making,
for the one preſuppoſeth the proofe

of

of the other.

L.

*That no man hath feene God in
any forme , and that therfore his picture or I-
mage, cannot be
made.*

Contrary to the expreffe wordes
of their owne Bible , Gen. 3. 8.
where God appeared vnto Adam
walking in the garden of paradife , in
a corporall forme . And Gen. 28. 12.
13. to Iacob, *ftanding aboue the ladder,*
wheron the Angells afcended, and
defcended. For we muft know, that
it is only the outward fhape and
forme of the thinge, which is expreffed, ether in this or the like Image, &
not the inward fubftance therof,
which is not poffible for any pain-
ter to expreffe ; which though it expreffe not all that is therin , yet that
which it expreffeth is a truth: & thus
may God be expreffed to vs . Yea,
who may hinder to picture or expres
God in the fame maner , wherin he

G 5   him-

him selfe manifested him selfe to
mortall eyes? Therfore his picture
or Image may be made.

Exod. 33. 11. God appeared, and
spake vnto Moyses, *face to face*, as
a man speaketh vnto his friend.
To the prophet Isay 6. 1. 5. *Sitting
vpon a throane*. To Daniel 7. 9. *Sitting*, wearing *garments*, and hauing
haire on his head, like pure wolle. How
then can a wise man dout, but that
thinge may be lawfully set forth, or
expressed vnto vs in an outward
image, which necessarilye must
be conceiued by an inward? Therfore &c.

1. Kinges (we 3.) 22. 19. *I saw
the Lord sitting on his throane, and
all the hoste of heauen, standing by
him, on his right hand, and on his
left*. One would thinke that en-
nough hath now bene said to proue
this point. But if they shall yet
answere, that God commandeth
vs to heare his word, and the histories which speake of his appari-
tions,

tions , but not to paint them . I
anſwere , that ſeeing we learne by
our eies, as well as by our eares,
there is no reaſon, why that may
not be painted before our eyes,
which may be preached to our eares. Againe , ſeeing he that can
reade the holye ſcriptures , muſt
needes finde the aforeſaid viſions
and hiſtories in the Bible, why not
as well ſee them in a picture on the
church wall, as in a booke of white
paper? Therfore &c.

LI.

That bleſſing or ſigning with the ſigne
of the Croſſe , is not founded in
holie ſcripture.

C Ontrary to the expreſſe wordes
of their owne Bible. Reuelations 7.3. Where one Angell, ſaid
to four other Angells . *Hurt not the*
earth , nether the ſea , nor the trees,
till we haue ſealed (we reade , *ſigned*)
the ſeruants of our God in their fore-
heads. Therfore &c.

Marc. 10. 16. *And hee tooke them*
G 6   *vp*

vp in his armes, put his handes vpon them, and blessed them. Therfore blessing is founded in holy scripture.

Luc. 24. 50. *And he led them out as far as to Bethanie, and he lift vp his handes, and blessed them.* Therfore &c.

See Fathers that affirme the same. Dionis. Areopagita cap. 4. 5. 6. eccles. Hier. Tertul. lib.de corona milit. Origen in Exod. cap.5.hom. 6.5. S. Cyrill. Cat.1. S. Basil lib. de spir. sanc. cap. 37. S. Chrysost. hom. 55. in Mat. cap. 16.

LII.

That the publique seruice of the Church, ought not to be said, but so as all the assistants may vnderstand it.

Contrary to the expresse wordes of their owne Bible, Luc. 1. 8. *And it came to passe, that while he executed the priests office before God, in the order of his course, according to the custome of the priests office, his lot was to burne incense in the temple of*
the

the Lord ; *and the whole multitude of
people were praying without, at the time
of incense* . Where note 1. that this
was the common cuſtome. 2. All
the people were without , and the
prieſt within , how then did they
vnderſtand him ? Therfore the pu-
bliq ie ſeruice of the church may be
ſo ſaid , as all the aſſiſtants vnderſtand it not.

Leuiticus 16. 17. *And there ſhal be
no man in the Tabernacle of the congregation, when he goeth in to make an
attonement in the holy place, vntill he
come out, and haue made an attonement
for him ſelfe, and for his houſ-hould,
and for all the congregation of Iſraell.*
Therfore &c.

What ſhall I neede to produce
authorities of Fathers , when the
practiſe of the whole Chriſtian
world, for theſe many hudred yeares
toge her, is directly contrary to Reformers in this point: againſt which
to diſpute (as S. Aug. ſaith) were inſo-
lent madnes. See. Rhe. Teſt. p. 463.

What

But for that much cauilling and wrangling is made by many, againſt the practiſe of the Church herein, I will therfore enlarge my ſelfe a litle theron, and ſolue what the aduerſaries doe ſay againſt it. Out of ſcripture, their probableſt place, is this which followeth. 1. Cor. 14. 16. *When thou ſhalt bleſſe with the ſpirit, how ſhall he that occupieth the roome of the vnlearned, ſay Amen at thy giuing of thankes, ſeeing he vnderſtandeth not what thou ſayeſt? For thou verely giueſt thankes, but the other is not edifyed.*

We anſwere hereto, that there be two kindes of prayers, or giuing of thankes, in the Church. The one *Priuat*, which euery man ſayes by him ſelfe alone. The other *Publique*, which the Prieſte ſayth, in the name & perſon of the whole Church. As cōcerning *Priuat* prayers, no Catholique denies, but it is very expediēt, that euery man pray in his owne tongue, to the end he may vnderſtād
what

what he fayes. But as touching the *Publique* prayers of the Church, it is not necessarie that the cōmon people vnderftand them, becaule it is not they who pray, but the Prielt in the name of the whole Church: For as it was enough for the people of the old law, to vnderftand, that in fuch a facrifice confifted the worfhip of God, although they had not fo cleare an vnderftanding of euery thinge that was done therin (as hath bene faid:) euen fo in the new law, when the people afift at the facrifice of the Maffe, acknowledging therby that God is worfhipped, and that it is inftituted for the remembrance of Chrifts death & paffion, although they vnderftand not the Latin tongue, yet are they not wholie deftitute of the vtilitie and fruict therof: befides the helpe of the godly ceremonies, which doe inftruct them in the whole.

Next, this place alleadgeth ferueth nothing to the purpofe, but is rather

ther repugnant to the same, yea proues, that the common seruice of the Church, was not then in the vulgar language, which euery man vnderstood, but in another láguage, which was not so comon to euery one. For S. Paul saying. *How shall the that occupieth the roome of the vnlearned, say Amē at thy giuing of thāks, seeing he vnderstādeth not what thou sayest?* shewes that such giuing of thankes, was not acustomed to be in the vulgar tógue: and requires, or rather supposes, that in the seruice of the Church, there should be some other to supply the place of the vnlearned, that is, one that should haue further vnderstanding of that tongue, in the which the seruice of the Church is said. But had the seruice bene in the vulgar tongue, there needed no man, to haue supplied, the place of the Idiot that vnderstandeth not. So that S. Paul shewes most clearly, that such seruice was not exercised in a vulgar tógue, but in another which was not common

mon

mon to the whole people (such as the Latin tongue is in England, as alfo thorough the whole East) and yet was not, in the contrary extremitie, that is to say, wholly ftrange, or vtterly barbarous.

And feeing they haue this place continually in their mouthes, and deceiue therby the fimple people, I fhall fhew vnto you, that this faying of S. Paul, is altogether peruerted by the Reformers them felues, becaufe where the Greeke and Latin text hath. *He who fupplies the place of an Idiot, how shall he say Amen?* The Minifters of Geneua, in many of their Bibles, haue turned the fame moft deceitfully and malitioufly, thus. *He that is an idiot, how shall he say Amen?* As if there were no difference betwixt an Idiot, and he who fupplies the place of an Idiot?

Moreouer, the thankfgiuing, to which S. Paul fayeth, Amen fhould be anfwered, is at all not practifed in many of your Reformed Churches,

ches, where nether your Idiots, nor
those who supply the place of your
Idiots, doe answere Amen, as S. Paul
willeth, but haue altered Amen, into
So be it, which is plainly repugnant
to his meaning, as also to the practice
of the whole Church: for they can
not say for their excuse, that S. Paul
wrote to those, who spake the Hebrue tongue (as Amen is Hebrue) for
he wrote to the Corinthiās, who had
their publike seruice in Greeke, and
not in Hebrue: a sufficient argumēt,
that the word Amen, ought to be re-
tayned in all languages, as it hitherto
hath euer bene amōgst all Christians,
before the dayes of our Reformers; in
so much that the most learned S. Au-
gustin writeth, that it is not lawfull
to turne Amen, into any other vulgar language, without the sclander of
the whole whole Church. Aug. epist.
118. & 2. de Doctrina Christ. cap. 20.

To conclude, I cannot but much
muse at the great simplicitie of the
common people, who notwithstanding

ding the great light of their reformed
golpel, lee not the lolenelle and va-
nitie of this their leaders cauill. For,
are ether the masters, or schollers,
so exceeding senfles as to say, that
their owne seruice, cõsisting in part,
of the pralmes of Dauid (the hardest
part of all the Bible) and partly of
lessons extracted out of the ould and
new Testament, that all the assistants
(I say) doe vnderstand them? Sure I
am the greatest deuines that euer
were in all christendome, neuer durst
say so much of them felues: how
wrongfully then, doe they wrangle
with vs about this matter? But perhaps they will say, that though the
simple vnderstand not the hard places, contayned in their psalmes and
seruice, yet that to their confort, they
vnderstand at least some part therof:
euen so say we of the Masse, and of
our simple who asist therat. And so
conclude as I begunne, in the title of
this booke. *By thine owne mouth I
iudge thee, naughtie seruant.*

LIII,

LIII.

That it is both superfluous, and superstitions, to repeate one and the same prayer, sundry times.

COntrary to the expresse wordes of their owne Bible. The Angells in the prophet Isay cap. 6. And the Beastes in the Reuel. cap. 4. which rest nether day nor night, doe thrice repeate one word to the honor of God, saying. *Holy, holy, holy, Lord God of Saboth.*

Againe, Christ him selfe, praying in the garden, repeated one and the same speeche, three feuerall times. Luc. 22. & Mat. 26. 36.

Finally, we reade, that the three children in the fornace, in lauing and praising almightie God, did in euery verse (being many in number) repeate a certaine halfe verse.

See Fathers that affirme the same. Lactantius lib. 4. diuin. instit. cap. 28. S. Amb. lib. de spir. sancto cap. 20. S. Aug. lib. 1. de serm. Dom in monte cap. 5. & lib. de doctrina Christiana

ftiana cap. 7. S. Greg. hom. 19. in
Ezech. & lib. 1. Moral. cap. 28.

A TABLE OF THE

CONTROVERSIES

contayned in this Trea-
tises.

The Table.

The Table.

44. Of

The Table.

Faults escaped.

Pag. 8. numb 5. line 11. & 12. after, *Chriſt our Lord.* ad, *his Apoſtles, or their ſucceſſors.* pag. 32. in ſome copies, for Iſay 9. 7. read, Iſay. 35. 9. pag. 37. line 17. and Church, read, and the Church. Ibid. line 20. *for you heauen,* read, *for you in heauen.*